BIKE

Wild Ride!

The Illustrated History of the Denver Broncos

Alex Marvez

Edited and Designed by
Bob Moon, SporTradition

Taylor Publishing Company
Dallas, Texas

Riddell
BRONCOS
DAVIS

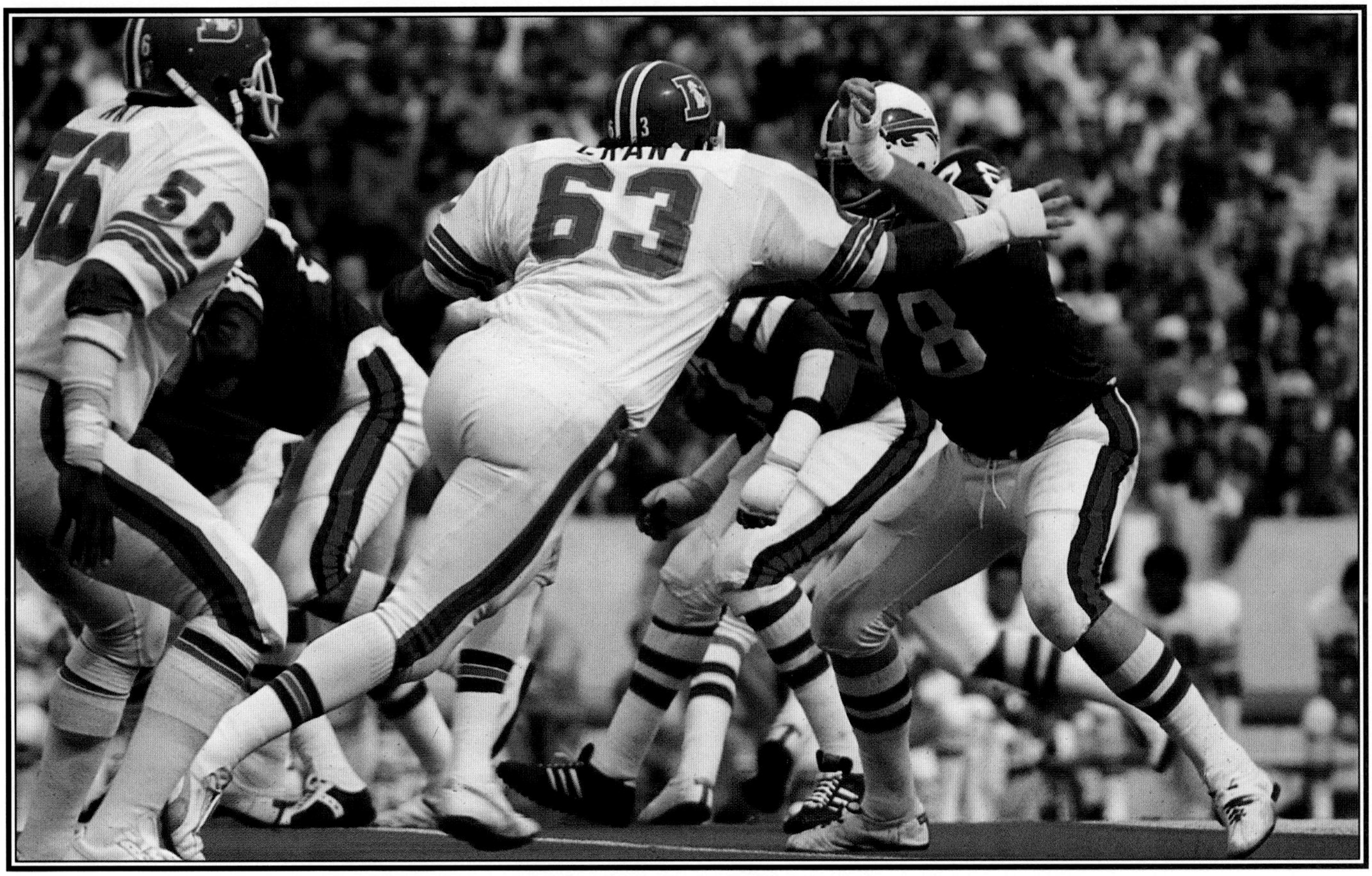

Published by Taylor Publishing Company
1550 West Mockingbird Lane
Dallas, Texas 75235

Edited, Designed and Produced by
Bob Moon, SporTradition Publications
798 Linworth Rd. East
Columbus, Ohio 43235

Library of Congress Cataloging-in-Publication Data
Marvez, Alex.
Wild ride! the illustrated history of the Denver Broncos / written by Alex Marvez.
p. cm.
1. Denver Broncos (Football team)—History.
2. Denver Broncos (Football team)—Pictorial works. I. Title.
GV956.D37M36 1998
796.332'64'0978883—dc21 98-34191
CIP

PHOTOS (i–vi and page 1):

(i) The menacing stare of Karl Mecklenberg. (ii-iii) John Elway hands off to Terrell Davis in the Broncos' playoff win over Jacksonville in 1997. (iv, above) John Grant uses hand combat against the Bills. (vi) Jerry Inman nails the Chicago Bears' Jim Grabowski. (1) Otis Armstrong gains ground on the Rams during his 1,407-yard season of 1974.

Contents

vi
Acknowledgments

1
Introduction

2
Chapter 1
Vertical Climb
1959–1960

8
Chapter 2
Slippery Footing
1961–1969

28
Chapter 3
Higher Altitude
1970–1976

44
Chapter 4
Red and Orange
1977–1980

64
Chapter 5
Arrival and Revival
1981–1985

80
Chapter 6
Drive to the Top!
1986–1989

100
Chapter 7
Rockier Roads
1990–1994

112
Chapter 8
Summit Salute!
1995–1997

132
Chapter 9
Elway and Company
The Offense

165
Chapter 10
A Crushing Experience
The Defense

188
Chapter 11
Upchurch Downfield!
Special Teams

200
Chapter 12
Shootouts in the AFC
The Rivalries

215
Denver Broncos
Records and Statistics

Acknowledgments

This book would have been a Wild Ride were it not for the help of some people who are special to me.

I want to thank Bob Moon at SporTradition Publications for giving me the opportunity to complete this project, which has given me an even better understanding of who the Denver Broncos are. I also want to thank Barry Forbis, Kevin Huhn, Sam Adams and Clay Latimer of the *Rocky Mountain News* for their help, as well as Jim Saccomano, Richard Stewart and Paul Kirk of the Broncos media relations office.

This book is dedicated to the people who have helped me achieve more than I could have ever imagined as a sports writer: My family, Phil North, Tom Wright, Don Peffly, Mike Rosenthal, Bill van Smith, Tom Archdeacon, Eric Rodriguez, Kim Wood, Dave Meltzer and most of all, my lovely wife Sherry for her understanding and patience in a very demanding field.

— Alex Marvez, May 3, 1998.

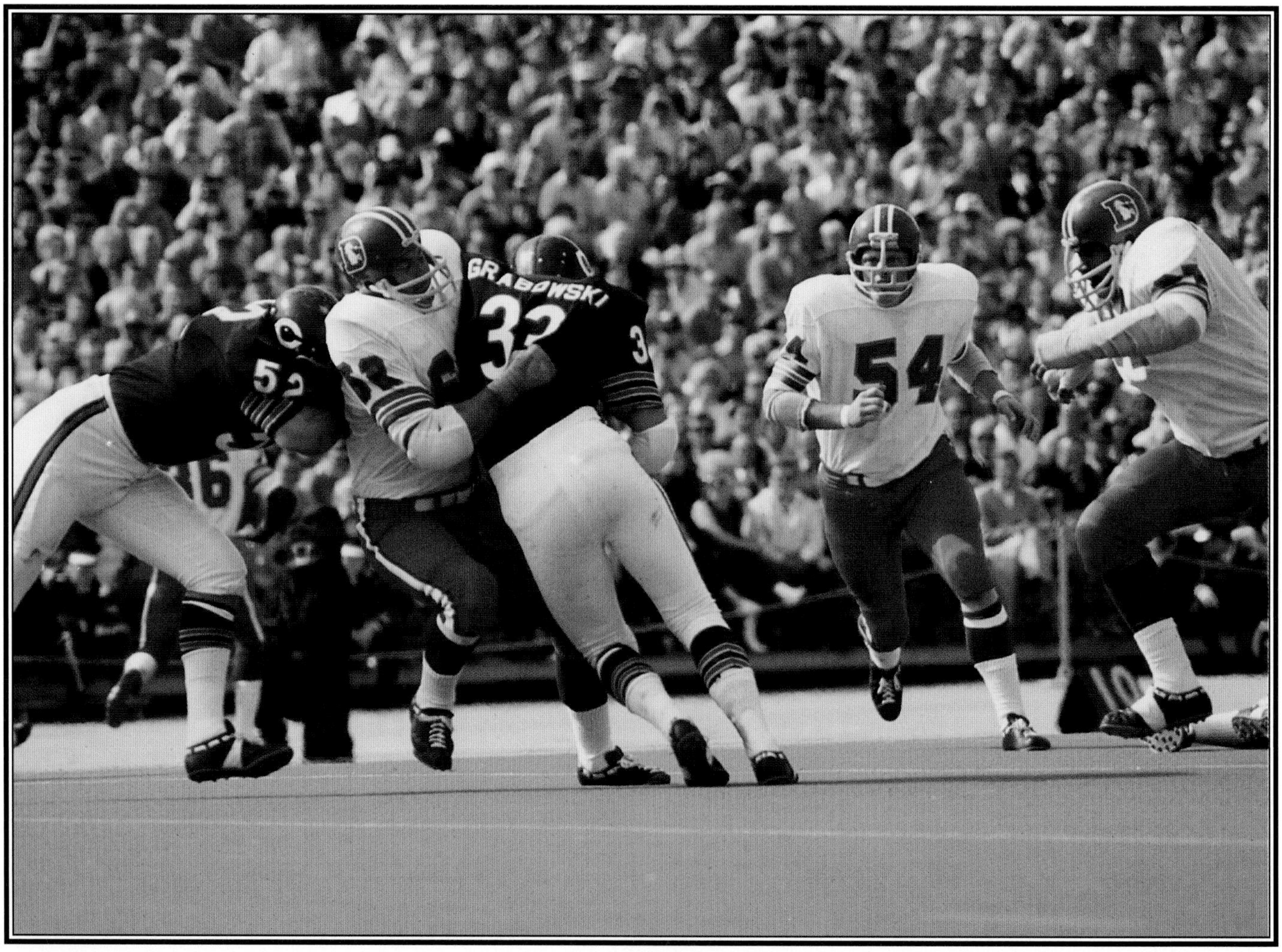

Introduction

I received my first introduction to Broncomania in July 1997, when more than 70,000 fans poured into Mile High Stadium—for an exhibition game. There may be no NFL team with a more rabid fan following than the Denver Broncos. Whenever the Broncos play on a Sunday, the entire city seems to shut down for three hours. The local television ratings for the Broncos are the highest for any NFL team. And more than 650,000 fans lined the streets of downtown Denver on January 27, 1998, to honor the team that finally won its first world title with a 31-24 victory over Green Bay in Super Bowl XXXII, a game considered by many to be the most exciting in the history of professional football's penultimate game.

But for the Broncos to become the ruling sports franchise of the Rocky Mountains wasn't easy. In fact, the team struggled so badly to gain fan support in the early 1960s that the Broncos almost were moved to another city looking to procure an AFL franchise.

Even after the Broncos were embraced by the city, their fans had to show an inordinate amount of patience. Denver never had a winning season in its first decade of play and did not make the playoffs during its first 17 seasons. Even when the Broncos finally became a legitimate contender, four Super Bowl losses had their fans wondering if the team would ever win a world championship.

Wild Ride! chronicles the 38 years of ups and downs preceding the team's first Super Bowl title. There are anecdotes about the greatest players ever to don a Broncos uniform, such as John Elway, Lionel Taylor, Billy Thompson and Terrell Davis. There are stories about the rivalries between Denver and its most hated foes, notably the Oakland Raiders and Kansas City Chiefs. And there's an in-depth look at the tales that helped shape the Broncos, such as the public burning of the team's original uniforms, the meeting of the Dirty Dozen, the trade that brought Elway to Denver and more.

So sit back and enjoy the Wild Ride!

—Alex Marvez.

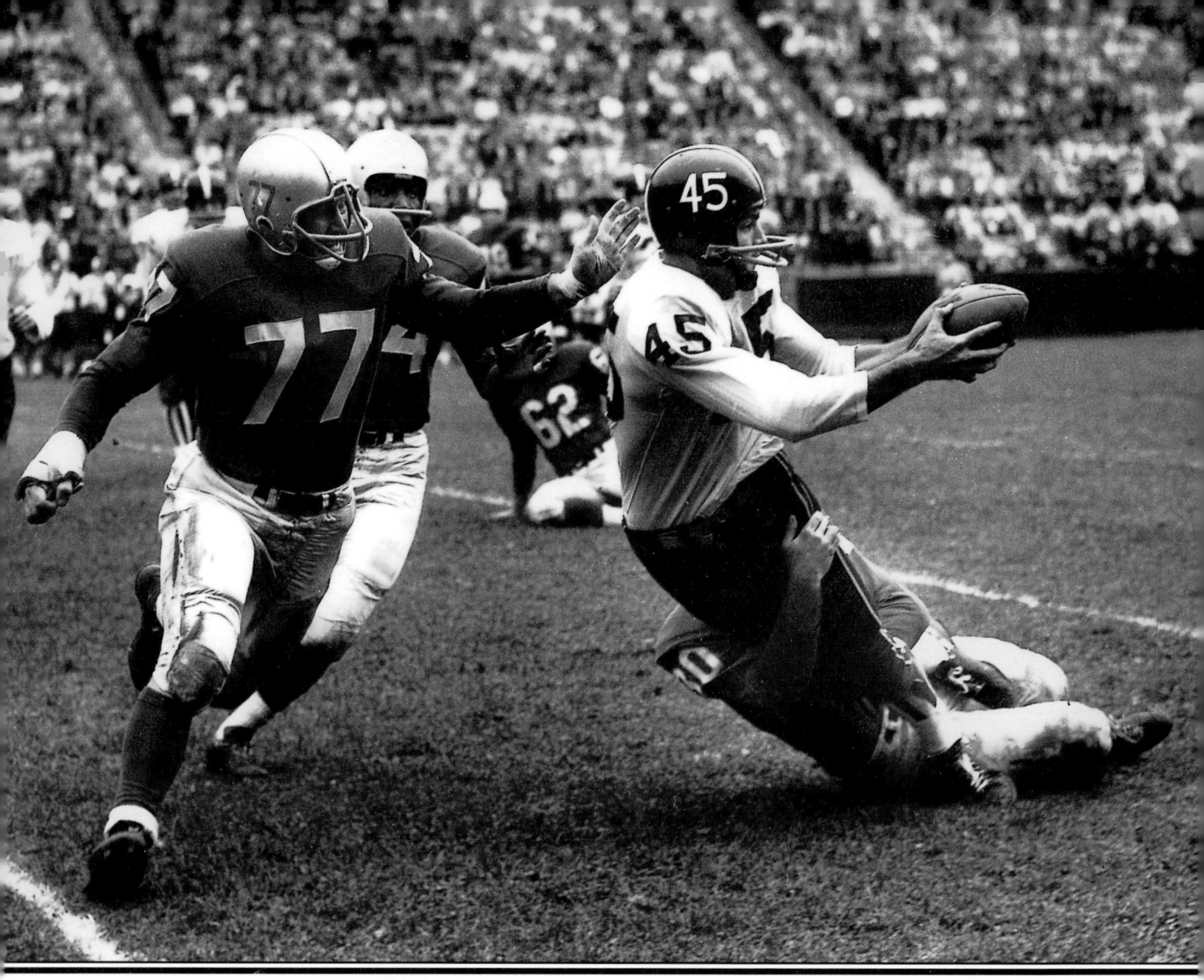

Safety Austin "Goose" Gonsoulin was an early Denver standout, intercepting this pass in a 27-21 win over Buffalo on Sept. 18, 1960. His four interceptions that day and 11 for the year remain Broncos single-season records.

Ever since the 1997 Denver Broncos won the first league championship in franchise history, a city that was already ga-ga about its football team has become even more crazed. Broncomania—the phrase coined in the 1970s to describe the adoration heaped upon the team—has manifested itself in everything from T-shirts to bumper stickers to a custom sign at Denver International Airport celebrating the Broncos' 31-24 victory over the Green Bay Packers in Super Bowl XXXII.

But when the team was founded, it was hard to imagine such a love affair between Denver and its Broncos would ever develop. In fact, it's almost miraculous that the Broncos now have what is arguably the most hard-core fan following in the National Football League.

The Broncos began playing in the upstart American Football League in 1960. The league was the brainchild of Texas millionaire Lamar Hunt, who had been previously rebuffed in his attempts to land an NFL franchise in Dallas.

Bob and Lee Howsam could relate. The brothers had attempted to procure an NFL franchise before the AFL was formed, but discovered little interest in what was, at the time, a small market. Therefore, it was no surprise that the Howsams became the first ownership group outside of Texas to apply for a membership in the AFL.

The Howsam brothers were no strangers to sports. They already owned the Denver Bears, an extremely successful minor league baseball franchise, and had controlling interest in Bears Stadium, the facility where the team played. Because of the popularity of the Bears, the Howsams believed a second baseball team could also succeed in Denver. So they applied to become members of the new Continental League, a potential third major league that was forming in the late 1950s.

Chapter 1

1959–1960

Vertical Climb

With their bargain-basement uniforms and players to match, it would be all uphill for the first-year Broncos.

To gain membership, the Howsams were required to expand Bears Stadium from 17,500 seats to 25,600 seats. The project forced them to take out a mortgage on the stadium, but they felt the money would be well spent if the Continental League was as successful as projected. The league, however, never got off the ground.

That left the Howsams with an expanded stadium and just one tenant, which would not generate enough revenue to pay the mortgage. Facing serious financial difficulties, the brothers sought an alternate sports team to fill those extra seats.

On August 14, 1959, the AFL was officially founded at a meeting in Chicago. The six charter members were Dallas, Denver, Houston, Los Angeles, Minneapolis and New York.

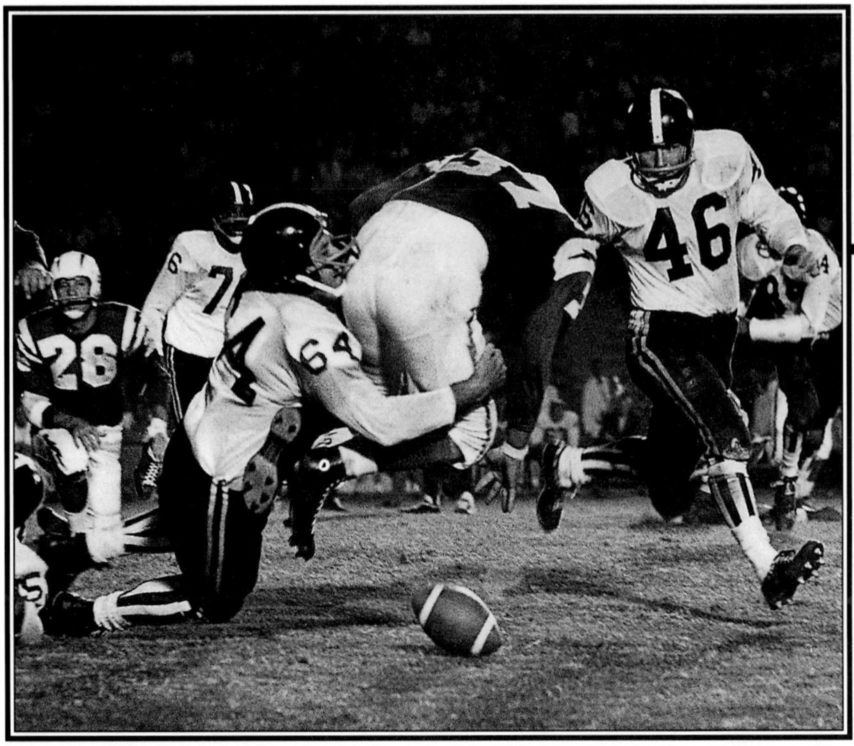

Defensive tackle Bud McFadin forces a fumble on L.A. Chargers fullback Howie Ferguson. The Broncos lost all five 1960 preseason games, including the final contest against the Chargers. No. 46 is linebacker Hardy Brown, known for his devastating shoulder tackles while with the 49ers in the 1950s.

Minneapolis, however, later withdrew from the league after its backers were offered an NFL expansion franchise for 1961. But the AFL then added Boston, Buffalo and Oakland to form an eight-team league that would begin play in 1960. Denver was placed in the AFL's Western Conference along with Dallas, Los Angeles and Oakland.

The nickname "Broncos" was selected from a mail-in name-the-team contest. The winning entry was submitted by a fan from nearby Golden, Colo.

The first AFL draft was held in November 1959 and the Broncos made center Roger LeClerc of Trinity their first selection. But in a pattern that would haunt the Broncos throughout their early years, LeClerc decided to sign with the Chicago Bears as Denver could not offer a lucrative contract. LeClerc did play one season with the Broncos in 1967, but that was no consolation to a team that needed as much help as it could get during its formative years.

On December 1, the Broncos named Dean Griffing the team's first general manager. Griffing held the same position with the Saskatchewan Roughriders of the Canadian Football League for the seven previous seasons, which is why he was familiar with Frank Filchock. So it was little surprise that exactly one month later, Filchock became the first head coach in Broncos history.

The hiring of Filchock raised some eyebrows in the sporting world because of his checkered past. When he was a player with the New York Giants, Filchock, along with the New York Police Department and teammate Merle Hapes, was reportedly involved in an attempt to fix the 1946 NFL Championship game against the Bears. Filchock was allowed to play in the game, but was reprimanded for not reporting the bribe attempt. He was then suspended after the season, prompting him to play in the CFL the next three seasons before he was reinstated. Filchock was named the Canadian Player of the Year in 1949 when playing for Montreal.

But while he was a winner as a player, the 43-year-old Filchock faced major obstacles as a head coach. His first problem was the Broncos' limited budget. Because the Howsams were having financial trouble from the stadium expansion, the Broncos couldn't compete for top-notch players. Like other AFL teams, they filled their roster with signable collegians, NFL castoffs and CFL transplants.

The Broncos could not hire a complete coaching staff and were forced to purchase second-hand uniforms that were among the most hideous ever worn in professional football. They were purchased from officials at the Copper Bowl in Tucson because that collegiate post-season game was going out of business. The gold jerseys

> ***"In the first year, we had only 35 players, three coaches and one trainer. I would give anything to play today with the equipment and trainers and money the players get."***

and brown pants could be worn for both home and away games. Even uglier were the brown-and-gold vertically-striped socks.

The Broncos' first training camp opened in July 1960 at the Colorado School of Mines, a small college nestled in the foothills of Golden, Colo. That also was an adventure for the players. On the first day of camp, the team was placed on the fourth floor of an Army-style barracks. There were no partitions or closets, so players were forced to hang their clothes on long pipes and live out of their suitcases. Hash was served as the usual meal of the day, with steak on Friday nights. Most of the Catholic players would have preferred fish on Friday, but after having to eat the hash all week, any change was welcome.

The equipment used by the Broncos was purchased from a local college. Because the team lacked an equipment manager, Filchock would repair the equipment as well as serve as the only offensive coach. Dale Dodrill was the defensive line coach and Jim Cason the secondary coach.

"It was a new experience to come from the Navy into this little, desolate small town," said Gene Mingo, a Broncos running back from 1960-64. "At least that's what it appeared like when I first came in. We had 125 guys staying in one gymnasium. We didn't have the best of equipment. As a matter of fact, we didn't even have weights like they have today.

"There are almost more coaches on the coaching staff today than we had players on the team. In the first year, we had only 35 players, three coaches and one trainer. I would give anything to play today with the equipment and trainers and money the players get."

Because the Broncos were too cash-strapped to sign a quality quarterback, Frank Tripucka was recruited from the CFL to serve as a player/coach. The "coach" title was later dropped after the 32-year-old Tripucka proved he was better than any other quarterback in camp. Tripucka, a former Notre Dame quarterback, had last played in the NFL with the Dallas Texans in 1952 before moving on to the CFL.

As expected from a team with a revolving door of players, the Broncos lost all five of their exhibition games. Also as expected, the Broncos made little splash in the local community. Only 2,600 season tickets were sold in the team's first season, further compounding the Howsams' financial woes.

But then a funny thing happened—the Broncos actually won the first regular-season game in American Football League history.

The Boston Patriots had hammered the Broncos in the first game of the preseason, 43-6. The same was expected when Denver ventured to Boston for the season opener on Friday night, Sept. 9, 1960. Instead, a crowd of 21,597 Patriots fans—many attending out of curiosity about the new league—went home stunned.

Tripucka connected with Al Carmichael on a 59-yard scoring pass, the first regular-season touchdown in AFL history. Mingo, who was inserted to return kicks after an injury felled the regular starter, scored the game-winning touchdown on a

Frank Filchock was a 43-year-old former NFL quarterback when he became the Broncos' first head coach. He lasted two seasons with an overall record of 7-20-1.

The vertically-striped Broncos won the first-ever regular-season game in AFL history, beating the Patriots in Boston on Sept. 9, 1960. Above, Patriots halfback Larry Garron is pursued by Chuck Gavin (61), Bud McFadin (64) and Al Romine (42) in the first quarter of the 13-10 Denver victory.

76-yard punt return. Toss in two interceptions by safety Au*stin "Goose" Gonsoulin and the Broncos were able to post a 13-10 victory.

"I'll never forget halftime of that game," said Mingo who doubled as Denver's place-kicker. "It went on a heck of a long time. I was sweating and wondering whether I would have to run back a punt. I can't explain the feeling when I reached the end zone. My legs felt like rubber bands because they had tightened up. When it came time to kick the extra point, I couldn't get my leg up. I kicked a divot.

"I can't describe the feeling when we won the game," he added. "I think some of the guys didn't even think we were going to win or had any hope of winning. We were very skeptical because of the beating they had given us before. But it was a different situation when the game started."

The victory signified the start of Broncomania—sort of. The Broncos could not consistently crack the front pages of the local newspapers, with the Denver Bears grabbing the biggest headlines.

Still, the Broncos were off to a promising start. Denver won its second game at Buffalo, 27-21, and hung tough in a 28-24 loss against the host New York Titans.

When the Broncos returned for their first home game, a crowd of 18,372 attended a 31-14 thumping of the Oakland Raiders. The crowd grew by about 1,000 fans the next week when Denver lost a heartbreaker to the eventual Western Conference champion Los Angeles Chargers, 23-19.

But shortly thereafter, the bottom fell out. While the Broncos had some talented players like Mingo, Gonsoulin, Tripucka and wide receiver Lionel Taylor, the team went 0-7-1 in its final eight games to finish with a 4-9-1 mark for the season.

"We started to have too many injuries," Mingo explained. "We just couldn't do it. We didn't have the bench strength other teams had."

Even more disheartening to the Howsams was the lack of fan interest after the Broncos began to slump. The Broncos only drew a total of 13,646 fans for their final two games. By the time the season ended, the franchise had reportedly lost $400,000, largely due to startup costs. Those losses prompted the Howsams to sell their share of the team in May 1961 to a syndicate headed by Denver businessmen Cal Kunz and Gerald Phipps.

Mingo recalls that his salary for that season was $6,500, which was $124,500 less than the minimum salary NFL players earned in 1997. Because the Broncos weren't as well known, Mingo said a local bank questioned the players when they tried to deposit their checks.

"When we first came in, they really had to verify who we were, especially me," he said. "There was another family in town whose last name was Mingo that had caused quite a bit of problems around the time. They didn't believe I was Gene Mingo the Broncos player, and they thought I had forged the check. They had to call the Broncos to make sure."

Frank Tripucka came from the Canadian Football League to become the Broncos' first quarterback. The 32-year-old veteran led the AFL in passing in 1960 with 3,038 yards, joining Jack Kemp and Johnny Unitas as the first quarterbacks in pro football history to break the 3,000-yard barrier.

But not all was gloom and doom. Mingo led the league in scoring with 123 points. Tripucka and Taylor were an exciting quarterback-wide receiver tandem. Tripucka (3,038), Jack Kemp of the Los Angeles Chargers (3,018) and Johnny Unitas of the Baltimore Colts (3,099) became the first pro quarterbacks to pass for more than 3,000 yards. Taylor caught a league-leading 92 passes for 1,235 yards and 12 touchdowns. Gonsoulin led the league with 11 interceptions. Taylor, Gonsoulin and defensive tackle Bud McFadin were named to the first official All-AFL team.

The NFL, though, found the most apt way to title Denver's first two seasons in the AFL—"The Early Futility." A plaque at the Pro Football Hall of Fame in Canton, Ohio, has a photo of Houston running back Billy Cannon playing against the Broncos, as well as one of the vertically-striped socks that symbolized the franchise's growing pains.

The plaque reads: "Heisman Trophy winner Billy Cannon signed with the Houston Oilers for 1960! Meanwhile, the Denver Broncos were playing in second-hand uniforms made famous by the vertically-striped socks that were later burnt in a public ceremony. Thus, the AFL's great hope and its early futility are graphically portrayed as Cannon gains yardage against the Denver team."

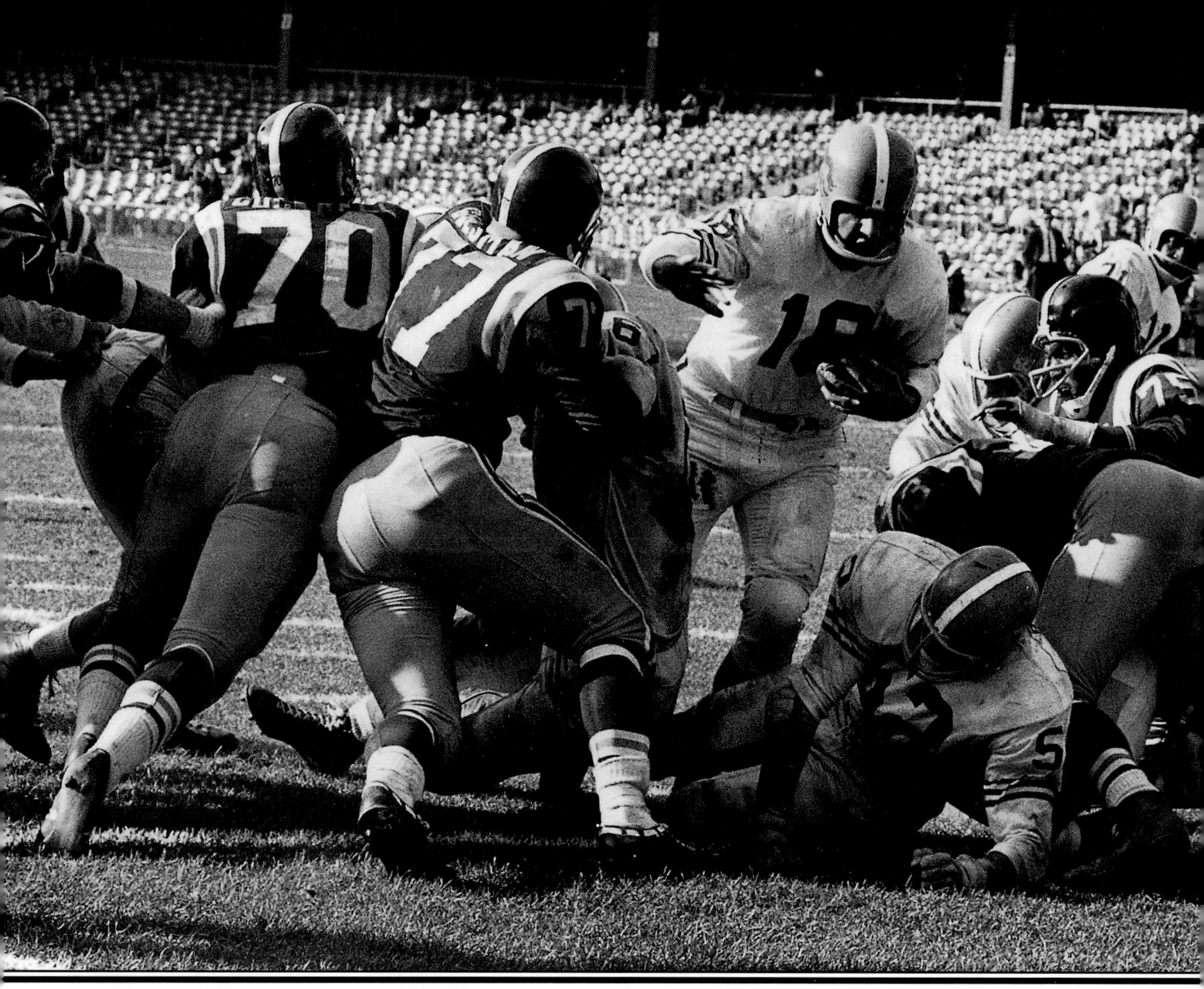

Quarterback Frank Tripucka scores against the New York Titans in a 32-10 victory at the Polo Grounds in 1962. The Broncos won seven of their first nine, but in a pattern that would plague them throughout the decade, they lost their last five to finish at 7-7.

They could have easily become the San Antonio Broncos. Or the Atlanta Broncos, Philadelphia Broncos, Cincinnati Broncos. Even the Birmingham Broncos was a possibility at one point. The early 1960s were the most unstable years in the history of the Denver Broncos. The team came perilously close to leaving Denver on several occasions, only to be saved by those who believed the city needed to have an NFL team to transform itself from what outsiders believed was a "cow town" to a thriving metropolis.

The Broncos drew 91,333 fans to their seven home games in 1960, which translated into a paltry average of 13,047. That was not enough to keep the Howsams financially afloat, so it came as no surprise when the brothers began listening to an offer from a group of investors from San Antonio that hoped to buy the team and move it to Texas.

Calvin Kunz did not want that to happen. In spring 1961, he engineered a deal that kept the Broncos in Denver. Kunz gathered a group that included three members (Gerald H. Phipps, Ben F. Stapleton Jr. and Edward

Hirschfield) of Rocky Mountain Sports, Inc.—the corporate owners of the Broncos franchise which the Howsams controlled—and six other financial backers (Walter C. Emery, William Grant, Robert T. Person, Allan Phipps, Charles W. Schoelzel and James E. Stokes) into purchasing the franchise from the Howsams. In June of 1961, the group became known as Empire Sports, with Kunz appointed president.

While the sale was great news for Broncos fans who wanted their team to stay in Denver, things actually grew worse for the franchise during the following season. Not feeling there was enough time to make a change before the 1961 campaign, the Broncos remained basically the same unit as the team that finished 4-9-1 in their inaugural season.

Chapter 2

1961–1969

Slippery Footing

Despite their annual long, slow slides to the bottom of the AFL standings, the Broncos (and their fans) survive the '60s.

The Broncos dropped to 3-11 in 1961 with the same late-season swoon that haunted the franchise the previous campaign. After opening the season 3-4, the Broncos lost their remaining seven games by an average margin of 36-14. Wide receiver Lionel Taylor was about the only bright spot, becoming the first receiver in professional football history to catch 100 passes in a season. Taylor finished the year with 1,176 receiving yards and four touchdowns.

But there still was not much local interest in what Taylor or his teammates were doing on the gridiron. Attendance dropped sharply from the 1960 season to an average of just 10,644 fans at Denver's seven home games. A change was needed if the Broncos were going to survive. So as soon as the season ended, Frank Filchock became the first casualty when he was fired as head coach.

Gene Mingo dives for yardage against the Houston Oilers in 1962. Under new coach and general manager Jack Faulkner, the Broncos scrapped their brown-and-gold uniforms to sport a new orange-and-blue look for '62.

General manager Dean Griffing also didn't return for a third season. The man who assumed both roles was Jack Faulkner, a former assistant coach with the San Diego Chargers. Faulkner's two-and-a-half-year coaching reign is remembered more for his taste in fashion than any on-field accomplishments.

Faulkner hated the Broncos' brown-and-gold uniforms about as much as the players hated wearing them. So Faulkner decided he would hold a public burning of the striped socks, which had become a symbol of the team's ineptness. He was then given permission to purchase new uniforms because the Broncos had been given an infusion of capital when purchased by Empire Sports. The new jerseys were orange and became the team's trademark until a navy blue jersey was introduced in 1997.

"I was a Cleveland Browns fan, and I wanted burnt orange uniforms like they wore," said Faulkner in the 1978 book, *Orange Madness*, by Woodrow Paige Jr. "But the manufacturer sent us bright orange instead."

Faulkner, though, didn't complain. The uniform change seemed to ignite a surge in the team's popularity. When the Broncos played host to San Diego in the 1962 season opener, almost 28,000 fans crowded into the University of Denver Stadium. Obviously inspired, the Broncos posted a 30-21 victory against a Chargers team that had finished 12-2 and reached the AFL title game the previous season.

That game also marked the first time that fans in the south end zone began earning a reputation as some of the most crazed spectators in sports. When the Broncos moved to Mile High Stadium, the fans would make so much noise in the south end zone that the goalposts would shimmy when an opposing kicker would attempt a field goal.

Quarterback Frank Tripucka remembers how the "South Enders" would support the team during his Broncos career (1960-63).

"That group would bombard the other team with anything and everything when they went to the locker rooms, which were under the south stands," he said in *Broncos: Three Decades of Football* (Joseph Hession and Michael Spence, 1987). "If we were ahead, they would give us the greatest ovation. That group there was very fun. . . . I have a soft spot in my heart for them."

The Broncos weren't soft on the field for the first part of the '62 season. Denver sped to a 7-2 record and appeared headed toward the first winning campaign in franchise history.

But once again, the team could not avoid a collapse in the second half of the season as five consecutive losses ended any playoff hopes. That string included heartbreaking losses to the Boston Patriots (33-29), New York Titans (46-45) and Dallas Texans (17-10 in the season finale).

Jack Faulkner coached the Broncos to their only non-losing season of the 1960s. The 7-7 mark in 1962 earned him AFL Coach of the Year honors.

Still, however, progress was being made. Faulkner was named AFL Coach of the Year despite his team's late-season slide. Gene Mingo led the league in scoring (137 points), Tripucka led in passing (240 completions for 2,917 yards), Lionel Taylor led in receptions (77) and Jim Fraser led in punting with 55 punts and a 43.6 average per punt. Taylor, offensive tackle Eldon Danenhauer, and safeties Goose Gonsoulin and Bob Zeman were named to the All-AFL team.

And most importantly, fan interest had finally begun to blossom. The Broncos set a Denver sports attendance record when 34,496 fans witnessed a 20-10 victory over Houston on Oct. 21. Overall attendance jumped to 178,485, which is an average of 25,497 fans per game. Things were so upbeat that the Broncos finally managed to sign one of their top draft choices—with a little political help.

Denver's first three first-round draft choices—center Roger LeClerc of Trinity (1960), halfback Bob Gaiters of New Mexico State (1961) and defensive tackle Merlin Olsen of Utah State (1962)—had spurned the Broncos for more lucrative offers in the National Football League.

The downward spiral began immediately with a 59-7 loss at home to the Kansas City Chiefs in the season opener. Not even during the Broncos' formative years was Denver handed such a lopsided defeat.

Olsen would have been a great help. He was named to 14 straight Pro Bowls with the Los Angeles Rams and elected to the Pro Football Hall of Fame in 1982.

The Broncos were so desperate to sign their high draft choices in 1963 that the team enlisted Colorado governor Steve McNichols to write letters to two of their top three picks—Texas fullback Ray Poage and Miami (of Ohio) offensive tackle Tom Nomina, both of whom were selected in the second round. Nomina was impressed enough that he signed with the Broncos.

After making strides in Faulkner's first season, there were, for the first time in franchise history, expectations that the Broncos would do well in 1963. That's what made the team's collapse even more painful than its 2-11-1 record.

The downward spiral began immediately with a 59-7 loss at home to the Kansas City Chiefs in the season opener. Not even during the Broncos' formative years was Denver handed such a lopsided defeat. After a 20-14 loss to Houston the following week, Tripucka decided he had enough and retired.

Frank Tripucka hangs up his jersey after two straight Denver losses to open the 1963 season. His reason for retirement: "Two bad games." The Broncos struggled to replace him and finished at 2-11-1.

Two days later, ex-Minnesota Vikings quarterback John McCormick was signed and inserted into the lineup for that week's game against Boston. McCormick led Denver to a 14-10 win, then threw three touchdown passes in a 50-34 victory over the Chargers the following week. The Broncos appeared to have found a gem, but one week later against Houston, McCormick injured a knee and was out for the year. The Broncos lost, 33-24, and were on their way to an 0-9-1 skein in their last 10 games. To make matters worse, McCormick's replacement, Mickey Slaughter, was injured the following week at Boston and replaced by Don Breaux.

Lionel Taylor, Goose Gonsoulin and new running back Billy Joe were the best things Denver had going in 1963. Taylor won his fourth consecutive receiving title with 78 catches for 1,101 yards and 10 touchdowns, while Gonsoulin was the only Broncos player to earn All-AFL honors. Joe was named the AFL Rookie of the Year after tallying 649 yards and four touchdowns on 154 carries.

A shakeup was needed for 1964. So Broncos management engineered the biggest trade in AFL history with the New York Jets. Denver sent linebacker Ed "Wahoo" McDaniel, wide receiver Gene Prebola, defensive tackle Gordy Holz and defensive back Bob Zeman to the Jets for defensive end Ed Cooke, defensive tackle Dick Guesman, defensive tackle Charlie Janerette, linebacker Jim Price and guard Sid Fournet. Every player but Fournet made the squad, with Guesman, Cooke and Janerette becoming starters on the defensive line in 1964.

Linebacker Jim Fraser (55) and cornerback John McGeever (47) pile on Buffalo halfback Ed Rutkowski on Nov. 3, 1963. The losses, however, soon piled on the Broncos. The 30-28 defeat was the first of seven to close out the season.

In another unusual off-season trade, the Broncos acquired (or borrowed)

Lionel Taylor reaches the end zone in 1964 for one of his seven TD catches that season. His 76 receptions was second behind Houston's Charley Hennigan (101), the first time Taylor did not lead the AFL.

quarterback Jacky Lee from Houston for Bud McFadin and a 1965 first-round draft choice. The deal called for Lee to return to the Oilers after two seasons. (He did.) Lee and Mickey Slaughter combined to have a dismal 1964 season, throwing 31 interceptions and just 14 touchdowns. Lionel Taylor had the lowest yardage total (873) of any of his first five seasons in Denver. And Billy Joe failed to recapture the magic from his rookie season, finishing with 415 yards rushing, second behind Charlie Mitchell's 590.

After the first four games, it became apparent the Broncos were in worse shape than ever. Denver lost to the New York Jets, Buffalo, Houston and Boston by a combined score of 137-46. So it was no surprise when Jack Faulkner was fired following a 39-10 loss to the Patriots on Oct. 4.

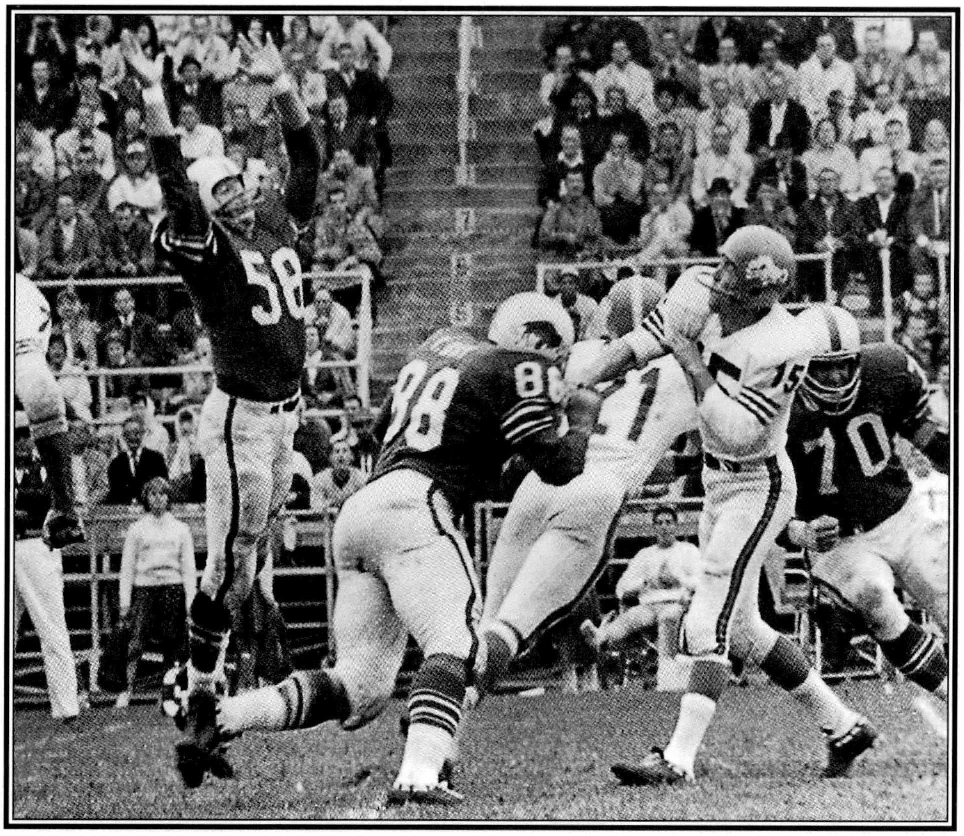

Faulkner's interim replacement was Broncos wide receivers coach Mac Speedie, whose enthusiasm initially rubbed off on the players. Speedie was so determined to get fan support that he led the crowd in cheers during his first game as head coach against Kansas City. He also opened practice sessions to the public.

Such exuberance gave the Broncos a lift in a 33-27 upset of the Chiefs on Oct. 11. The Broncos, though, won only once more in 1964, a 20-16 victory over the New York Jets before a sparse crowd of 11,309 fans.

On the bright side, Speedie did show enough talent to be named the permanent head coach on Dec. 12, two weeks after the Broncos forged a 20-20 tie against Oakland. Jim Fraser also won his third consecutive AFL punting title with a 44.6-yard average, while defensive back Willie Brown was named to the All-AFL team.

Denver's second consecutive 2-11-1 mark was devastating off the field. The average attendance in 1964 dropped to 16,894 fans a game, leading to even more financial woes for Empire Sports. The syndicate had reportedly lost $2 million since buying the team in spring 1961.

Jacky Lee throws over the arms of Buffalo linebacker Mike Stratton in 1964. Denver's ongoing quarterback search found Lee being loaned to the Broncos in a deal with Houston that required him to return to the Oilers after two seasons. The Broncos, however, could barely borrow a victory in '64, finishing at 2-11-1.

Fullback Billy Joe breaks between two New York Jets in the 1964 season opener at Shea Stadium, won by the Jets, 30-6. Joe was the 1963 AFL Rookie of the Year with 649 rushing yards, but his total dropped to 415 in 1964 and he was traded to the Buffalo Bills in '65 for fullback Cookie Gilchrist.

With no on-field turnaround in sight, Kunz decided he wanted to sell the team to Cox Broadcasting for $4 million. Cox would then move the Broncos to Atlanta, a growing city seeking a professional football franchise.

Kunz was never able to follow through with his plan because of Gerald and Allan Phipps. The brothers refused to sell their share of the team stock, which scared off potential suitors who wanted full control of the team. Philadelphia and Cincinnati were two other cities looking to get their hands on the Broncos.

When the Cox deal fell apart, Kunz agreed to sell the 52 percent of the stock he controlled to the Phipps brothers for $1.5 million. The deal was completed in February 1965.

Said Gerald Phipps: "We are trying to attract industry to this community. Nothing would hurt us more than headlines around the country saying that Denver had lost its football team. I would be cutting my own throat if I did something that would set back the community. If we can sell 20,000 season tickets, we can break even financially."

Such a show of civic loyalty was rewarded. Gene Mingo remembers that during his five years in Denver (1960-64) he once walked the sidewalks with other Bronco players trying to sell season tickets. "I marched up and down Broadway and Colfax asking for donations to keep the team here," Mingo said.

But the impact of Phipps's purchase was felt immediately. The day after the sale, the Broncos sold a franchise-record 143 season tickets. That record was shattered on March 5 when the Broncos sold 941 season tickets in one day. Local banks designed a program that would allow fans to purchase tickets through an interest-free loan.

By April 1, more than 20,000 tickets were sold, a figure that rose by 2,000 in the following month. Attendance also never dipped below 20,000 fans again for a Broncos home game.

Broncos fans continued to support the team despite an inept on-field product. The team didn't show much improvement in 1965, finishing 4-10 with yet another late-season swoon. This time, the Broncos failed to win in their final four games for the sixth consecutive season. The only highlight during that skid was Lionel Taylor becoming the first AFL player to catch more than 500 passes in his career. He finished with 85 receptions for 1,131 yards and six touchdowns.

Besides Taylor, Eldon Danenhauer and fullback Cookie Gilchrist—an off-season acquisition in 1965—were named to the All-AFL team. Abner Haynes also led the AFL in kick returns with a 26.5-yard average. And most importantly for the Phipps brothers, the Broncos averaged 31,398 fans a game.

Speedie, the starting left end for Paul Brown's Cleveland Browns championship teams from 1946-52, did not show the same coaching confidence as his Hall-of-Fame mentor. Instead, Speedie became a scapegoat for Denver's losses. He would gesture to the stands for fan responses when a critical coaching decision needed to be made, such as whether the Broncos should go for it on fourth down. The fans always shout-

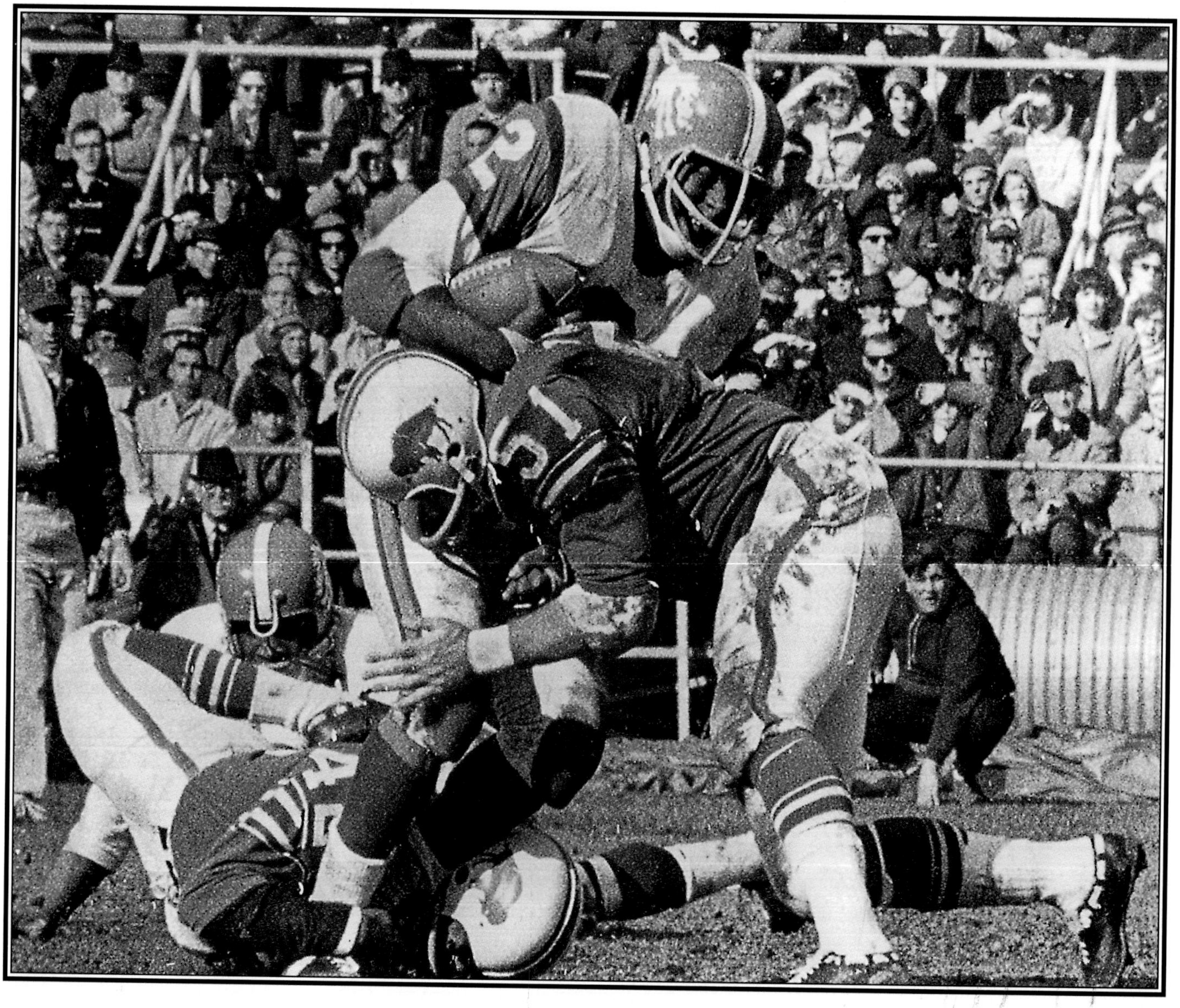

Cookie Gilchrist is crumbled on a short gain in a 31-13 loss to Buffalo on Oct. 24, 1965. He led the league in rushing for the '64 AFL-champion Bills, then joined the Broncos in a trade for Billy Joe. Gilchrist gained 954 yards in '65 before being dealt again to the expansion Miami Dolphins.

ed yes, which prompted Speedie to usually eschew a punt or field goal. When the Broncos gained a first down, the fans cheered. But when the Broncos were stuffed (which is what usually happened), Speedie would become a target for fan abuse.

It became obvious that Denver needed a coaching change after being spanked by Houston, 45-7, in the 1966 season opener. The Broncos were embarrassed like no other team in AFL history. Denver failed to make a first down and gained only 32 yards of total offense. The Broncos also set an AFL record by completing just two of 20 passes for minus 2 yards.

After a 24-10 loss to Boston in the second game, Speedie was fired and replaced by assistant coach Ray Malavasi. Speedie's final coaching record with Denver was 6-19-1, giving him the lowest winning percentage (.250) of any head coach in Broncos history. But, of course, no Broncos coach had a winning percentage in the '60s.

Malavasi didn't fare much better, although he proved to be a credible coach elsewhere by taking the Los Angeles Rams to Super Bowl XIV during the 1979 season. Malavasi faced a lack of offensive talent as quarterback remained a major weakness, with John McCormick and Max Choboian combining to throw 27 interceptions and just 10 touchdowns. The rushing game also suffered after Cookie Gilchrist was dealt to the expansion Miami Dolphins. Gilchrist, who gained 954 yards in 1965, had been involved in a dispute with management over a friend he had brought to training camp not being given a tryout.

Taylor finished with career lows in receptions (35), yardage (448) and touchdowns (one), while Gonsoulin failed to record an interception. Gonsoulin, though, did join linebacker John Bramlett, guard Jerry Sturm, and wide receiver/punter Bob Scarpitto as selections to the AFL All-Star contest after the season ended.

The low point of the season came on Oct. 23 during a 56-10 loss to visiting Kansas City. With a huge fourth-quarter lead, Chiefs coach Hank Stram wanted to end the game without running up the score even further. So he instructed placekicker Jan Stenerud to squib a kickoff to Denver's 30-yard line so the Broncos could recover. The plan worked flawlessly except for one problem. Actually, it was a major problem because the ball bounced off the knee of a Denver player and the Chiefs recovered. Fans thought Stram was trying to score even more points, prompting a stream of debris being thrown at Chiefs players trying to leave the field.

"After the game, we walked off the field with our helmets on because they were throwing beer cans and everything at us," Chiefs defensive end Jerry Mays said. "Doak Walker, who was a scout for the Broncos, walked over to me and said, 'Jerry, I'll give you $300 for the use of your helmet for 10 minutes.'"

Someone was needed to stop the bleeding for 1967. The Phipps brothers thought they had found their man in Lou Saban, who was considered one of pro football's top coaches. Saban was the first coach of the Boston Patriots and later won back-to-back AFL championships with the Buffalo Bills (1964-65). That was enough to earn Saban a 10-year contract to serve as Broncos head coach and general manager. Saban also was given a new practice facility with a full-length field and locker rooms. The previous field the Broncos practiced on was only 60 yards long.

"I think he was very influential in helping the Broncos solidify who they were initially," said ex-Broncos defensive back Billy Thompson, who began playing under Saban in 1969. "He kind of set the organization on the path of where we are now.

"When I got here in 1969, they were reeling. The team had started in 1960 and didn't have any kind of base or direction. They were floundering a little bit. He grabbed them and said, 'OK, we're going to do it this way.' It was a bit archaic, but that's what he had. He kind of brought them some legitimacy from a head coaching standpoint, and stability, early on."

Abner Haynes was acquired from Kansas City in 1965 for linebacker Jim Fraser. Haynes was the first AFL rushing champion in 1960 for Dallas. He made his mark with Denver as a kick returner, leading the league with 901 yards in 1965.

Lou Saban brought his fiery brand of leadership to Denver in 1967. He coached Buffalo to consecutive AFL titles in 1964 and '65, then had quick success with the Broncos when they beat Detroit, 13-7, in the '67 preseason to become the first AFL team to defeat an NFL squad.

The Broncos also were about to reap the many benefits of the 1966 merger between the AFL and NFL. One of the agreements called for a single draft rather than the individual ones that were being conducted separately by the leagues. The situation often led to bidding wars for players, many of whom the Broncos failed to sign.

Denver struck gold immediately in the first AFL-NFL draft when they chose Syracuse halfback Floyd Little in the first round. Little had expected to be selected by the New York Jets because of a pre-draft understanding, something that was common in that era of football. But the common draft changed the rules—official or otherwise—and Little was required to play for the Broncos, becoming the first-ever No. 1 choice to sign with the team. Little proceeded to lead the Broncos in rushing for seven consecutive seasons, setting most of the team's rushing records in the process. As a rookie, Little also led the league in punt returns with a 16.9-yard average.

Thompson laughs when remembering the love-hate relationship Saban had with Little. "He [Little] would tell the story about when he fumbled the ball late in a game and Lou Saban fired him," Thompson said. "Lou would fire half the team about every other game. He was that kind of coach. He was very emotional. He would fire Floyd before the game even started sometimes."

The Broncos, though, had to deal with more off-field turmoil. The merger agreement required teams to play in stadiums that could seat at least 50,000 fans. Because Bears Stadium wasn't big enough, voters in Denver were asked to support a $25 million bond issue to build a new stadium. The issue was voted down in March 1967, triggering rumors that the Broncos would be moving to Birmingham, Ala.

But by this time, the Broncos had solid fan support despite still not having posted a winning record in the franchise's first seven seasons. A non-profit fan group began its own fund-raising drive, resulting in $1.8 million in donations being given to purchase Bears Stadium. Empire Sports Inc. then sold it to the group in 1968 which, in turn, donated the stadium to the city of Denver for renovations. The facility was renamed Mile High Stadium in 1968 as construction included the building of a 16,000-seat upper deck to raise the capacity to over 50,000 for the '68 season.

Even with Saban at the helm, the 1967 season was as forgettable as the previous seven. The Broncos finished with a 3-11 record. At one point, the Broncos lost nine straight games, including a brutal 51-0 thrashing at Oakland.

The only players to receive post-season honors were wide receiver Al Denson, defensive tackle Dave Costa, center Larry Kaminski and cornerback Nemiah Wilson. All four, along with Saban and his coaching staff, represented the West team at the AFL All-Star game in Jacksonville, Fla.

Denson, assuming the role of Denver's top receiver after Lionel Taylor was traded to Oakland, led the Broncos with 46 catches for 899 yards and a league-high 11 touchdowns. Bob Scarpitto led the AFL in punting for a second straight season with a 44.9-yard average, a feat made even more incredible considering he punted a team-record 105 times in just 14 games. By comparison, Broncos punter Tom Rouen punted 60 times in a 16-game schedule in 1997.

Saban also made a mistake by trading cornerback Willie Brown and quarterback Mickey Slaughter to Oakland for defensive tackle Rex Mirich and a draft choice. Brown played 12 seasons for the Raiders, earning all-league honors from 1968-73.

Bob Scarpitto (left) was a wide receiver who made his mark as a punter, leading the AFL in 1966 and '67. Cornerback Willie Brown (right) played four seasons in Denver (1963-66) before being dealt to Oakland where he continued his Hall-of-Fame career through 1978.

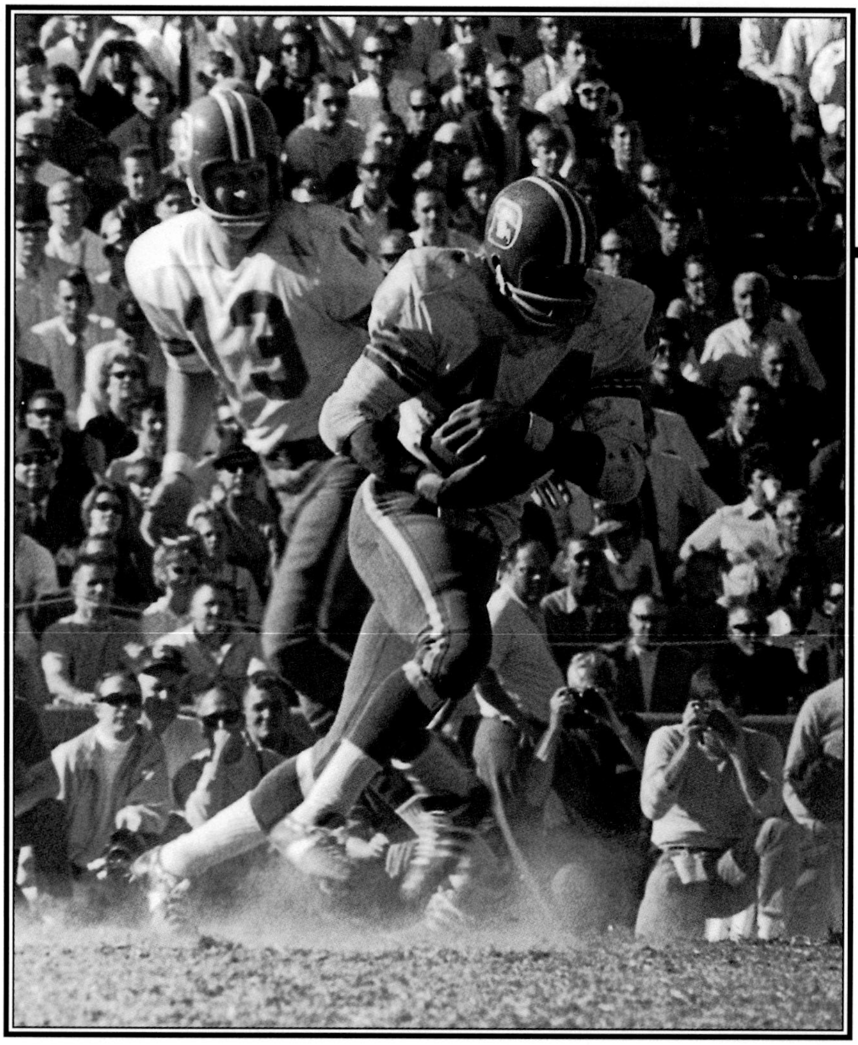

The Lou Saban era saw an influx of talent in 1967. Floyd Little (No. 44, above) was a first-round draft choice who became the Broncos' all-time leading rusher. Defensive tackle Dave Costa (above right) was acquired from Buffalo and became a three-time AFL All-Star.

He was inducted into the Pro Football Hall of Fame in 1984, an honor that no player who spent the bulk of his career in Denver has earned before or after the trade.

At least the 1967 Broncos can take pride in this—they became the first AFL team to defeat an NFL team. Before Detroit was scheduled to play Denver in the preseason, Lions defensive lineman Alex Karras said he would "walk back to Detroit" if the Broncos won. If Karras was a man of his word, he may still be walking today. Before a crowd of 21,228 at the University of Denver Stadium, the Broncos forged a 13-7 victory over the Lions on Aug. 5 in a game that saw Karras ejected for fighting.

The Broncos, though, paid a heavy price in the victory because Cookie Gilchrist's first game back in a Denver uniform became his last. Gilchrist, who had been reacquired in a trade with the Dolphins, suffered a serious knee injury and never played in Denver again.

The Broncos' 1968 season featured a little magic, as in Marlin "The Magician" Briscoe, who became the first black athlete in AFL-NFL history to garner extensive playing time at quarterback.

Defensive end Rich Jackson was acquired from Oakland in 1967. A dominating defensive force, Jackson became a two-time AFL All-Star and the first Bronco to record four sacks in a game on Oct. 19, 1969, versus the Cincinnati Bengals (right).

BENGALS
87

13

A rookie from Nebraska-Omaha, Briscoe also became the first starting quarterback in Broncos history to finish the season with more touchdown passes (14) than interceptions (13). Briscoe replaced Steve Tensi, who became the target of frustrated Broncos fans after being acquired from San Diego for first-round draft choices in 1968 and '69. Tensi had garbage regularly thrown on his lawn, his kids were harassed at school, and he frequently received obscene phone calls.

Briscoe's magic could only take the Broncos so far. Their 5-9 record included three losses to open the season and three losses to close the season.

Tensi managed to regain his role as the starter for the 1969 season, but the Broncos fared about the same as always. They opened at a respectable 4-4, but then the bottom dropped out once again. They won only one of their last six, a 27-16 victory over the Cincinnati Bengals, a second-year expansion team, in the season finale. Denver finished with a 5-8-1 record, giving the team a 39-97-4 record during the 1960s. The Broncos also became the only original AFL team not to qualify for a playoff berth during the entire 10 years of the league's existence.

Quarterback Marlin "the Magician" Briscoe brought his act to the Broncos in 1968. At 5-11, 178 pounds, he needed more than hocus-pocus to escape the likes of San Diego's 6-4, 270-pound defensive end Houston Ridge (above).

But the 1969 season can be considered a success on this account—the team landed a player whose leadership and ability would help the Broncos for years to come. Billy Thompson was a third-round draft choice from Maryland State, one of three cornerbacks selected with Denver's first four picks as the Broncos tried to shore a secondary with more leaks than the Titanic. Thompson immediately helped in that area by leading the Broncos with three interceptions in 1969.

He also became the first player in pro football history to lead the league in punt returns (11.5-yard average) and in kick-off returns (28.5). More importantly, he added enthusiasm to a Denver team that was understandably down in the dumps.

Steve Tensi battled through tense times in Denver. Acquired from San Diego in 1967 for two first-round draft choices, he was expected to lead the offense for years. But after four frustrating seasons, he retired at age 28 in 1970.

Running back Tom Smiley can't find the handle on this play in 1969. The Broncos couldn't find the handle on winning during the 1960s, finishing with a losing record nine out of 10 seasons and in the basement of the AFL West six times.

"I was always optimistic because I came from a team that won," Thompson said. "I was used to winning all my life, even in high school. It was very frustrating for me that we never won at first, but I never gave up hope. I thought if I played to my potential all the time, I could live with that. I was just hoping as time went on we could better ourselves as a team and eventually go to and win the Super Bowl."

Thompson fulfilled part of his dream eight seasons later when the Broncos finally reached the Super Bowl after the 1977 season. He also earned his championship ring, albeit not for his on-field work. Thompson, who in 1998 is the Broncos' Director of Player Relations and Alumni Coordinator, was one of the members of Denver's front office who was presented a championship ring after the franchise defeated Green Bay in Super Bowl XXXII.

Rookie Billy Thompson steals a pass from Boston's Charley Frazier in 1969. Thompson became an immediate starter at cornerback, but his main claim to fame that season was leading the AFL in both punt and kickoff returns.

Otis Armstrong became a symbol of success for the Broncos in the 1970s, breaking the 1,000-yard rushing barrier in 1974 and in 1976 (above).

No team can lose forever. The Cleveland Indians—one of the most disgraced franchises in recent sports history—turned their luck around in the 1990s and reached the World Series twice. Even the Tampa Bay Buccaneers, long known as an NFL laughingstock since the team's 1976 inception, got on the right track in 1997 and reached the playoffs for the first time in 15 years.

It was inevitable that the Broncos would eventually end their 10-year swing of losing records that began in 1960. But the franchise and its fans would still have to endure three more sub-.500 seasons before finally becoming a legitimate playoff contender.

The Broncos were continuing to gain a rabid following at the start of the decade, receiving a franchise-record 43,584 season-ticket orders (an increase of 12,000 from 1969). Much of the enthusiasm was generated by Denver joining the new American Football Conference Western Division that also included the team's three biggest rivals—Oakland, San Diego and Kansas City. But such rising popularity also raised the expectations in

Denver, which is why fans began to grow disgruntled with coach Lou Saban and his players.

Six-year veteran quarterback Steve Tensi continued to receive the most abuse. The player the Broncos traded two first-round draft picks to acquire played in just seven games during the 1970 season and retired afterward at the age of 28. His reason: "Football isn't fun anymore."

The Broncos weren't making it much fun for their fans either with yet another late-season malaise. They opened the season at 4-1, but slid to 5-7 with two games remaining. Hopes of a .500 record ended in a game against San Diego.

Chapter 3

1970–1976

Higher Altitude

Good trades, outstanding draft choices and a new coach send the Broncos closer to the top of the AFC West standings.

With the score tied, 17-17, and 11 seconds remaining, Denver quarterback Alan Pastrana ran to San Diego's 35-yard line to set up what could have been the game-winning field goal. Pastrana, though, was knocked unconscious. Being the only player authorized to call a time out, the clock expired and Denver was on its way to a 5-8-1 record.

About the only high point in the second half of the season came when Floyd Little won the first of back-to-back AFC rushing titles with 901 yards. It was also the first season in which Little stayed free of injury to play in all 14 games.

Saban tried to shake up his roster in the off-season by obtaining 12 new players via trade. But the only one who would make a lasting impact was kicker Jim Turner, who set the franchise's all-time record for scoring with 742 points during his nine years in Denver.

Already on thin ice entering the season, Saban finally sealed his fate during the 1971 regular-season opener with a decision that some say exemplified his entire legacy in Denver.

The Miami Dolphins, a team on the rise under future Hall of Fame coach Don Shula, entered Denver favored to crush the Broncos. It didn't happen. The Broncos—in particular the defense—played so well that the score was tied, 10-10, when Denver's offense received the ball deep inside its own territory with less than a minute to play.

But rather than try to score and win the game, Saban told his offense to run out the clock and settle for a tie. The record-crowd of 51,228 fans—47,500 of whom were season ticket holders—went berserk. Saban was pelted with snowballs as he left the field.

Saban attempted to justify his decision during a post-game news conference with the media: "We didn't want to throw from our own territory, especially when we had to work out of the muck," Saban said, referring to the sub-par field conditions that day at Mile High Stadium. "Half a loaf is better than none."

From that point, Denver's beleaguered coach was known as "Half a Loaf Saban." Fans were furious with Saban's reasoning. No victory—not even a 27-0 win over Cleveland midway through the season that marked the first time the Browns were held scoreless in the regular season since 1952—would appease them. Until Saban resigned with the Broncos holding a 2-6-1 record, he was booed, hung in effigy and threatened. He couldn't even leave home unless escorted by a Broncos staff member.

Saban's coaching record from 1967-72 was 20-42-3, which translated into less than "half a loaf"—a 33.1 winning percentage. He resigned as Denver's general manager after the 1971 season ended.

Offensive line coach Jerry Smith assumed the coaching reigns from Saban for the final five games of the season and did a respectable job, with Denver posting a 2-3 record. But Broncos management knew that if the fan support was going to remain high, they would need a hot head coach with a track record of winning.

The Broncos won their first game in the American Football Conference, beating the Buffalo Bills, 25-10, on Sept. 20, 1970. Above, O.J. Simpson dives over the top of Denver's goal-line defense for a score.

Enter John Ralston. Only days after leading Stanford to a victory in the Rose Bowl, Ralston was named Denver's seventh head coach. Later that off-season he became the general manager, which is where his skill in assessing talent would immediately shine through for the Broncos.

One of the biggest acquisitions Ralston made was obtaining quarterback Charley Johnson from Houston for a third-round pick. The Broncos finally had their first legitimate starting quarterback since Frank Tripucka in the team's formative years.

Ralston also sent wide receiver Dwight Harrison to Buffalo for Haven Moses, who was considered a project at the time. That "project" would develop into Denver's best receiver since Lionel Taylor. An equally productive acquisition was making University of Houston tight end Riley Odoms the team's first-round pick. Odoms proceeded to lead the Broncos in receiving four times during the 1970s.

Fans liked the moves Ralston was making. So much so that for the first time in franchise history, the Broncos did not make season tickets available to the public. In March 1972, the Broncos announced that all but 1,000 of the team's 47,500 season ticket holders would be renewing their seats. Those same fans also exercised their option for 8,000 additional seats, making a ticket to a Broncos game harder to find than an alligator in the Rocky Mountains.

Frustration showed on the face of head coach Lou Saban (left), who resigned after nine games of the 1971 season and a 2-6-1 record. Happier days were ahead for John Ralston (right), who would lead Denver to its first winning campaign in 1973.

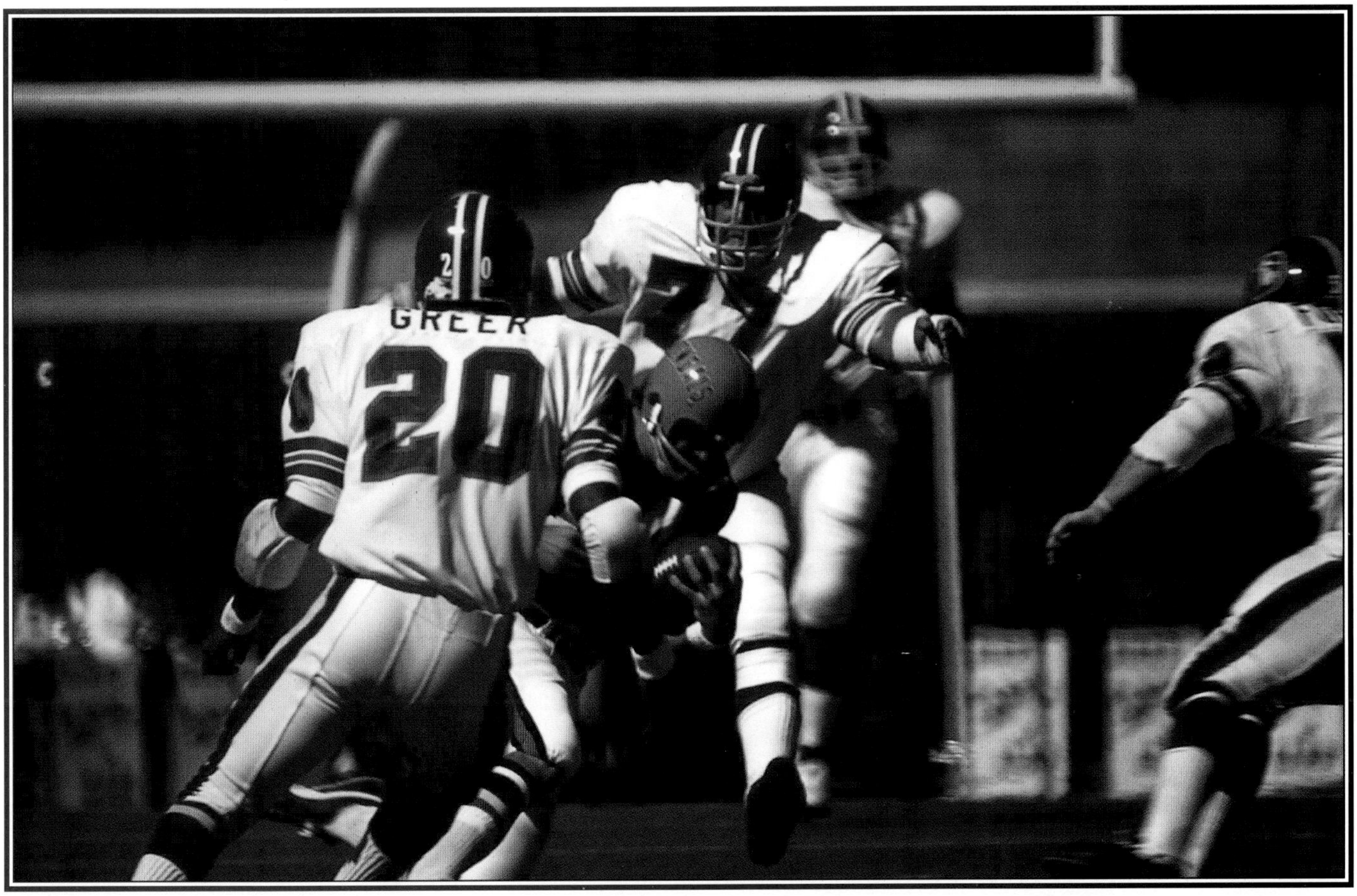

Although the 1972 Broncos finished with a 5-9 record, it was becoming obvious that Ralston was assembling a team that would be a winner soon. Charley Johnson and Steve Ramsey added stability to the quarterback position, combining to throw for 2,833 yards with 17 touchdowns and 23 interceptions—a much better touchdown-to-interception ratio for the Broncos than in previous seasons. Floyd Little, who led the NFL in rushing in 1971 with 1,133 yards, remained a serious threat in '72 with 859 yards and nine touchdowns on 216 carries. And the Broncos finished strong, with victories in their final two games for the first time in franchise history.

Defensive end Lyle Alzado (77) was a 1971 fourth-round draft choice who brought an emotional style of play to the Broncos. Alzado anchored the right side of the line through 1978 before being traded to the Cleveland Browns.

Sensing something good was coming, Broncos fans with season tickets weren't about to surrender them. In the spring of 1973, only 200 of the team's 48,000 season ticket holders decided not to renew their orders. Once again, season tickets were not made available to any new buyers through the Broncos.

Riley Odoms became one of pro football's best tight ends of the 1970s. Denver's first-round draft choice in 1972, Odoms spent his rookie season learning the ropes (left), then became a Pro Bowl selection four times in his 12-year career.

Ralston also hit pay dirt in the draft once again. Purdue running back Otis Armstrong was the Broncos' first-round selection, which was a bit surprising considering Little was still considered a top-flight starter. Armstrong, though, would eventually win the starting job from Little and post 1,000-yard rushing seasons in 1974 and '76.

Even more important for Denver's eventual success were the defensive players Ralston landed. Second-round pick

Bobby Anderson (11) breaks downfield behind guard Larron Jackson (68) and center Larry Kaminski (59) in 1972. The 6-0, 208-pound fullback from the University of Colorado was Denver's top draft choice in 1970. He joined Floyd Little in the backfield through 1973 and also returned kickoffs.

Barney Chavous would quickly become a starter at defensive end and remain with the team for 13 seasons. Louisville linebacker Tom Jackson—who earned fame in the 1990s as an NFL analyst for ESPN—was a fourth-round selection who became one of the cornerstones in Denver's "Orange Crush" defense.

Five of Ralston's 16 other draft choices—Brigham Young guard Paul Howard (third round), Notre Dame linebacker Jim O'Malley (12th), Washington cornerback Calvin Jones (15th), and defensive tackles John Grant of Southern Cal (seventh) and Ed Smith of Colorado (13th)—would become starters within their first two years in the NFL.

Broncos safety Billy Thompson, who spent his entire NFL career in Denver from 1969-81, believes such acquisitions were the keys to the team's turnaround. Thompson, though, also said that continuity helped contribute to Denver's success. Keeping a team together for several seasons is something that is almost impossible to accomplish in the 1990s era of free agency, where players hop-scotch from team to team on a yearly basis.

"It was definitely the talent, but it was also a different time," Thompson said. "We had time to mold a team. Now, you can buy a team. Back in those days, you drafted a player and we were able to bond into a competitive team. It's just a little

bit different today. It's almost like chasing a dollar today. Loyalties are very slim. The loyalty is to the money."

The 1973 Broncos were different from any other team in franchise history, as they started the season slowly but finished strong. As a result, Denver finally had a winning football team.

After a 1-3 start, the Broncos would finish the year with a 6-2-2 streak. The turnaround began in the fifth game with a 48-20 victory at Houston. During that contest, Charley Johnson—returning to the city where he had played in 1970 and '71—became the 18th quarterback in NFL history to pass for more than 20,000 career yards. Johnson riddled the Oilers for 214 passing yards and threw three touchdown passes to wide receiver Haven Moses.

Haven Moses catches a second-quarter pass from Charley Johnson against Kansas City at Mile High Stadium on Nov. 25, 1973. Denver's 14-10 victory was the sixth of its first-ever winning season.

Charley Johnson throws over the top of Detroit's pass rush on Nov. 28, 1974. It was the first appearance for the Broncos in the annual Thanksgiving Day game. Denver won, 31-27.

Then came what was arguably the biggest game in franchise history, one that would be played on a night dubbed by fans and media as "Orange Monday." In their first appearance on "Monday Night Football," the Broncos rallied for a 23-23 tie against Oakland. A 35-yard field goal by Jim Turner with four seconds remaining helped Denver avoid what would have been a devastating loss. Fans who weren't thrilled with Saban's attitude toward tie games were pleased by Ralston's take on the finish. "Well," he said, "It's better to be the tie-or than the tie-ee."

Riding high on the momentum from that game, Denver would win four of its next five and forge a 17-17 tie at St. Louis in the other. On Dec. 9, the Broncos ensured a winning season with a 42-28 victory at San Diego.

But by this point, the Broncos no longer cared about finishing above .500. There were bigger goals in mind. The playoffs would become a reality if the Broncos could travel to Oakland and beat the dreaded Raiders in the season finale.

What happened was one of the most heartbreaking losses in franchise history. The Broncos were trailing, 14-10, in the third quarter and facing a fourth-and-10 from their own 49-yard line. Ralston, known as a gambling coach, decided to call a fake punt. The Broncos, though, tipped their hand so badly that the Raiders were waiting for the play. Joe Dawkins—who was the blocking back on the punt—bobbled a direct snap and was buried for a 1-yard loss. The Raiders scored three plays later and Denver was unable to get into the end zone again until the final minutes of the fourth quarter. Final score: Oakland 21, Denver 17.

Despite the loss, Denver's first winning season (7-5-2) was well rewarded. Ralston was voted AFC Coach of the Year. Four Broncos—Floyd Little, Haven Moses, Riley Odoms and defensive tackle Paul Smith—were selected for the Pro Bowl.

Rookie linebacker Randy Gradishar (above) and second-year defensive end John Grant (left) were two of the young standouts in the Broncos' improving defense in 1974.

Expectations were never higher entering the 1974 season, especially after another nice series of off-season acquisitions by Ralston. He obtained fullback Jon Keyworth from the Washington Redskins for sixth- and 11th-round picks. First-round pick Randy Gradishar would not only reach the Pro Bowl seven times in a 10-year career, but he proved to be Denver's "Iron Man" by never missing one of his 145 career starts. Third-round pick Claudie Minor would also start at either left or right tackle for the next nine seasons.

Ralston wasn't shy about how well he thought Denver would fare in 1974. On Ralston's desk and mirror were signs reading, "Finish 12-2, go to and win the Super Bowl." Fans bought into Ralston's optimism, especially after a 4-2 record during the

Pittsburgh's Mean Joe Greene slams into Charley Johnson on Sept. 22, 1974, in the third quarter of the first regular-season overtime game in NFL history. Johnson's shoulder was injured on the play. Neither team could score in the sudden-death period, resulting in a 35-35 tie at Mile High Stadium.

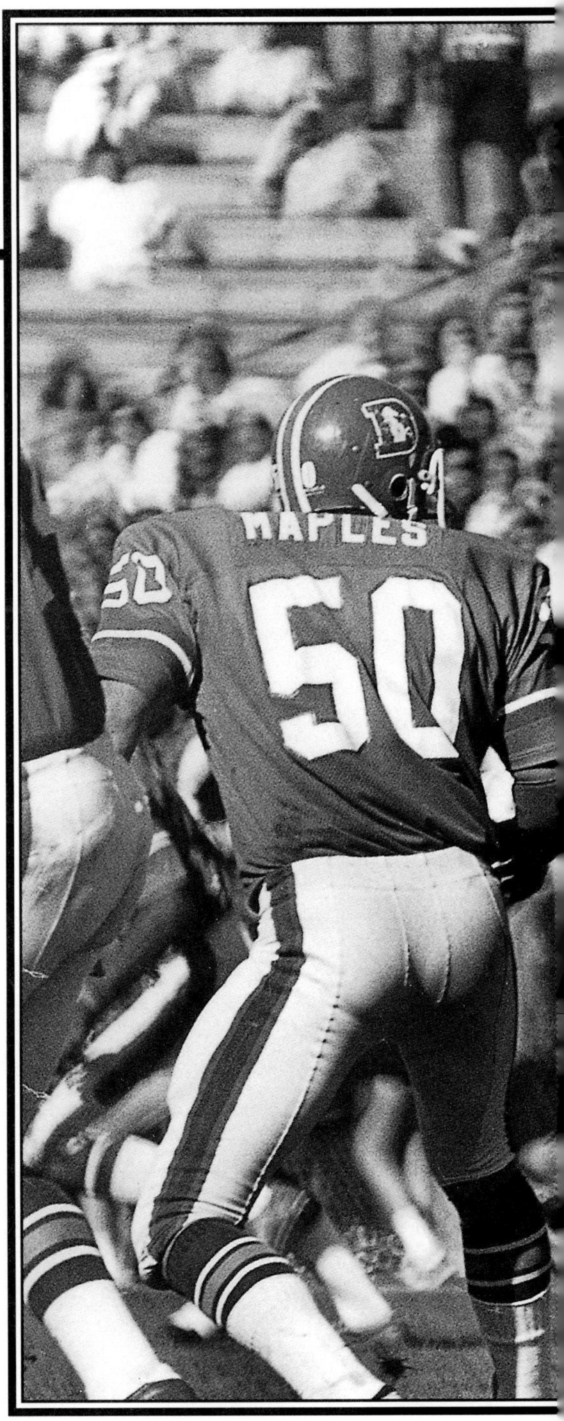

exhibition season. So it was no surprise when a $25 million bond issue was approved by Denver voters just before the start of the regular season. Mile High Stadium would expand from 50,000 to 75,000 seats, which was good news for the 25,000 fans on the team's waiting list for season tickets.

Ralston's optimism, however, would only take the Broncos so far. In fact, many of the players were growing wary of Ralston's hands-off coaching style. The team finished with a 7-6-1 record, swell compared to the past, but not reflective of the team's talent.

Otis Armstrong replaced Floyd Little as Denver's featured running back and set franchise records for yards in a game (183 against Houston on Dec. 8) and season (1,407). At the time, Armstrong was one of only six players in pro football history to average more than 100 yards a game for an entire season. Charley Johnson enjoyed his best season in Denver with 1,969 passing yards and 13 touchdowns, while tight end Riley Odoms earned his second Pro Bowl berth by leading the Broncos with 42 receptions for 639 yards and six touchdowns.

Being the team that scored the first points in AFL history and the first AFL team to defeat an NFL team, it was no surprise when the 1974 Broncos made football history once again. This time, the Broncos played in the NFL's first overtime regular-season game. The result was a 35-35 tie against Pittsburgh.

Despite the grumblings of his players, Ralston continued to assemble quality talent through the draft. In 1975, Denver landed cornerback Louis Wright, wide

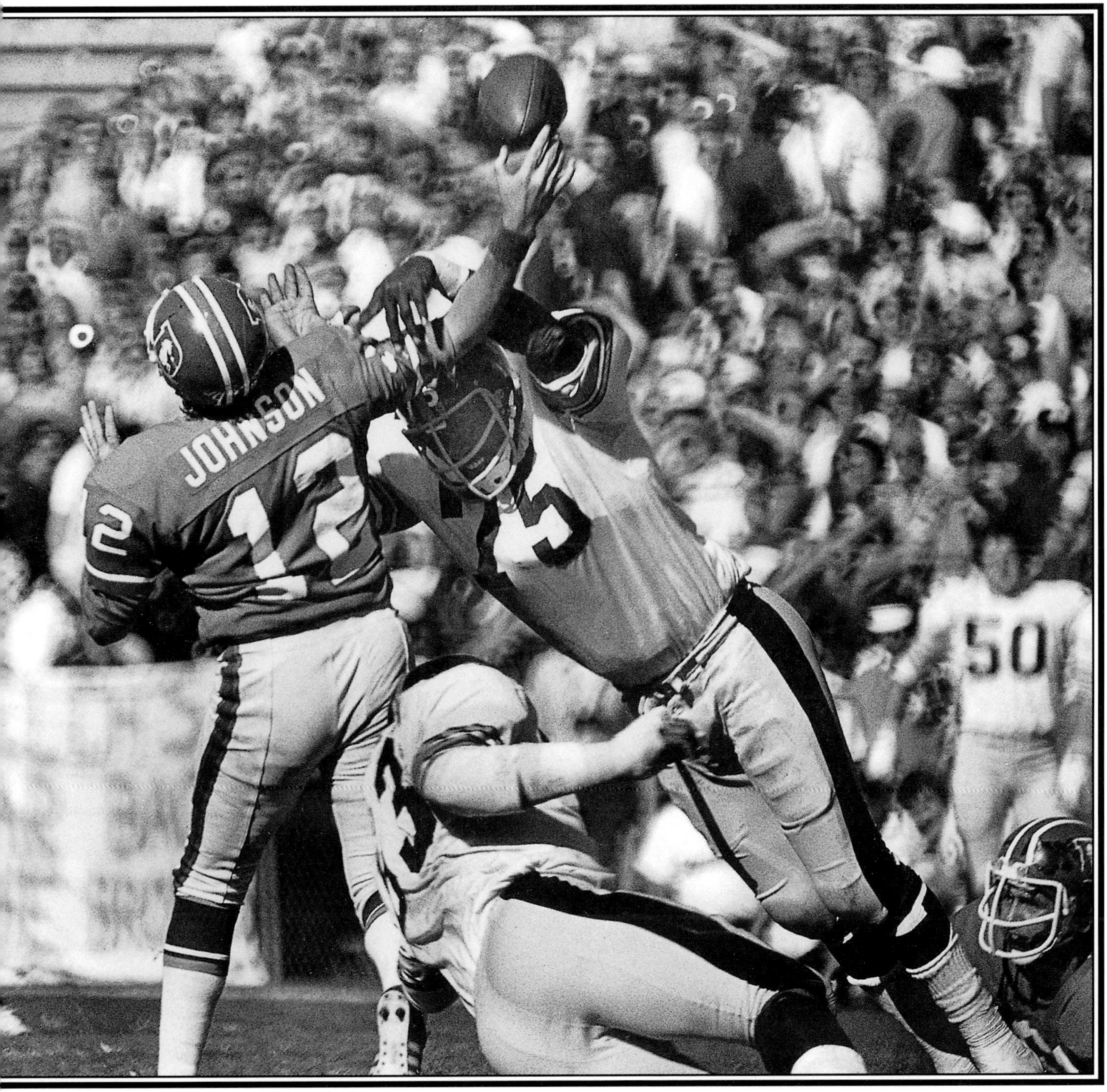

receiver Rick Upchurch, defensive tackle Rubin Carter and cornerback Steve Foley. All would play key roles in Denver's drive to Super Bowl XII three seasons later.

But despite his prowess as an assessor of talent, Ralston's troops continued to underachieve on the field. With Armstrong injured for much of the season, the Broncos took a step back in 1975 with a 6-8 finish. The only real highlight came in the home season finale against Philadelphia when Floyd Little tallied 150 total yards and two touchdowns in the final home game of his nine-year career.

Quarterback Charley Johnson also retired after the 1975 season, having grown disgusted with Ralston's Dale Carnegie style of coaching. Several small groups of players approached Broncos owner Gerald Phipps about their dissatisfaction with

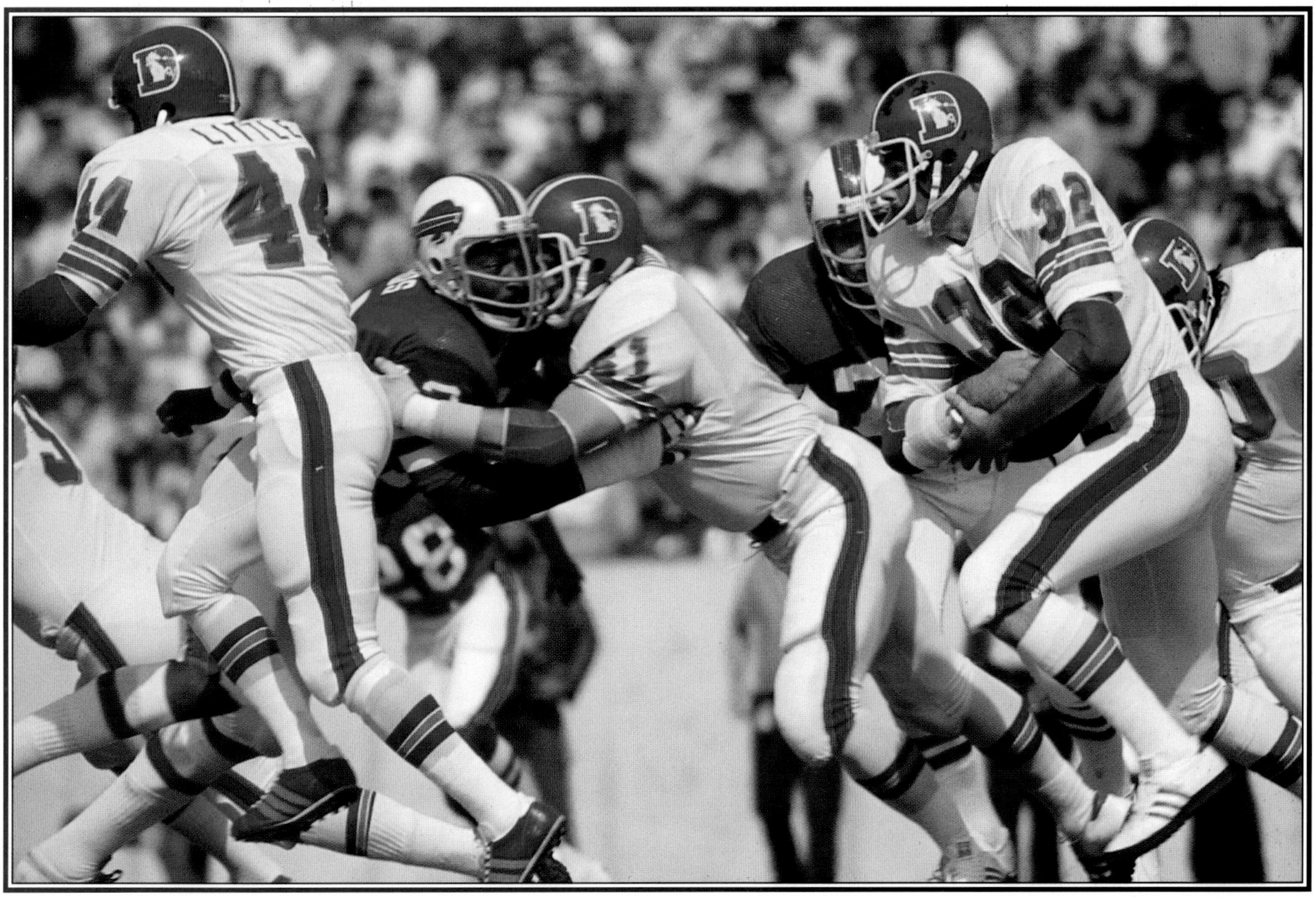

Ralston. But Phipps, who signed Ralston to a five-year contract extension at the end of the 1974 season, gave his coach a vote of confidence.

Ralston, though, probably caused his own unraveling before the 1976 season even began. First, he asked some of his players during the off-season to meet with him and voice their complaints. The move backfired as players became upset if Ralston did not fix what was requested. He also made the mistake of bad-mouthing quarterback Steve Ramsey. Ralston had told players that he planned to trade for New England quarterback Jim Plunkett, who would later lead the Oakland Raiders to victory in Super Bowl XV. But the deal fell through, leaving Ralston with a starting quarterback that he personally had ripped. When Ralston tried to pitch Ramsey as a quality quarterback at the start of training camp, players lost even more confidence.

Jon Keyworth (right) became a starter in the backfield in 1974. The 6-3, 230-pound fullback from the University of Colorado carried the load in 1975 (above) after an injury to Otis Armstrong. Keyworth led the Broncos in rushing with 725 yards.

Ralston then lost any support he had left after an Oct. 10 contest at Houston. The day before the game, offensive coordinator Max Coley became hospitalized with stomach problems. That required Ralston to run the offense and review the game plan, both of which he knew very little about. The Broncos lost, 17-3, and a revolt was quickly brewing.

Veteran backup quarterback Steve Ramsey replaced the retired Charley Johnson in 1976. Ramsey completed 128 of 270 passing attempts with 11 touchdowns for the 9-5 Broncos. He was traded to the Giants in 1977 for Craig Morton.

There was no question that the Broncos were among the AFC's most talented teams, especially when playing at a Mile

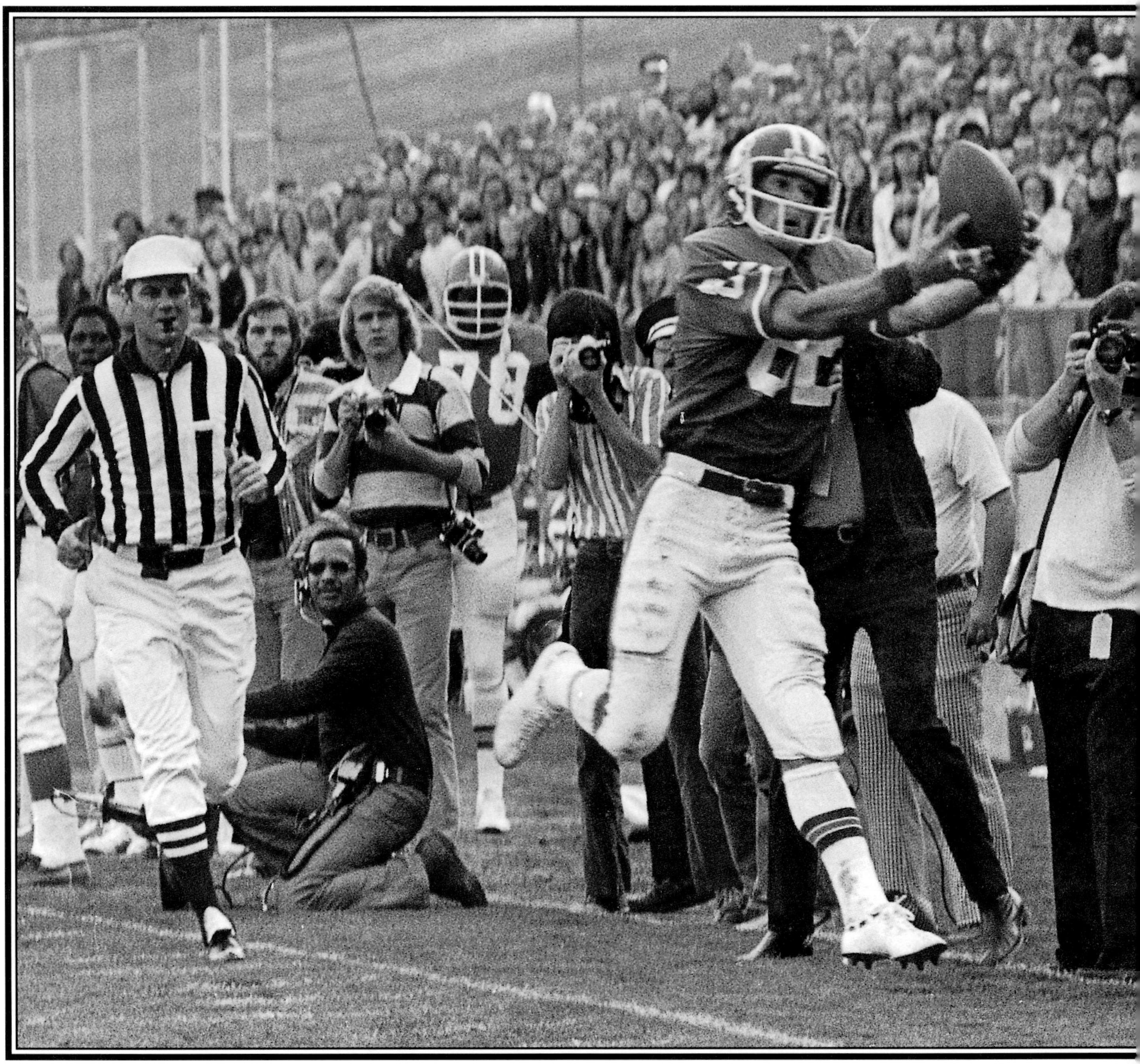

High Stadium that was expanded to 63,500 seats. The defense was the stingiest in team history, allowing more than 17 points in a game just three times.

Rick Upchurch emerged as a dangerous punt returner, tying the NFL's single-season record with four touchdowns. He also tied a league record with two returns for scores in a 44-13 victory over visiting Cleveland. Kicker Jim Turner was a special teams threat as well, becoming only the fifth player in NFL history to surpass 1,200 points. And Otis Armstrong finished the season with 1,008 rushing yards.

A 17-16 victory over Kansas City on Dec. 5 gave the Broncos a franchise-record eight victories. Denver also ended the season on a high note with a 28-14 win at Chicago. But once again, a post-season berth eluded the Broncos. Oakland won the AFC West with a 13-1 record, while New England claimed the conference's lone wild-card berth with an 11-3 mark.

Although unsettled at quarterback, the Broncos assembled one of pro football's best sets of game-breaking clutch receivers by 1976. It included Riley Odoms, Haven Moses, Rick Upchurch and Jack Dolbin (left). Dolbin averaged nearly 15 catches a season during his first four years in Denver.

Armstrong seemed to reflect the feelings of every Broncos player when he said, "That record doesn't mean a thing. The *worst* we could have done with that schedule was 9-5."

Something needed to change and Lyle Alzado was not afraid to say so. Emerging as one of the league's best defensive ends after being drafted in 1971, Alzado missed most of the '76 season with a knee injury. He grew so disgusted watching the Houston defeat that he slammed a crutch through his television.

Twelve players—Alzado, Armstrong, John Grant, Tom Jackson, Jon Keyworth, Jim Kiick, Tommy Lyons, Haven Moses, Carl Schaukowitch, Billy Thompson, Rick Upchurch and Billy van Heusen—met in late December to discuss a plan of action, according to *Orange Madness*, a book detailing Denver's Super Bowl season of 1977. What emerged was a petition to oust Ralston that was signed by 32 of the 43 players on the roster. The plot was then leaked to the media in hopes of putting more pressure on Ralston to resign.

Ralston held onto his head coaching position for five more weeks until Phipps and new general manager Fred Gehrke decided a change was needed. Ralston was out and ex-Broncos assistant Red Miller was hired as the new head coach. Although Ralston was vilified by his players, there is no denying that it was his acquisitions that helped Denver become one of the best teams of the late 1970s.

"I won't criticize anybody about what happened," Ralston said in *Orange Madness*. "I don't think in negatives. We made some real progress here. This town accepted losers when I came. Not anymore."

With his leadership, personality and coaching abilities, Red Miller took the Broncos to Super Bowl XII.

There is an old adage in football that a team's personality is usually a reflection of its head coach. If that is true, the Broncos made the right decision by hiring Robert "Red" Miller for the position on February 1, 1977. Under Miller, the '77 Broncos developed the personality of a champion, winning their first-ever AFC title before falling to Dallas in Super Bowl XII.

The son of a coal miner, Red was one of 10 children in the Miller household. The family struggled financially to the point that he sometimes left the dinner table hungry as a child. He also missed an entire year of elementary school with double pneumonia.

But determined to escape a fate of working in the coal mines, Miller turned his entire focus to sports. He earned a scholarship to Western Illinois, where his determination helped him move from 16th on the depth chart at guard to a starter in his first season. Miller was selected three times as his team's Most Valuable Player, a remarkable accomplishment considering he was an interior lineman.

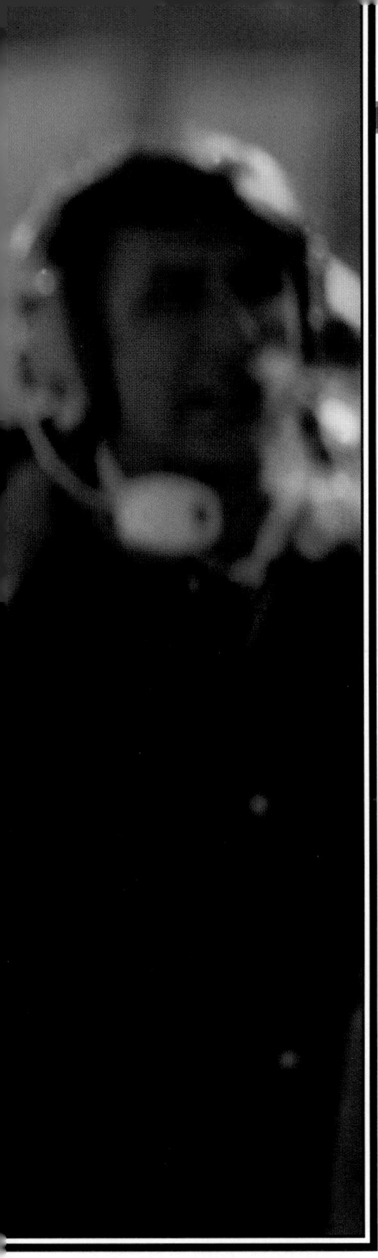

Miller then turned to coaching and landed a job in the American Football League with Lou Saban at Buffalo in 1962. Miller next moved on to Denver where he was the Broncos' offensive line coach from 1963-65.

When Miller departed, he thought he would not return to coach the Broncos again. He continued to bounce from job to job in the NFL as most assistants are forced to do in the 1990s. Then Miller's big break came when he was hired by former University of Colorado head coach Chuck Fairbanks to join the staff of the New England Patriots in 1973.

Chapter 4

1977–1980

Red and Orange

With Miller, Morton and a crushing defense, the Broncos make miracles happen all the way to Super Bowl XII.

Miller became New England's offensive coordinator and helped turn the Patriots into a powerhouse. Although the Patriots didn't post a winning record in their first three seasons under Fairbanks, New England turned the corner in 1976 with an 11-3 record and the second-highest point total (376) in the NFL. The Patriots not only defeated Denver that season, but also claimed the AFC's lone wild-card berth.

That meant the Broncos were shut out of the post-season for the 17th consecutive season since the franchise's inception. Shortly thereafter was the meeting of the Dirty Dozen—the 12 players who met to plot the ouster of John Ralston as head coach.

Miller thought he would never have a chance to become an NFL head coach. He was approached about becoming Denver's offensive coordinator after the 1976 season, but was happy in New England.

"I knew Red from way back," Broncos general manager Fred Gehrke said. "We all lived in Broomfield [a city located northwest of Denver] when he had coached here, along with Mac Speedie and Ray Malavasi.

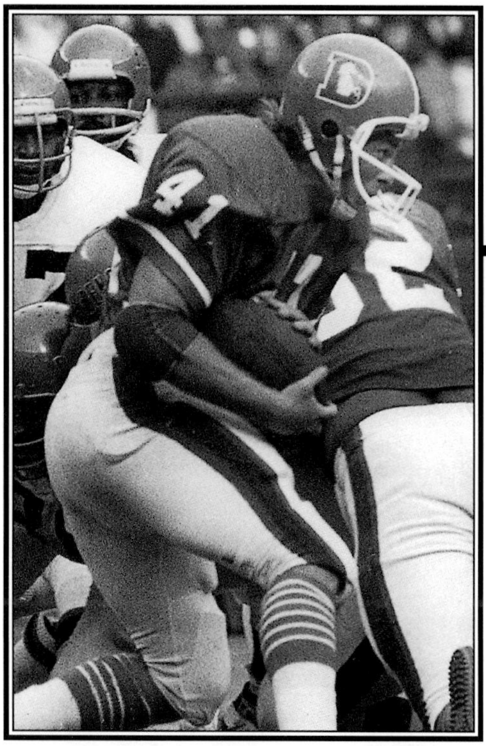

Rob Lytle assembled the Broncos' 1977 rookie talent show that received an unexpected performance from rookie coach Red Miller.

"I knew of his coaching ability and what a strict coach and good manager of the team he was. I went after him when I decided that John Ralston was not doing the job. I was trying to help out by bringing Red in as offensive coordinator to help John, but he wouldn't come. He said the only way he would come is if it was as head coach. So I told Gerry [Phipps, the Broncos' owner] that we've got to do something because we'll have another players strike if we don't.

"We had to let John go and get Red. [He] was in control of players and they appreciated that and looked up to him, whereas John was a very nice guy who just wasn't tough enough with these guys.

"That's all we needed was a guy like Red to come in and take control of those people," Gehrke added. "The players were already tight knit and together. It was just that John, during a game particularly, didn't have control of the team. They lost confidence in John. Red turned out to be great and had the material there as players, that's for sure. That helps a lot."

But while Miller knew he was inheriting a talented yet underachieving team, he had to earn the trust of a cynical group of players. Miller set the tempo immediately by calling the Broncos together for a mini-camp. It was there he began setting new team rules, including one that had bugged him from the onset. Players were known for bringing soda into team meetings. Under Miller, that would stop. He also called each player into his office for an individual meeting telling them what he expected if they were to remain a Bronco.

Miller and Gehrke, though, knew that even discipline on a quality team wouldn't necessarily help the Broncos win the Super Bowl. As Cincinnati Bengals president/general manager Mike Brown has said, the biggest key to fielding a winning team is having a quality quarterback. So Miller and Gehrke put their heads together trying to figure out which direction the Broncos should turn.

Enter Craig Morton. A collegiate superstar at the University of California, Morton appeared headed for fame as the successor to Don Meredith as quarterback of the Dallas Cowboys. Morton, though, was eventually beaten out by future Hall of Famer Roger Staubach and traded to the New York Giants in 1974 after nine and a half seasons in Dallas. Morton didn't have nearly as much success in New York and found himself heavily booed by Giants fans during the 1976 season.

The Giants and Morton were looking for a new direction just as badly as Denver and quarterback Steve Ramsey. So shortly after Miller was named head coach, the Broncos sent Ramsey—the player Ralston bad-mouthed and was trying to trade before the 1976 season—and a fifth-round pick in 1978 to New York for Morton.

"Craig Morton was all we needed," Gehrke said. "I think he made a great impact. He was a leader and he could throw the ball. Players had confidence in him. He was good at playing injured. Sometimes, he held onto the ball too long before he got rid of it and he went down a lot. In fact, when we went to the Super Bowl, he was black

and blue from his neck to his ankles. But he was a tough guy and a great guy. The trade was just a deal we got going. I think he wanted to leave New York and come back nearer to his home, which was on the West Coast."

Miller and Gehrke weren't done wheeling and dealing after acquiring Morton. Bernard Jackson was obtained from Cincinnati for two draft picks and immediately became the starting safety opposite Billy Thompson. Center Mike Montler (Buffalo) and offensive tackle Andy Maurer (San Francisco) were two other acquisitions who earned starting spots in their first season in Denver. The Broncos also sent a mid-round draft pick to Dallas for fullback Jim Jensen, who became a starter in 1979.

All Miller needed now was the respect of his players. He earned it during one Saturday night in training camp—albeit it in an unusual fashion. Miller assigned running back Rob Lytle to assemble the annual "Rookie Talent Show," where Denver's first-year players are forced to perform in front of their teammates as a rite of passage. In most cases, rookies were required to sing their college alma mater or the equivalent to appease the veterans.

Before leaving to begin organizing the event, Lytle asked Miller if he should also participate in the show because he was their rookie head coach. Rather than scoff at the offer, Miller told Lytle to find a piano. "Ragtime Red" proceeded to pound out tunes on the piano as his players laughed and clapped along. It showed the Broncos that while Miller was a strict disciplinarian, he also could be their friend. And on that 1977 team, no player wanted to take advantage of that special relationship.

"Chemistry was the key," said Miller in *Orange Madness*. "That was it. I tried to create an atmosphere to be a team. It was all about team. My style was being [a player's coach]. I coached 33 years of football, 23 years in the pros, and I used it all the way through. There was a lot of background going into that."

Miller, who was known earlier in his career for hoisting a few beers with his players after practice, cemented a positive player-coach relationship one day in practice when he was demonstrating a pass-blocking technique to tackle Claudie Minor. A

Red Miller leads his Broncos across the Riverfront Stadium turf on Oct. 23, 1977, before a game against Cincinnati. Denver won, 24-13, for its sixth straight win to open the season.

cut opened above Miller's eye after he was inadvertently belted by Minor. The coach's response: "No problem."

Here's how Broncos wide receiver/kick returner Rick Upchurch described Miller: "First of all, Red was personable in that he would sit down and talk with you. He would shoot straight from the hip to let you know exactly how he felt about you and your situation. That's one thing we really respected about him. He would not ask any more of you than he would ask of himself. He was a hard-working person and he would expect the same from you.

"He would tell us about his [amateur] wrestling days at Western Illinois and how he was a leatherneck playing football. He just seemed like a real hard-nosed, tough guy. You could go into an alley with that guy watching your back and you would come out in pretty good shape.

"It was 180 degrees different than before, because John Ralston was more of a Dale Carnegie type guy. He could talk his way into getting you to believe you could do things. But with Red, he would go out and demonstrate it. He would wrestle with players and do all those things a tough guy would do to back it up."

Craig Morton was a missing piece for Denver's puzzled offense. Acquired from the Giants for Steve Ramsey and a draft choice, the 13-year-veteran quarterback was named AFC Player of the Year after the Broncos' first-ever Super Bowl appearance.

The players respected other coaches on Miller's staff as well. Defensive coordinator Joe Collier, a former Buffalo Bills head coach (1966-68), was so quiet that some believed his demeanor better suited him to be a college professor than an NFL coach. But nobody questioned Collier's knowledge of the game.

Miller made the wise move of keeping Collier—a coach in Denver since 1969—as his defensive coordinator after Ralston was fired. Safety Billy Thompson said Collier's schemes probably helped Denver reach Super Bowl XII about as much as Miller being named head coach.

"The one coach who was a constant throughout all of that was Joe Collier, who deserves a mountain's share of the credit," said Thompson, who entered the NFL in the same year Collier began coaching in Denver. "He was the guy, I think, that was very instrumental in the team developing like it did. When you're good, you're confident. We were very confident in what we could do. Everybody knew the scheme.

"Joe was probably the best coach I've been around who could use the people he had in a way that was just incredible. He was a mastermind at taking the talent he had and putting it into position to win."

Finally, the Broncos were in a position to win. That became evident when Denver steamrolled to a 5-1 preseason record. Denver's defense allowed a total of only 27 points in the team's five victories, with the only sub-par performance coming in a 28-24 loss at Philadelphia.

The biggest question mark was—as usual—Denver's offense. Most on the team felt that if Morton and Co. could produce just a respectable number of points, the Broncos would at least reach the playoffs. Odds-makers in Las Vegas had installed Denver as a 20-to-1 long shot to reach the Super Bowl, and most preseason predictions called for the Broncos to finish with an 8-6 record.

That's why Denver's season-opening game against St. Louis would be regarded as the harbinger for the year to come. The Cardinals were coached by Don Coryell, whose teams were known for their high-powered offense. In the 1980s, Coryell would establish his coaching legacy by fielding a San Diego Chargers squad with future Hall-of-Fame selections Dan Fouts, Kellen Winslow and Charlie Joiner. But on a 70-degree September afternoon in Denver, Coryell found himself helpless against the Broncos' defense. With the team's stadium expansion complete, a record 75,002 fans poured into Mile High Stadium to watch the Broncos shut out the Cardinals, 7-0.

Uncertainties abounded in the 1977 Broncos offense that ranked 17th in the NFL. Otis Armstrong (above) followed his 1,008-yard 1976 season with just 489 in '77 as Rob Lytle saw increased playing time.

In the first quarter, linebacker Randy Gradishar—who had predicted that the Cardinals would not score—made the tackle that stopped St. Louis on fourth-and-one from the Denver 4-yard line. Late in the game, St. Louis was stuffed again after reaching Denver's 7-yard line. Otis Armstrong rushed for Denver's only touchdown, which was all the Broncos needed to win.

"That set the tone for the whole year," said Thompson, who registered a team-high five interceptions in 1977 en route to a Pro Bowl berth. "We [the defense] just said, 'We don't care what the offense does. We're going to play like there was no tomorrow for every game.' It bonded us as a team."

Pretty soon, the rest of the NFL would begin to receive a taste of Orange Crush—the nickname given the Broncos' dominating defense. Denver allowed a total of only 26 points in its next three victories over Buffalo, Seattle and Kansas City. The Broncos were 4-0 for the first time in franchise history.

Skeptics, though, felt that streak would end at the hands of the Oakland Raiders, who had won Super Bowl XI the previous season. Since the 23-23 tie on "Monday Night Football" in 1973, the Raiders had beaten the Broncos in six of the last seven regular-season meetings.

But Oakland's recent dominance ended in a fashion nobody could have envisioned. After falling behind 7-0 on the Raiders' first possession, the Broncos scored 30 unanswered points in a 30-7 win at the Oakland Coliseum. Quarterback Kenny Stabler was intercepted seven times and the Broncos scored on a fake field goal, exorcising the ghosts of the blown fake punt that probably cost Denver a victory in 1973.

"We had always believed in ourselves, which is why I believe we won six straight games," Rick Upchurch said. "We knew the type of team we had. Some people would say we did not have a good offense, but we had Morton and Riley [Odoms] and Haven Moses and Otis Armstrong. When you have those guys, you're able to move the ball and not put our defense in a bad situation.

"It's hard to describe that team and what it was like. We were just a team that felt we could go out and do anything."

At this point, Broncomania was just about to shift into fifth gear. When the team flight landed at Stapleton Airport after the Raiders game, approximately 10,000 fans were waiting to greet the team. Another type of "Orange Crush" occurred when several fans were sent sprawling down an elevator in the midst of a frenzy that ensued when the team stepped off the plane.

Sadly, it was not the first time that Broncos fans had taken their love of the team too far during that era. After a 33-14 Broncos loss to Chicago in 1973, a fan committed suicide because he was so dismayed that Denver fumbled five times. The suicide note said, "I have been a Broncos fan since the Broncos were first organized and I can't stand their fumbling no more."

Tight end Riley Odoms bolts over two Houston defenders for a second-quarter touchdown in the Astrodome on Dec. 4, 1977. The 24-14 victory was the Broncos' 11th of the season, clinching the first playoff berth in franchise history. They beat San Diego one week later to win the division crown.

At one Denver-area bar, a patron named Rick Savage wanted to dance with his girlfriend. But he played the jukebox during a Denver-Baltimore game—a faux pas that cost him his life. Savage was shot and killed in an alley behind the bar while his girlfriend was injured. At first, the gunman expressed no regrets for his action.

By and large, though, most Broncos fans worshipped their team in a non-violent way. Among the goofier stories about Broncomania in 1977:

• One prisoner asked that his jail transfer be delayed because the Broncos were playing that day on television.

• Newborn babies were wrapped in orange swaddling blankets.

• A local manicurist painted orange football helmets on her clients' fingernails.

• Police officers would carry AM radios to listen to Broncos games while on patrol. After all, there was almost no crime to worry about when the Broncos were playing. More than 88 percent of the televisions in Denver were tuned in for every Broncos game, giving the team the most rabid following in the nation. A shopping center was even forced to close its doors on Sunday due to a lack of clientele.

As one Detroit newspaper columnist wrote after the Raiders game, "The townspeople [display] a permanent extended finger to the rest of Pro Football America. It's not the finger folks customarily use for such gestures, but rather the index finger. Number One."

The Broncos, though, had more work to finish before claiming that honor. The Raiders avenged the loss to Denver two weeks later with a 24-14 victory at Mile High Stadium. The Broncos' hopes of a perfect season had ended after a 6-0 start, but Denver didn't fade like in the past.

Denver proceeded to rip off another six-game winning streak en route to finishing the season 12-2 and claiming their first AFC West title. In that string, the Broncos defeated the Baltimore Colts, 27-13, in a game pitting the teams with the NFL's

Otis Armstrong scores on a 10-yard run to put the Broncos ahead in the second quarter of the 1977 AFC Divisional playoff game against Pittsburgh at Mile High Stadium. The Broncos defeated the Steelers, 34-21.

two best records. A 24-14 victory against the Houston Oilers on Dec. 4 ensured the Broncos would reach the playoffs for the first time in franchise history. Denver also ended the regular season with the AFC's best record, earning the Broncos home-field advantage throughout the playoffs.

For their first playoff game, the Broncos and their fans were treated to an early Christmas present. On Dec. 24, Denver defeated Pittsburgh, 34-21, before the largest crowd (75,011 fans) ever to watch a sporting event in Colorado. The game was tied at 21-21 in the fourth quarter until a 44-yard field goal by Jim Turner put the Broncos ahead for good.

Denver linebacker Tom Jackson intercepted Steelers quarterback Terry Bradshaw twice, the latter of which set up a 34-yard touchdown pass from Craig Morton to wide receiver Jack Dolbin in the final two minutes.

Riley Odoms outruns two Pittsburgh defenders to pay dirt for a third-quarter Denver touchdown in the 1977 AFC Divisional playoff game. The 30-yard pass from Craig Morton gave the Broncos a 21-14 lead.

Defeating the Steelers moved the Broncos within one game of reaching Super Bowl XII. But in Denver's way was its biggest rival—the Oakland Raiders. The Broncos not only had to avenge an earlier loss to the Raiders at Mile High Stadium but prove they could come through when the chips were down.

Before the AFC Championship game even began, Rick Upchurch had a good feeling about Denver's chances. "The first thing I remember is that it was cold as heck," said Upchurch, referring to the 18-degree temperature at kickoff. "When we were standing for the national anthem, our fans had these posters they were holding up. When it was over, the fans turned the posters over and the whole place just turned orange. When I saw that, I thought, 'Boy, these guys are in for it today.'

"The atmosphere when you're playing the defending world champions is do or die. When we stepped out on that field, we believed we could win that game and we

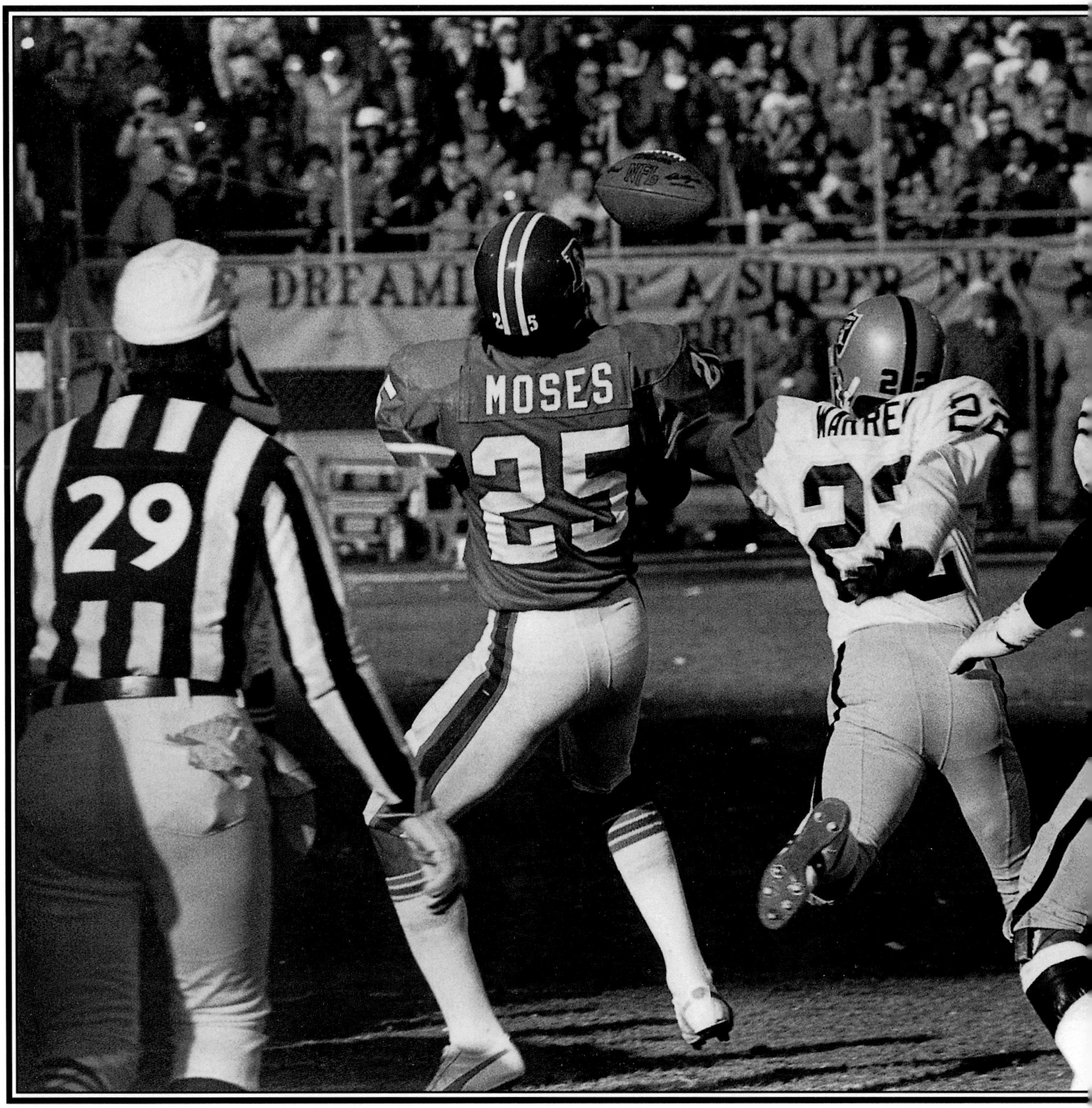

did. Our offense kept the ball out of [quarterback Kenny] Stabler's hands and we played a total game on offense and special teams. It was just overwhelming."

The Broncos took a 7-3 lead on their first series when Morton connected with Haven Moses on a 74-yard touchdown pass.

Denver then capitalized on two Oakland turnovers. A fumble recovery by defensive end Brison Manor led to fullback Jon Keyworth scoring on a 1-yard run. With the Broncos holding a 14-10 lead, linebacker Bob Swenson intercepted a Stabler pass and returned it to the Oakland 14-yard line. Morton then connected again with Moses for a 12-yard touchdown pass, giving the Broncos a 10-point lead midway

Haven Moses steps past Jimmy Warren to catch a 74-yard first-quarter touchdown pass from Craig Morton in the 1977 AFC Championship game at Mile High Stadium. Moses also caught a 12-yard TD pass in the fourth quarter of the 20-17 Broncos victory.

through the fourth quarter. Moses, playing in his 10th pro season, grabbed five passes against the Raiders for 168 yards.

The Raiders closed the score to 20-17, but the Broncos then controlled the ball for the final 3:08 to earn a trip to New Orleans to battle the Dallas Cowboys in Super Bowl XII.

Pandemonium gripped the city after the victory. Fans flooded onto the Mile High Stadium turf and began swinging on goalposts and dancing in celebration.

"I was driving home that night on the highway and people were honking at me," Billy Thompson said in *Orange Madness*. "They just saw me and knew me. Everybody in the neighborhood was cheering. When I came home, there was an orange stripe painted all the way up the street and all the way to my house."

As expected, tickets for the Super Bowl were in such great demand that the Broncos probably could have filled a million-seat stadium. But the team only had about 9,000 tickets to allocate among its 73,000 season-ticket holders. Demand for seats in Dallas was just as high, with fans who couldn't score Super Bowl tickets rioting when told the Cowboys' allotment was sold out.

Even when Denver fans knew tickets were unavailable, they traveled to New Orleans anyway—some still searching for a way to see the game, others simply to partake in the festivities. The city's entire allotment of hotel rooms was sold out as additional flights to New Orleans were added from Denver to accommodate the demand for airplane tickets. About 150,000 fans lined the streets of downtown Den-

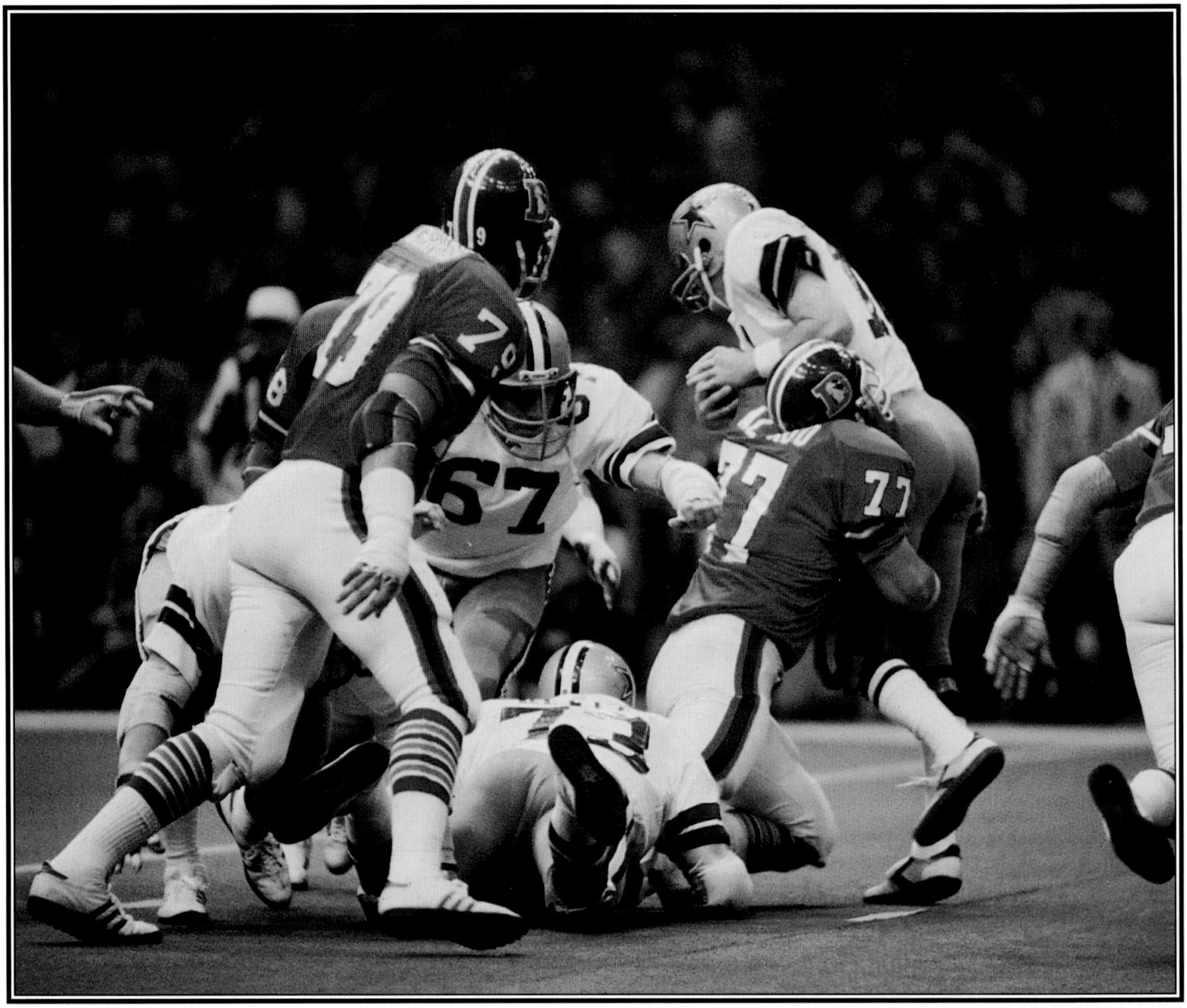

Lyle Alzado sacks Roger Staubach in Super Bowl XII at the Louisiana Superdome. The Orange Crush defense registered five sacks, but it was the Broncos who were crushed, 27-10.

ver to wish the team luck before the Broncos departed for New Orleans, while another 20,000 traveled to the Bayou.

The Broncos soon faced another type of crush—a swarming media contingent that was interested in seeing if Morton had anything controversial to say about the Cowboys and his former coach, Tom Landry. Morton also was trying to recover from a bruised hip that almost sidelined him for the AFC Championship game against Oakland. As it turned out, there wasn't much trash-talk before the game. But afterward, it was Dallas linebacker Thomas "Hollywood" Henderson who crumpled an orange cup, threw it at Denver fans and shouted, "There's your Orange Crush."

Before 90 million viewers worldwide—the largest audience ever to watch a sporting event—the Broncos fell to Dallas, 27-10, on Jan. 15, 1978. It was a particularly ugly game for Denver's offense, which was responsible for four interceptions (all thrown by Morton), four fumbles and just 156 net yards of total offense.

The Cowboys led 20-3 in the third quarter after Roger Staubach threw a 45-yard touchdown pass to Butch Johnson. But Rick Upchurch returned the ensuing kickoff 67 yards to the Dallas 26. Two plays later, Morton was benched in favor of Norris Weese, who then led Denver to a touchdown—a 1-yard run by Rob Lytle—to cut the

> ***"People don't really realize how hard we played in that game. I think the most critical statistic is time of possession. If your defense is playing 75 percent of the game, that says something about your [offense]."***

margin to 10. The Cowboys clinched the victory in the fourth quarter when running back Robert Newhouse threw a 29-yard option pass to wide receiver Golden Richards for a touchdown.

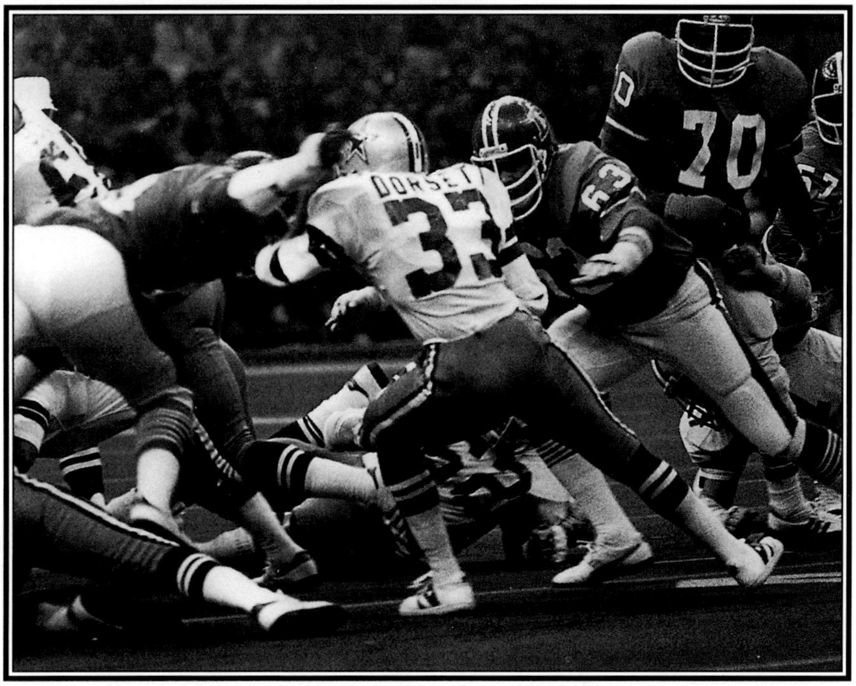

After a 3-yard first-quarter touchdown run, the Orange Crush slammed the door on Tony Dorsett in Super Bowl XII. The future Hall of Famer finished with just 66 rushing yards.

"If we hadn't turned the ball over so many times, I honestly believe we could have won that football game," Rick Upchurch said. "We had several opportunities that we didn't capitalize on. Had we done that, we would have won because the Orange Crush was so tough. People remember that in the fourth quarter it was 20-10 and we were gaining momentum. There was a whole lot of time left in that game. We could have been world champs the first time out."

The loss was especially painful for the Denver defense, which sacked Staubach five times and held star running back Tony Dorsett to 66 rushing yards. But the defense was on the field for almost 39 minutes, a time of possession statistic that Billy Thompson said happened too frequently during the 1977 season.

"People don't really realize how hard we played in that game," said Thompson, who had five tackles and two passes defended against the Cowboys. "I think the most critical statistic is time of possession. If your defense is playing 75 percent of the game, that says something about your [offense].

"If you look at that 1977 team, it felt like we were breaking every record in the history of football. If we would have had the offense we had [in 1997] coupled with that defense, we probably would have been like the Pittsburgh Steelers [in the 1970s]. When they won, they were very well balanced. They were loaded all the way through. We weren't like that at all. But I think it made us better. We knew what white-knuckle defense was."

The people of Denver still loved their Broncos after the loss, giving the team a standing ovation after the Super Bowl ended. In March 1978, only 143 season-ticket holders didn't renew their orders for the upcoming season.

But unfortunately for the Broncos, the magic just wasn't the same during the 1978 season. The defense remained as nasty as ever, allowing 21 or more points in only three contests during the NFL's new 16-game schedule and intercepting an average of almost two passes a game. The offense, though, actually struggled even more than the previous season. Denver averaged only 17.6 points a game, a drop of two points a game from the 1977 team.

Denver was good enough to finish 10-6 in 1978, but not good enough to secure home-field advantage in the playoffs. So the Broncos were forced to travel to Pittsburgh and face the team the Broncos had defeated in the 1977 playoffs.

The Steelers gained their revenge with a 33-10 rout at Three Rivers Stadium. Denver's defense actually deserves much of the blame for this loss, as Terry Bradshaw threw for 272 yards with two touchdowns and running back Franco Harris galloped for 105 yards and two touchdowns on 24 carries. As expected, the Broncos' offense wasn't good enough to offer much support. The Broncos were limited to 87 yards rushing and 168 yards passing, with quarterback Norris Weese getting sacked five times.

"We had more injuries that year, and that plays a big part in the success of a team," said Upchurch, who led the Broncos in punt returns for the fourth consecutive season. "I also think every team was like, 'Here comes Denver.' They played their heart out against us and we couldn't sneak up on people. People knew if they were going to get to the championship, they would have to go through Denver."

By the end of the decade, the Broncos had begun a search for Craig Morton's successor. One trade found backup Craig Penrose (above) being sent to the Jets in a deal for Matt Robinson, who lasted just one season.

The 1979 season was almost a mirror image of the previous campaign, except it became apparent that age was taking its toll on the Denver defense. The Broncos allowed 262 points, 114 more than the Orange Crush unit surrendered two seasons earlier in a 14-game schedule and 64 more than in '78. Just like in 1978, the Broncos finished the '79 season with a 10-6 record. Just like in 1978, the Broncos didn't finish with a good enough mark to land a playoff game at Mile High Stadium. And just like in 1978, the Broncos lost their first playoff contest largely because of an anemic offense.

Playing the wild-card game against Houston in the Astrodome, the Broncos could only tally 216 yards of total offense as Craig Morton was sacked six times. Trailing by six points in the final two minutes, a Denver drive reached Houston's 27-yard line before fizzling. The Oilers won, 13-7, and the Broncos went home a loser once again.

It became apparent that Miller's magic had finally faded during the 1980 season. As brilliant as the trade for Craig Morton was three years earlier, the acquisition of quarterback Matt Robinson from the New York Jets was exactly the opposite. Denver sent its first- and second-round picks and backup quarterback Craig Penrose to the Jets for a player they thought would be able to replace the aging Morton. Robinson, though, was a bigger flop than Steve Tensi a decade earlier. Robinson completed only 48.1 percent of his passes in 1980 and had a miserable touchdown-to-interception ratio of 2-to-12. Morton, meanwhile, completed 60.8 percent of his attempts, but also had more interceptions (13) than touchdowns (12) for the second consecutive season.

Denver's hopes for a fourth consecutive playoff berth were dashed in December when the Broncos lost three consecutive games. A 25-17 victory over Seattle in the season finale was one of the few saving graces as Denver finished with an 8-8 record to avoid its first losing campaign since 1975.

"We were getting older and we had to rebuild," said Upchurch, who played through 1983. "We had a lot of veteran players on our team."

The end of the Red Miller era came when the Phipps brothers decided to sell their stake in the Broncos. Edgar F. Kaiser Jr. became the new owner in February 1981 and did not wait long to make sweeping changes in the team's front office. The next month, both Miller and general manager Fred Gehrke were fired and replaced by Dan Reeves and Grady Alderman respectively.

Craig Morton ponders defeat after the Broncos were beaten by Houston, 13-7, in an AFC Wild-Card playoff game on Dec. 23, 1979, in the Astrodome.

Miller's coaching record in Denver was 42-25 (including the playoffs) which gave him the best winning percentage in franchise history (.627) until Mike Shanahan led the Broncos to a 37-16 mark (.698) from 1995-97. Miller never again became an NFL head coach, and as of spring 1998, was working as a stockbroker in the Denver area.

Billy Thompson retired after the 1981 season without having won a Super Bowl. But he has no regrets, especially regarding a 1977 team whose theme was, "Make Those Miracles Happen."

"It was an incredible group that was unselfish and played for the love of the game," Thompson remembered. "We knew only one way to win—depend on each other and play together. The city was such a big part of it. I've never seen a city that excited about anything.

"Make those miracles happen. We did."

ELWAY
FOR
PRESIDENT

The Mile High Factor

How rare air and dedicated fans combine to spark the Broncos' winning tradition

No team in professional sports may enjoy more of a home-field advantage than the Denver Broncos. From 1974-97, the Broncos amassed the best home record (148-47-1) of any NFL team. That includes a franchise-record 16-game winning streak that began in 1996 and continued through the next season. Besides the Broncos fielding quality teams, there are two other reasons Mile High Stadium has caused so many opponents to feel so low: The altitude and the fans.

The stadium is aptly named, as Denver's elevation of 5,280 feet translates to exactly one mile above sea level. The air is thinner in Denver than in any other NFL city, which means opposing players often struggle to catch their breath if they are not in extremely good condition.

"The altitude either physically or psychologically affects a visiting team in the fourth quarter," said linebacker Karl Mecklenburg, who played for the Broncos from 1983-94, in his autobiography, *Meck for the Defense*. "Teams will say, 'We're tired now.' That's why we tend to win games at the end when we play at home. Other players from other teams hate to play in Denver because they get tired. I think that it's because they expect to get tired and then they actually do. It becomes a self-fulfilling prophecy. But that does give us an edge."

When Mike Shanahan became head coach of the Broncos in 1995, one of his first moves was to establish four different summer mini-camps before training camp even began. Besides promoting team camaraderie, Shanahan wanted to make sure his team was in condition so that the Broncos could exploit opponents in the mile-high atmosphere.

Orange-clad fans (left) display their feelings at Mile High Stadium in the 1980s. Un-crushable orange hair styles were on display for Super Bowl XII (above).

The regimen Shanahan installed paid dividends on the Broncos' march to the Super Bowl in 1997. When Jacksonville came to Mile High Stadium for a wild-card game, the Broncos controlled the ball for almost 41 minutes. By the fourth quarter, the Jaguars were so tired that Denver

Young fans can mask their faces, but not their enthusiasm for the Broncos at Mile High.

was able to run the football at will. Terrell Davis (31 carries, 184 yards) and Derek Loville (11 carries, 103 yards) spearheaded a 310-yard rushing attack in a 42-17 rout.

The Broncos concluded the 1997 season with a string of 23 consecutive victories when leading at halftime still intact.

"Anyone who says [the thin air] isn't a factor is kidding himself," said Greg Robinson, who became Denver's defensive coordinator in 1995. "Mike knows that and believes strongly that conditioning is very, very important to this football team."

As is fan support.

Broncos fans made a major splash on Oct. 23, 1966, at Mile High Stadium following a 56-10 loss to Kansas City. With the Chiefs holding a large lead late in the game, head coach Hank Stram ordered an onside kick and instructed his players to let the Broncos recover it. The Broncos, however, were so inept that they could not even accomplish that.

Fans thought the Chiefs were trying to run up the score. As the Chiefs left the field, fans pelted players with just about everything that wasn't nailed down. Stram thought he could be shielded from abuse by walking off the field with former Heisman Trophy winner Doak Walker, but the fans even pelted the beloved Walker in the head with a bottle.

"First they threw paper bags, then beer cans," Chiefs quarterback Len Dawson said. "[When] the game was almost over, [they threw] whiskey bottles. They had a good shot at us, too, because the south stands were only about eight feet from the field. I've never seen such emotional fans. It was no wonder they called the south stands the 'Snake Pit.'"

When Red Miller was named Broncos coach in 1977, he asked fans to turn Mile High Stadium into a "snake pit." They responded with an outpouring of support the city had never seen. "Broncomania" seemed to reach into the life of every Den-

> ***"Our fans stood up and gave the team a 10 or 15 minute ovation. I didn't know whether we had won or lost after that. It was the most emotional time that I've ever experienced when our fans started to cheer."***

ver resident. Kids who were sending their Christmas lists to Santa Claus instead asked if they could mail them to the Broncos. A reverend painted the trim on his church orange after quarterback Craig Morton praised the Lord following a victory over the Raiders. A senior citizens center even held a pep rally for the Broncos.

When the team reached the Super Bowl, more than 150,000 fans lined the streets of Denver for a send-off parade. And even though only 9,000 tickets to Super Bowl XII were available through the team's ticket office, more than double that amount traveled to New Orleans in hopes of finding a way to watch the Broncos defeat the Dallas Cowboys.

Although the Broncos lost that game, 27-10, it didn't end Broncomania. In fact, Denver safety Billy Thompson said he will never forget how Broncos fans responded after the game ended.

"Our fans stood up and gave the team a 10 or 15 minute ovation," Thompson said. "I didn't know whether we had won or lost after that. It was the most emotional time that I've ever experienced when our fans started to cheer. It was incredible. It was like they were ready for the game to go on more because we played hard.

"I think the Mile High fans are the greatest of all time. No question, hands down," he added. "I'm not just saying that because I played here. But they're with us, win or lose. You have some fans that are bandwagon people, but I think Mile High fans are the greatest."

Mile-high fatigue affects Broncos opponents in the fourth quarter, according to Karl Mecklenburg.

The adulation continued 20 years later when the Broncos finally brought home a Super Bowl trophy. The team's playoff games, as usual, drew the highest local ratings in the country. More than 20,000 fans met the Broncos at the airport after a 24-21 victory over Pittsburgh in the AFC Championship game. Two days after the Broncos posted a 31-24 victory against Green Bay in Super Bowl XXXII, an estimated 650,000 fans lined the streets of downtown Denver to honor their heroes.

And in what may be the most telling statistic of all, the Broncos' string of consecutive sellouts shows no signs of ending even though the city now has three other professional sports franchises. About 9,000 people remained on a waiting list for season tickets before the start of the 1998 campaign.

The purchase of the Denver Broncos by Edgar F. Kaiser Jr. in February 1981 was a stunning event. But it was only the first of a number of changes that would alter the direction of the franchise in the early 1980s. A new head coach and quarterback would follow and, by the middle of the decade, the Broncos were on their way to the best streak of success in franchise history.

When Gerry Phipps decided that he wanted to sell his two-thirds ownership of Rocky Mountain Empire Sports Inc.—the parent organization of the Broncos—he placed a call to only one suitor: Kaiser. Phipps was looking for a young, energetic owner who was willing to spend money to make the Broncos an NFL champion. Phipps found his man in the 38-year-old Kaiser, who was a successful international industrialist without a sports business background. At the time of the sale, the reclusive Kaiser said in a rare interview, "This is simply something I want to do because I think it will be fun." Kaiser was welcomed into the NFL as the league's only Canadian-born franchise owner.

Chapter 5

1981–1985

Arrival and Revival

A new owner and coach, then a promising new quarterback and once again the Broncos are sighting the Super Bowl.

The $30 million sale was so well kept under wraps that Broncos general manager Fred Gehrke heard the news while listening to the radio in his car. At first, it appeared Kaiser was leaning toward keeping Gehrke and head coach Red Miller in their respective positions. Shortly after buying the team, Kaiser said that he expected "my head coach and general manager to run [the Broncos] on a day-to-day basis." But one month after the sale was approved, Kaiser changed his mind. Gehrke and Miller were relieved of their duties.

Two factors seemed to contribute to Kaiser's decision. First, the Broncos missed the playoffs in 1980 despite having one of the NFL's most well-paid rosters. Two of their best players had also become the best paid at their positions.

John Elway, the rookie, faces the Raiders in 1983 at the L.A. Coliseum.

7
7

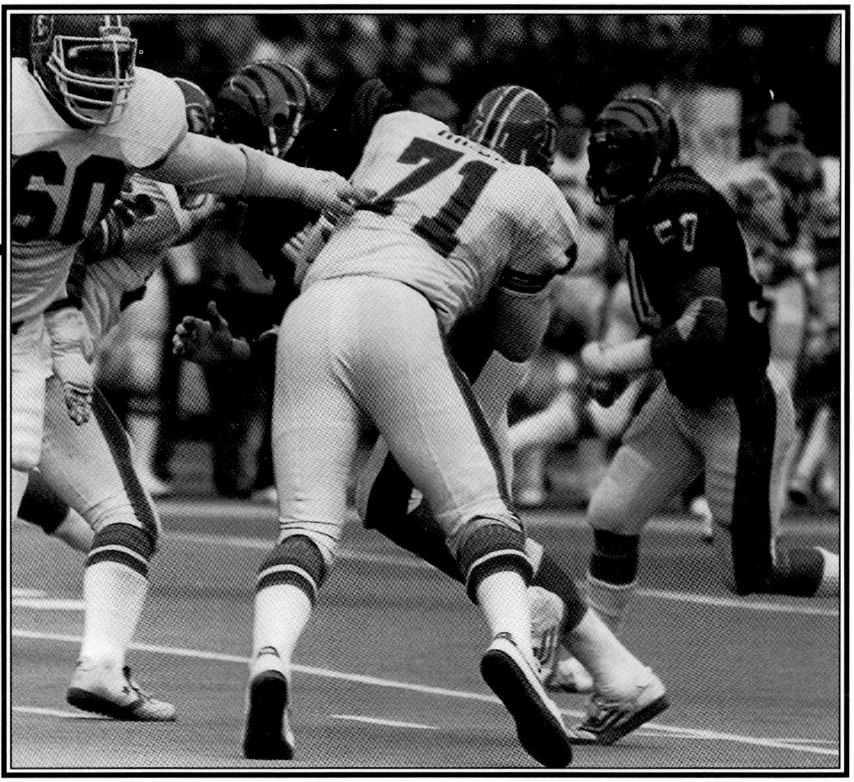

Escalating NFL salaries found Denver linebacker Randy Gradishar (left) and offensive tackle Claudie Minor (No. 71, right) the highest-paid players in 1980 at their respective positions.

Linebacker Randy Gradishar ($271,250) and offensive tackle Claudie Minor ($230,000) were the highest-paid players in pro football at their respective positions, while four other Broncos were close to gaining that ranking.

The second factor was Kaiser's desire to hire a younger coach. The person who fit the bill was 37-year-old Dan Reeves, who was considered one of the NFL's top assistant coaches after seven seasons with the Dallas Cowboys. As the Cowboys' offensive coordinator, Reeves had helped Dallas become one of the NFL's elite franchises. Kaiser hoped the coach would be able to achieve the same success with the Broncos that Dallas head coach Tom Landry had attained with the Cowboys.

"I feel like I'm ready to be a head coach," said Reeves, who had turned down that opportunity with the Atlanta Falcons in 1977 because he didn't feel the organization was ready to win immediately. "I don't think there's anything [available] in Dallas for a long time. Sooner or later, you have to leave home."

Reeves began his NFL career in 1965 with the Cowboys as a relatively unknown free-agent quarterback from South Carolina. He made the roster after being converted to running back, but later threw a 50-yard fourth-quarter touchdown pass against Green Bay in the legendary "Ice Bowl" game of 1967.

The Dan Reeves era opened with success when the Broncos defeated the Super Bowl champion Oakland Raiders, 9-7, in the 1981 season opener. Barney Chavous sacks Jim Plunkett while Randy Gradishar (53) provides reinforcement.

After becoming a Cowboys assistant coach, Reeves became acquainted with quarterback Craig Morton. That made it easier for Reeves to settle on Morton as his starting quarterback for the 1981 season, although he appeared to draft his quarterback of the future in Purdue's Mark Hermann.

A better selection, though, was Southern Cal safety Dennis Smith in the first round. Following in the footsteps of such legendary Broncos safeties as Goose Gonsoulin and Billy Thompson, Smith earned a reputation as being one of the NFL's biggest hitters during his 14-year career.

With Reeves installing a new offensive system, Morton needed the first two games of the '81 season to get comfortable. But once he did, Morton set a franchise record by throwing for four touchdown passes in consecutive victories against Baltimore and San Diego. Morton's favorite target?

An unheralded wide receiver from Temple University, Steve Watson caught only 12 passes in his first two seasons in Denver. But after the 12th game of the 1981 season, he had already caught a club-record 13 touchdown passes. Watson set the team's single-season yardage record with 1,244 on 60 catches, a mark that was still standing 16 years later. Morton set a team record for passing yardage with 3,195 (surpassed by John Elway's 3,891 in 1985) and an average gain of 8.50 yards per pass, second all-time to Jacky Lee's 8.65 in 1965.

Craig Morton's 1981 season was his last as a full-time quarterback, but resulted in his first 3,000-yard campaign. At age 38, Morton completed 225 of 376 attempts for 3,195 yards and 21 touchdowns.

But Morton and Watson would have traded all of their personal accomplishments for an appearance in the playoffs. Despite a 10-6 record, the Broncos were unable to reach the post-season. A 35-24 loss at Chicago in the final game of the regular season allowed the New York Jets and Buffalo Bills to slip into the playoffs instead.

Denver fans were disappointed, but they were convinced that Reeves would have the Broncos back in the Super Bowl soon. Only 49 season-ticket holders did not renew their orders for the 1982 season, ensuring the 13th season of consecutive sellouts in Denver.

Steve DeBerg was the expected successor to Craig Morton, but his first year as a full-time starter was the strike-shortened 1982 campaign. By '83, a quarterback named Elway had arrived and DeBerg was dealt to Tampa Bay in '84.

The Broncos had a promising new starting quarterback in 1982 in Steve DeBerg. The '82 draft had produced two running backs—Gerald Willhite and Sammy Winder—who would contribute for years to come. So why would the Broncos finish 2-7 in 1982? Blame it on the effects of a players strike that few thought would occur.

Sammy Winder (left) and Gerald Willhite (right) were 1982 draft choices and part of the influx of new talent under Dan Reeves that led to a berth in Super Bowl XXI. Winder and Willhite joined a Denver backfield that would add another new member a year later, John Elway.

The NFL Players Association was pushing for a free-agency system that would inevitably lead to an increase in salaries. When an agreement couldn't be reached, a strike was called after the second game of the season. For eight consecutive weeks, an eerie thing happened in Denver on Sunday afternoons. There were no games being played and no Broncos to cheer for.

When the strike finally ended with the NFLPA receiving only minor concessions in what would be regarded as an ineffective strike, Denver fans embraced the Broncos just like before. But it was obvious that the Broncos weren't the same team. Denver lost six of its final seven games, with the only victory a 27-24 nail-biter against the Los Angeles Rams.

The only memorable event following the strike was when Rick Upchurch returned a punt 78 yards for a touchdown in a loss to the Kansas City Chiefs. That enabled Upchurch to tie the NFL's all-time record for punt returns for touchdowns with eight.

Rich Karlis (left) raises a hand in victory after his 18-yard field goal with three seconds remaining beat the Super Bowl champion 49ers in the second game of 1982. Holder Steve DeBerg (17) and tight end Ron Egloff (85) join the celebration.

17

Despite the awful finish to the season, Broncos fans once again showed their loyalty when only 89 season-ticket holders failed to renew their orders for 1983. At the time, the Broncos were expected to field either Steve DeBerg or Mark Hermann as their starting quarterback.

Then came the trade that shocked the NFL and forever changed the history of sports in Colorado. With the first pick in the 1983 draft, the Baltimore Colts selected what may have been the most highly touted quarterback since Joe Namath in Stanford's John Elway. One of the most prolific passers in NCAA history on a mediocre college team, Elway was such a good athlete that he spent the summer of 1982 playing outfield for a Class A minor-league team in the New York Yankees' farm system.

With John Elway in the fold, head coach Dan Reeves was poised to guide Denver to six playoff trips from 1983 through '92.

Although there was no questioning Elway was the top player in the draft, the Colts knew they were taking a risk by drafting him. Elway had never publicly said he wouldn't play in Baltimore, but it was no secret that he might choose a baseball career rather than play for the Colts. Elway wanted to play football on the West Coast. He and his father, Jack, also were not fans of Colts head coach Frank Kush. In fact, John Elway wouldn't even accept Kush's call of congratulations on draft day.

One week after the draft, Colts owner Robert Irsay realized the war with Elway was not one he could win. So against the advice of Kush, the Colts traded Elway to the Broncos for Hermann, guard Chris Hinton (Denver's first-round pick in 1983) and a first-round choice in '84.

While at Stanford, John Elway set five NCAA Division 1-A and nine Pac-10 records. He completed 62.1 percent of his passes for 9,349 yards and 77 touchdowns. As a senior, he was a consensus All-American and Heisman Trophy runner-up.

"That was his right as an owner," Jim Irsay said of his father's refusal to give Elway a five-year, $5 million contract.

"But in defense of him, you have to remember this: He had concerns about the franchise's stability. He was in Baltimore, he had that old stadium and was clearly under financial duress with the lease and declining attendance.

"Maybe if Dad had been on better financial footing and maybe if there had

"Everyone talked about the media in the Super Bowl, but it didn't compare with my rookie year. The toughest thing about my rookie year was the media. They wore me out."

John Elway's biggest challenge as a rookie was not found on the field, but rather it was mastering Dan Reeves's complicated offense.

been a coach or a general manager or both pleading to get it done, things might have been different. The dynamics . . . were in place to make sure Elway wasn't going to be a Colt."

Still, the Colts will forever rue trading Elway, who has started 219 of 237 regular season games and won more of them (138) than any quarterback in NFL history in his first 15 NFL seasons. In that same span, the Colts started 16 different quarterbacks and have not won an NFL championship since Super Bowl V. But success would not come immediately for Elway. Were it not for an incredible amount of inner strength, Elway might have never reached the heights that will land him a spot in the Pro Football Hall of Fame.

Of all the players who have ever been shoved into the spotlight when joining a new team, Elway may have faced more pressure than any of them. First came the expectations generated by the multi-million-dollar contract Elway signed, something that still wasn't commonplace in professional sports. Baltimore fans were so angry at Elway—whom they considered a spoiled brat from California—that they sent 48 bags of hate mail in the months after the trade. Robert Irsay even went so far to say, "He'll never be any good. . . . We're going to get Elway."

Elway then had to face the media, which covered him not merely as an athlete, but like a rock star or president. Anything Elway did was sure to make at least one of the two local newspapers in Denver—the *Rocky Mountain News* or *Denver Post*—who were involved in an all-out circulation war. What Elway had for breakfast, lunch and dinner was news. Where Elway got his haircut was news. What he watched on television—"All My Children" was an early favorite—was news. What nightclub he attended and how many dancing partners he had was reported. "I don't read anything that says 'Elway,' because I've read it all before," Elway would say shortly after arriving in Greeley, Colo., for his first training camp.

Steve Watson, who would become one of Elway's closest friends, said, "John had the toughest first year of any player in the game. It was ridiculous to subject a guy to that." Elway, himself, would later say, "Everyone talked about the media in the Super Bowl, but it didn't compare with my rookie year. The toughest thing about my rookie year was the media. They wore me out. . . . During training camp, I was spending as much time on the playbook as I was with the press. That set me back, but at the time, I didn't realize it."

If Elway wasn't exhausted from being the center of attention publicly, learning Dan Reeves's offense sapped any remaining energy. Elway studied late into the night to learn a complex system that required the understanding of 90 to 100 plays a game. Watson called the offense the "Edsel" because "it was a Neanderthal system that focused on keeping guys in to protect instead of attacking a defense. Instead of getting five guys into routes, they get three guys so outlets were few and far between."

Elway, though, was such a good athlete that he could have starred while playing in a wishbone attack. He proved that in his first appearance in a Broncos uniform. Playing in the fourth quarter of a preseason game against Seattle, Elway completed five of six pass attempts and led the Broncos to a touchdown on a 10-play drive.

Fans and media immediately began believing that Elway was superhuman even though he was only playing against Seattle's third-string and rookie players.

As strange as it sounds, Elway would probably have been better off by performing poorly because Reeves named Elway his starting quarterback during the preseason, something he would later admit was a mistake. Elway was thoroughly confused by Minnesota's defense in a 34-3 loss in the preseason finale.

It got even worse in the Broncos' regular-season opener against Pittsburgh at Three Rivers Stadium. Facing a heavy Steelers blitz, a confused Elway completed only one of eight passes for 14 yards while getting sacked four times. Elway was mercifully yanked and replaced by DeBerg, who led Denver to a 14-10 victory.

It was just as bad for Elway the following week as the Broncos played at Baltimore, a city waiting to crucify the player who refused to become a Colt. Elway needed police protection because death threats were made before the game. Once again, Elway failed to distinguish himself in a nine-for-21 outing. The Broncos won, 17-10.

Elway started the first five games of the season, but threw only one touchdown with five interceptions. Elway was so rattled in the fifth game against Chicago that Reeves again benched him in favor of DeBerg, who was gaining support from some in the Broncos' locker room as the rightful starter.

At times, Elway did play well. His finest performance in 1983 came in the first of more than 40 fourth-quarter comeback victories he has orchestrated. With the Broncos trailing, 19-0, after three quarters, Elway threw three touchdown passes—including the game-winner to Gerald Willhite with 44 seconds remaining—to score a 21-19 victory over the Colts on Dec. 11.

Steve Watson, who once called the Broncos' offensive scheme an outdated "Edsel," produced big numbers at wide receiver nevertheless. He led the Broncos in receiving four times from 1981-85, averaging 57 receptions a season.

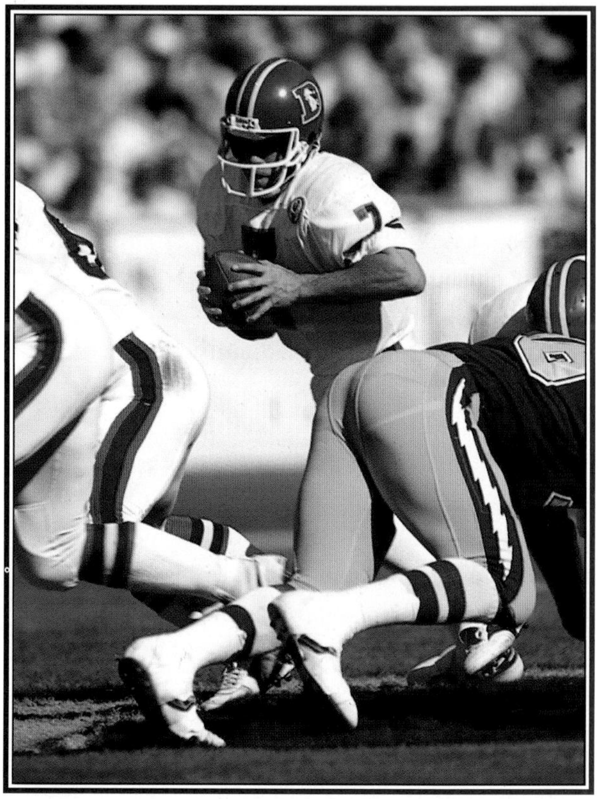

With Steve DeBerg (left) traded to Tampa Bay, John Elway took full-time control of Denver's offense in 1984. Three of his fourth-quarter comebacks occurred that season, including a 16-13 victory over the San Diego Chargers on Nov. 11 (right).

"I've seen this before," Reeves said after the game. "[Dallas quarterback Roger] Staubach got his reputation that way with great comebacks, and Danny White did it after him. Now our team is never really out of a game. That gains maturity for the whole club, and they will never quit."

Between Elway—who has said that in his childhood he would "run around the backyard imagining I'm Roger Staubach"—and DeBerg, the Broncos were talented enough to make the playoffs as a wild-card with a 9-7 record. Elway, though, returned to the bench for a wild-card game against Seattle after Reeves learned DeBerg was healthy enough to start again. The Broncos lost the game, 31-7, and Elway's rookie season was finally over. He finished with the NFL's lowest quarterback rating at 54.9, completed only 47.5 percent of his passes and threw twice as many interceptions (14) as touchdowns (seven). Making matters worse, Miami quarterback Dan Marino—who was selected 22 picks after Elway—was enjoying an outstanding rookie campaign with the AFC East champion Dolphins.

Some in the NFL were wondering whether Elway was the real deal, but not *Rocky Mountain News* beat reporter T. J. Simers.

"Remember what the first days of a new job brought for you and understand what it would have been like, performing before 70,000 screamers, TV cameras complete with instant replay and a horde of national media types," Simers wrote.

“Even boo-birds must understand the current John Elway is not the John Elway who will play for the next decade. This is a rookie quarterback, and the problems now figure to disappear with the passing of time.”

The Broncos knew that Elway was their future quarterback, so the disgruntled DeBerg was traded to Tampa Bay for two draft choices. His career continued through 1993 with additional stops in Kansas City and Miami.

Elway’s backup in 1984 became Gary Kubiak, an eighth-round draft pick in 1983 out of Texas A&M. The two would become close friends, a relationship that grew even stronger when Kubiak became offensive coordinator in 1995.

Even bigger news than the DeBerg trade was Edgar Kaiser deciding that he no longer wanted to remain an NFL owner. Kaiser sold the Broncos to Patrick Bowlen, whose enthusiasm for the team prompted him to dissolve almost all of his other business interests in the 1990s so he could concentrate on running the Broncos. Since Bowlen arrived in 1984, the Broncos have enjoyed more AFC West titles (six) and Super Bowl appearances (four) than any of the other four teams in the division. Bowlen acquired 100 percent ownership of the Broncos in 1985 and, one year later, oversaw the construction of 60 luxury suites at Mile High Stadium.

Anyone who doubted Elway after the 1983 season quickly became a believer in 1984. That’s because a much more composed Elway—along with a dominating defense coached by longtime coordinator Joe Collier—helped the Broncos win a franchise-record 10 consecutive games after a 1-1 start. During that stretch, Denver held five of its opponents to 13 or fewer points.

The Broncos finished the season with 13 victories—the most in team history—and Elway rebounded with a sound season. His touchdown-to-interception ratio improved to 18-to-15 and he completed more than 56 percent of his passes. Elway also received some help from Sammy Winder, whose 1,153 rushing yards made him Denver’s first 1,000-yard rusher in eight seasons.

The city of Denver was having Super Bowl dreams once more as the Broncos would have home-field advantage throughout the playoffs and would first face the team with the worst record, Pittsburgh (9-7), of any AFC playoff team.

Sammy Winder emerged in 1984 as one of the league’s top running backs. His career-high 1,153 rushing yards was third-best in the AFC, earning him a trip to the Pro Bowl.

Broncos linebacker Rick Dennison gets close, but cannot get a hand on Steelers running back Walter Abercrombie in a 1984 AFC Divisional playoff game in Denver. The improving Broncos were close to Super Bowl status, but lost this game, 24-17.

What transpired on Dec. 30 at Mile High Stadium, however, was a 24-17 loss that remained arguably the team's most disappointing post-season defeat until the 1996 Broncos dropped a 30-27 decision to Jacksonville, also at Mile High. The Broncos had two possessions in the game's final two minutes, but even Elway was unable to rally a team that was thoroughly outplayed by the Steelers before 74,981 dejected fans.

If someone would have told the Broncos before the 1985 season that they would finish with an 11-5 record, almost everyone in the organization would have been pleased. But as it turned out, Denver became one of the best teams not to reach the post-season in NFL history. The Los Angeles Raiders won the AFC West title with a 12-4 mark, a record bolstered by overtime victories of 31-28 and 17-14 against the Broncos. As for a wild-card berth, the Broncos found themselves losing a tie-break-

er to the New York Jets based on conference record and a tie-breaker to New England based on a better record against common opponents.

That fate ruined what was otherwise a banner year for Elway and linebacker Karl Mecklenburg. Elway shattered the team's single-season passing record with 3,891 yards, while Mecklenburg had a team-record 13 quarterback sacks. Denver's offense also enjoyed the most prolific campaign of its first 26 seasons with 5,496 total yards and 380 points.

In retrospect, maybe it was better that Denver didn't make the playoffs in 1985. That's because the Broncos became so hungry that they reached the Super Bowl in their subsequent two seasons.

John Elway is nailed by Bryan Hinkle in the '84 AFC Divisional playoff. The fourth-quarter comeback belonged to the Steelers this time. They scored the winning touchdown in the final two minutes.

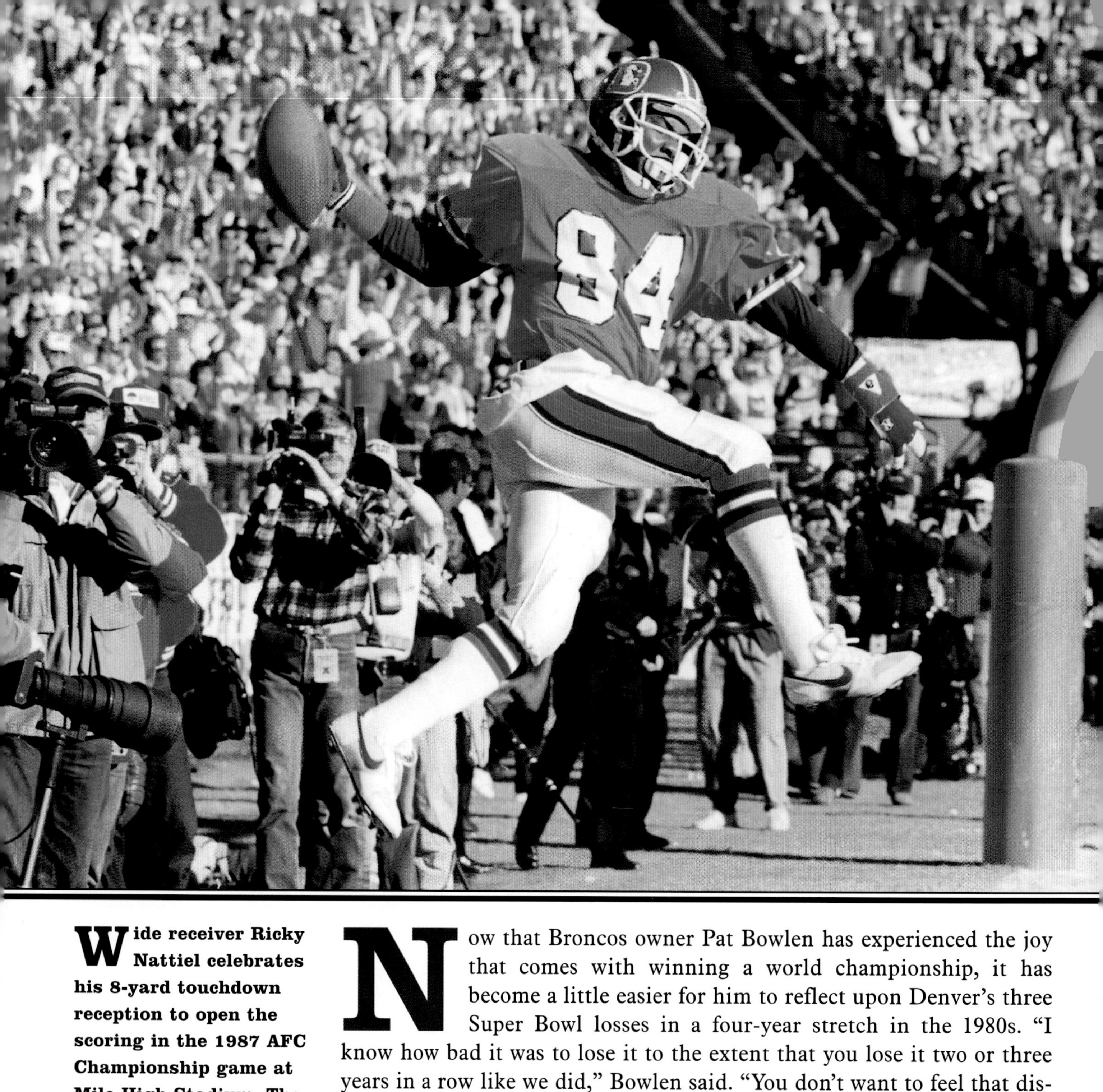

Wide receiver Ricky Nattiel celebrates his 8-yard touchdown reception to open the scoring in the 1987 AFC Championship game at Mile High Stadium. The Broncos held on to beat the Cleveland Browns, 38-33, and advance to Super Bowl XXII.

Now that Broncos owner Pat Bowlen has experienced the joy that comes with winning a world championship, it has become a little easier for him to reflect upon Denver's three Super Bowl losses in a four-year stretch in the 1980s. "I know how bad it was to lose it to the extent that you lose it two or three years in a row like we did," Bowlen said. "You don't want to feel that disappointment. I heard people say it: 'Let's not go to the Super Bowl because we're going to lose.'"

The Broncos of 1997 not only had to battle the defending champion Green Bay Packers, but also the ghosts haunting the AFC and previous Denver teams. Before Denver's 31-24 upset victory, AFC teams had lost 13 consecutive Super Bowls. The Broncos were on the wrong end of three such defeats, losing by bigger scores each time.

But if one goes back to the start of the 1986 season and the success Denver would experience over the next four years, it is hard to believe that the Broncos had to wait so long to become Super Bowl champions.

Denver opened the 1986 campaign with the best start in franchise history, rolling to a 6-0 mark after a 31-14 whipping of the San Diego Chargers on Oct. 12. The Broncos were living up to their preseason billing as the AFC favorite to reach the Super Bowl, but things got rocky the next week when they lost their first game to the New York Jets, 22-10, on "Monday Night Football." Despite rebounding to win the next two games, several mediocre performances followed. The most embarrassing was a 37-10 loss at Kansas City where John Elway threw four interceptions against the Chiefs.

Chapter 6

1986–1989

Drive to the Top!

With three AFC championships in four years, the Broncos climb higher than ever, but can't quite reach the Super Bowl summit.

At 10-4, the Broncos were still considered the favorite to gain home-field advantage throughout the playoffs. But both the Broncos and their fans were looking for a sign that the 1986 team was good enough to capture a world title. They received it thanks to Elway in a wild 31-30 victory over Washington on Dec. 13 at Mile High Stadium.

Denver scored just one touchdown before halftime, but Elway led the Broncos to 24 second-half points while completing 20 of 35 passes for 282 yards and a touchdown. The victory was especially significant because the Redskins entered the game as one of the NFL's best with a 10-4 record. "In the second half, this game came close to being playoff tempo," Broncos linebacker Tom Jackson said.

The Broncos were unable to carry the momentum into the season finale, a 41-16 loss at Seattle, a game in which Elway sprained an ankle and three offensive starters were injured. The defeat helped Cleveland score home-field advantage in the playoffs. But the Broncos weren't finished—and neither was Elway's brilliance in leading second-half charges.

Vance Johnson gestures to the crowd after his third-quarter scoring reception puts Denver ahead to stay in the AFC Divisional playoff game on Jan. 4, 1987, versus the Patriots.

In an AFC Divisional playoff game before a record crowd of 76,105 fans at Mile High Stadium, the Broncos found themselves deadlocked with New England at halftime, 10-10. But in the final two quarters, Elway connected on a 48-yard touchdown pass to Vance Johnson and All-Pro defensive end Rulon Jones sacked Patriots quarterback Tony Eason for a safety with 1:37 remaining to clinch a 22-17 Broncos victory. Elway only completed 13 passes, but chalked up 257 yards while also rushing for a 22-yard touchdown in the second quarter. Sammy Winder also became the first running back in Broncos history to post a 100-yard rushing game in the postseason, finishing with 102 yards on 19 carries.

Besides moving the Broncos to within one game of Super Bowl XXI, the playoff victory also was Denver's first since the 1977 season. Dan Reeves had lost both of his playoff games since becoming Denver's head coach in 1981. After defeating the Patriots, Reeves said, "I thought about this for six years now and what it would feel like to win a playoff game. But I underestimated it. I can't tell you how proud I am of our football team."

If Reeves was happy then, imagine his euphoria when the Broncos reached the Super Bowl with a 23-20 overtime victory over Cleveland in the AFC Championship game. Of all the game-winning fourth-quarter drives that Elway has conducted, the

Rulon Jones exits Mile High Stadium after the Broncos beat the Patriots. He sacked quarterback Tony Eason in the end zone for a safety to clinch Denver's 22-17 victory.

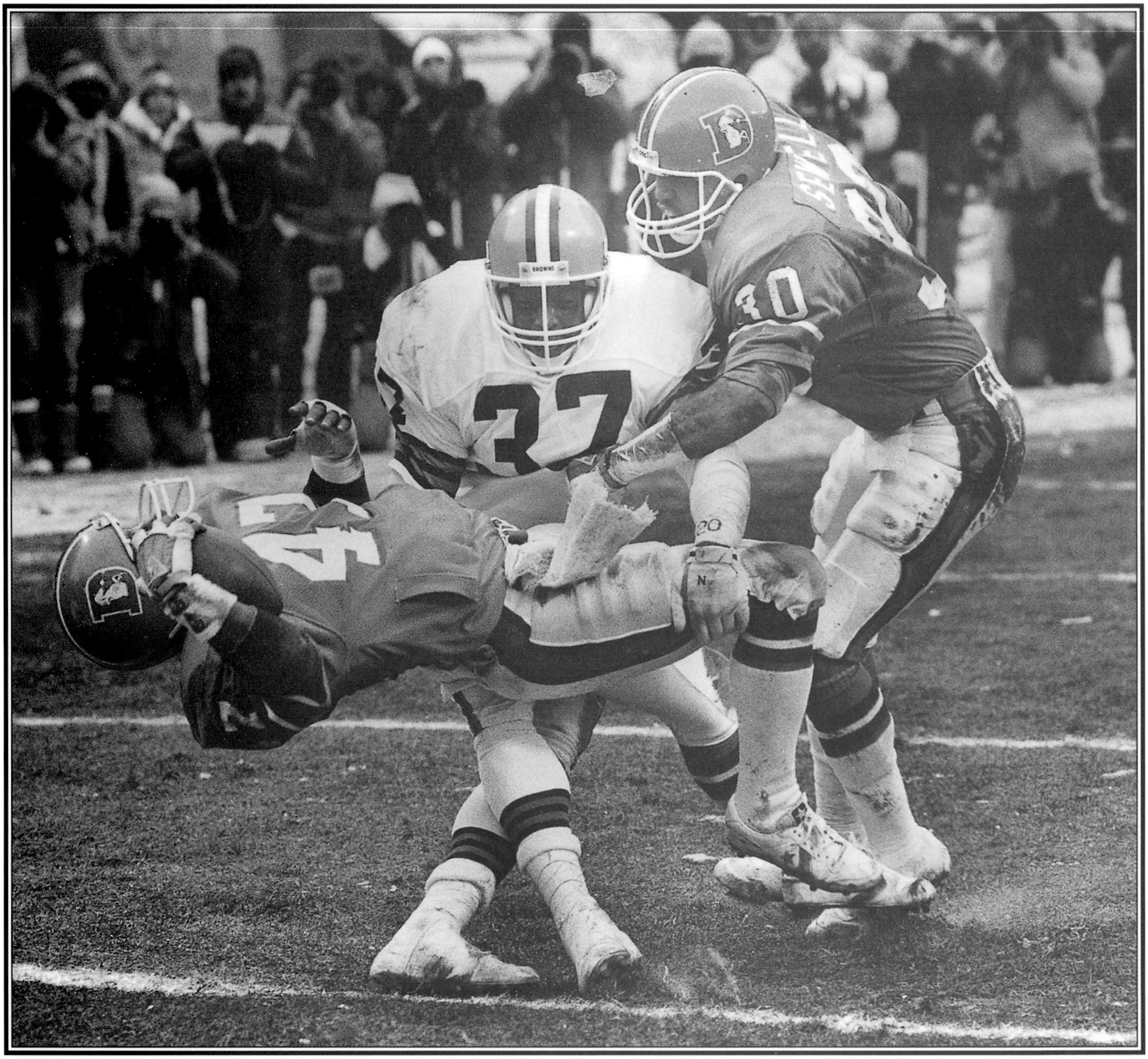

Before The Drive there was the dive. Gerald Willhite lands over the goal line for the Broncos' first touchdown in the second quarter of the 1986 AFC Championship game.

one in this game will be the most memorable for several reasons. First, the Broncos were playing before a Cleveland Municipal Stadium crowd of 79,915 fans determined to make as much noise as necessary to ensure the Browns would reach the Super Bowl for the first time in the franchise's history. That meant Elway would be forced to use hand signals to call plays and a silent count at the line of scrimmage.

"The Drive" had an inauspicious start. On the kickoff after the Browns had taken a 20-13 lead with less than six minutes remaining in the fourth quarter, the ball rolled to the 2-yard line where Broncos returner Gene Lang fell on it. That meant Elway needed to take the Broncos 98 yards for a score against a defense that had held the Broncos to a touchdown and two field goals through three quarters. Denver's previous two drives had ended with only 15 yards of total offense.

The Drive was almost stopped at its onset, but the Broncos converted on a third-and-two from their own 10-yard line after a 2-yard Winder run. The Broncos reached the Cleveland 40-yard line when the comeback try was almost foiled again.

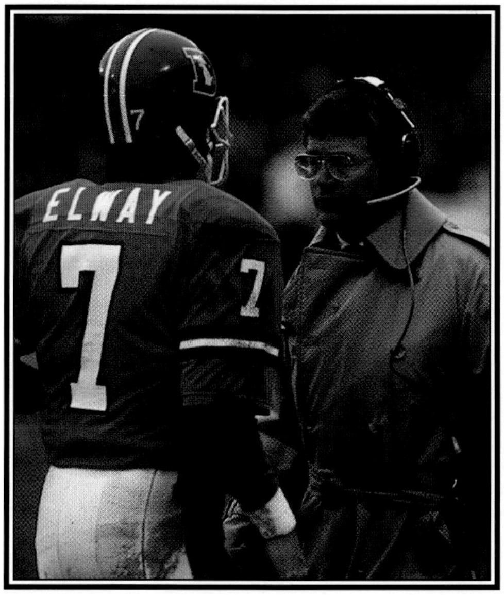

With about two minutes remaining in the game, Elway threw an incompletion on first down and was sacked for an 8-yard loss on the next play. It got even worse on third down when a shotgun snap to Elway accidentally deflected off wide receiver Steve Watson, who had gone in motion. But rather than panic, Elway scooped up the ball and rifled a 20-yard pass to Mark Jackson for a first down at the Cleveland 28.

Five plays later and with 37 seconds remaining, Elway and Jackson hooked up again on a 5-yard touchdown. Rich Karlis's extra point tied it at 20 and sent the game into overtime.

"We shut him down the whole game," Browns defensive end Sam Clancy said. "And then in the last minute, he [Elway] showed us what he was made of."

With an analysis like that, one can understand why Cleveland was emotionally spent when the overtime began. Even though they won the toss, the Browns were forced to punt on their first series when running back Herman Fontenot was stopped for no gain on a third-and-two inside Cleveland territory.

The Broncos regained possession on their own 25-yard line and quickly moved to win the game. Once again, it was Elway making life miserable for the Browns. Completions of 22 yards to tight end Orson Mobley and 28 yards to Watson put

Reeves and Elway (above left) confer during the 1986 AFC Championship game in Cleveland. Above, Elway fires one of his many clutch completions during The Drive.

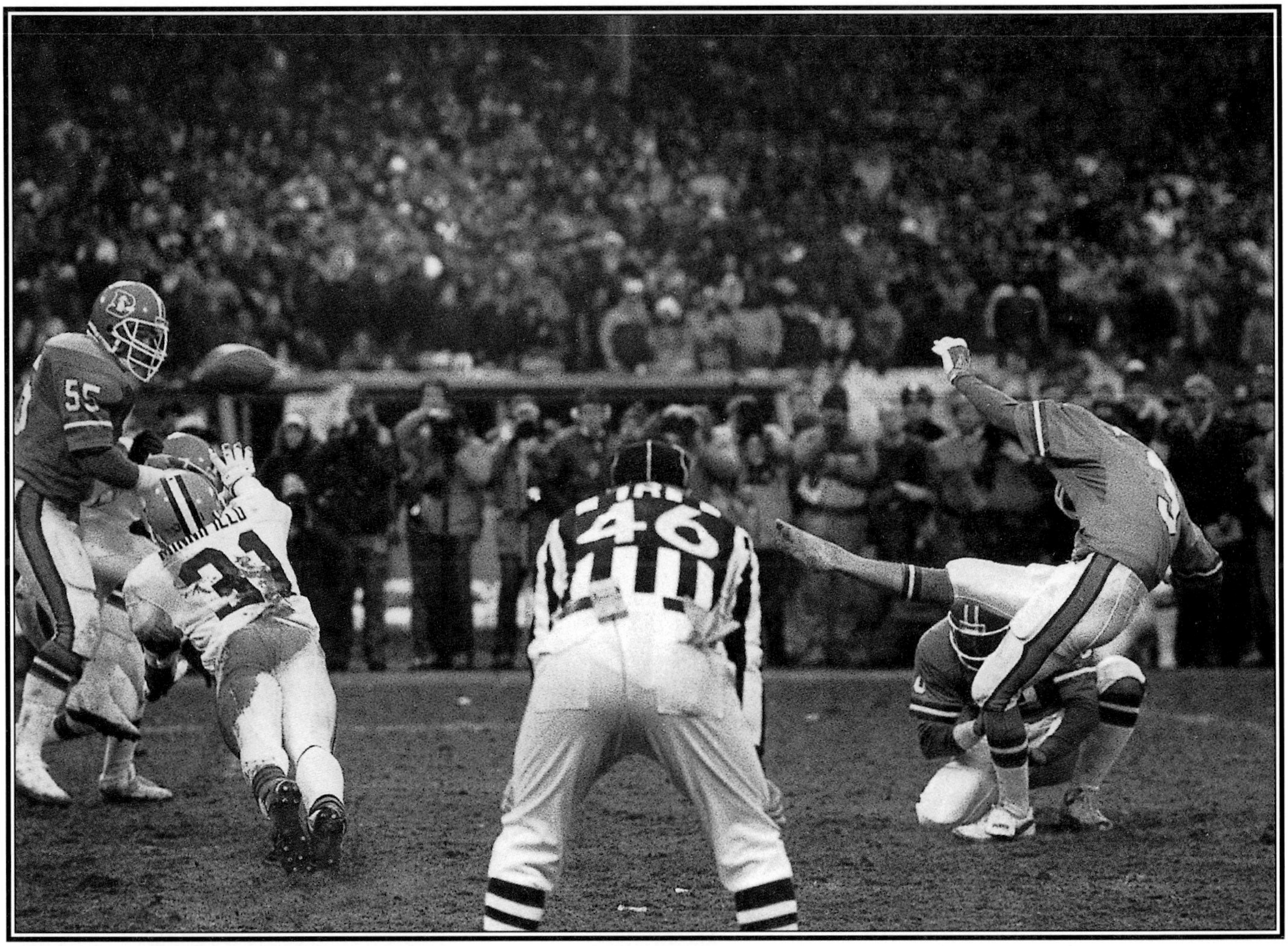

Rich Karlis delivers the kick heard 'round the Rockies, his 33-yard game-winner in overtime to give the Broncos a 23-20 victory over the Browns in the 1986 AFC Championship game in Cleveland.

Denver well inside Cleveland territory. After reaching the Browns' 15-yard line, Rich Karlis kicked his third field goal—this one from 33 yards—to win the game.

Elway finished the game with 244 yards on 22-of-38 passing with one touchdown and one interception. Even more impressive was Elway's elusiveness in the pocket as he rushed for 56 yards on four carries, including a 34-yard scamper that set up a touchdown to give Denver a 10-7 lead in the second quarter. As for The Drive, Elway said: "That drive is something I might not be able to do again. The day before the big game, you dream of doing things like that. But you never expect them to happen. That was the best drive I've ever been involved in."

Eleven years after "The Drive," Dan Reeves said it was still the most memorable series he had ever witnessed.

"It was the most exciting one I was a part of," Reeves said. "To have as much on the line. . . . You look at San Francisco against Cincinnati in [the fourth quarter of Super Bowl XXIII]. That was a good drive. I've seen some, but not with that much on the line for us. To go from your own 2-yard line to have to tie the score. . . . That was the biggest one in my career."

So off the Broncos went to Pasadena, Calif., to face the NFC champion New York Giants, a team that finished at 14-2 and had slipped by the Broncos, 19-16, in a November meeting at Giants Stadium. The Giants won behind a dominating defense led by linebacker Lawrence Taylor—who is generally regarded as the best pass-rusher of modern football—and a grind-it-out running attack.

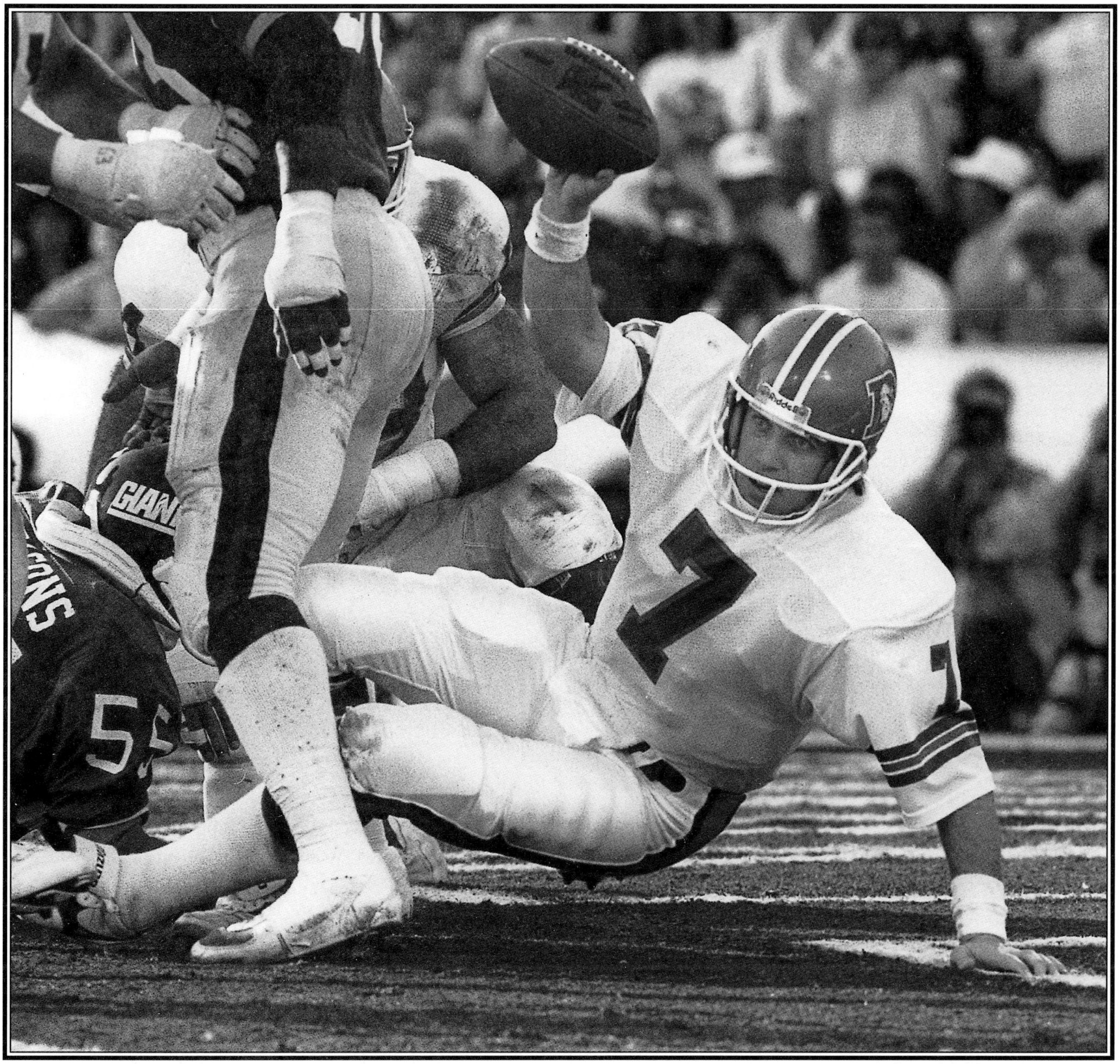

John Elway scores on a 4-yard run in the first quarter of Super Bowl XXI. Denver took a 10-7 lead, but the Giants then scored 26 unanswered points to take command, and an eventual 39-20 victory.

The Broncos took a 10-9 lead into halftime, but missed on two scoring opportunities that proved costly. Karlis, one of the heroes of the win over Cleveland, tied a Super Bowl record in the first quarter with a 48-yard field goal. But he then botched a 23-yard attempt—the shortest miss in Super Bowl history—and a 34-yarder before halftime.

"I don't think I lost any concentration," said Karlis, who had missed only one of 12 attempts between 20 and 39 yards during the 1986 regular season. "Hindsight is 20-20. If I had those kicks back, I probably could have made them. . . . It just shows that you can go from the penthouse to the outhouse real quick."

To completely blame Karlis would be unfair. The Broncos' secondary was riddled by Giants quarterback Phil Simms, who won Super Bowl XXI Most Valuable Player honors by competing 22 of 25 passes for 268 yards and three touchdowns. Simms was sacked only once and threw no interceptions in what Giants head coach

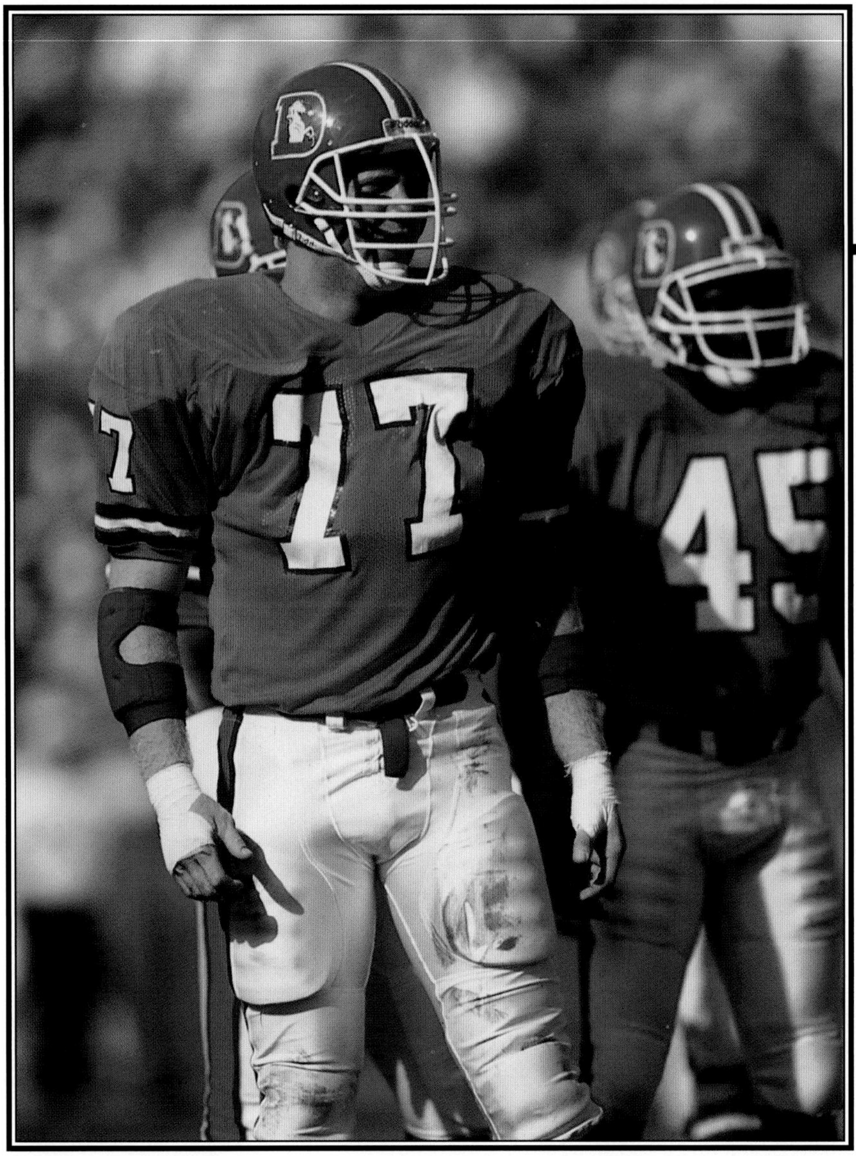

The conference champion Broncos featured the AFC Player of the Year in 1986. Linebacker Karl Mecklenburg (77) recorded 9.5 sacks to achieve the honor.

Bill Parcells called "as good a game as anyone has played in any game, not just this game."

"I had been looking at film of [the Broncos] for seven or eight weeks. I noticed they showed us no respect throwing the ball." said Simms. "They played us man-to-man [coverage], and I wanted to [attack the cornerbacks] if they were going to play us like that. They thought they could just bump us and play us man-to-man and they couldn't."

On the series where Karlis missed the 23-yard field goal, the Broncos had first and goal from the Giants' 1-yard line but lost five yards on three running plays. It was typical of just how much Denver relied on Elway to put points on the board.

In fact, Elway provided almost all of Denver's offense, completing 22 of 37 passes for 304 yards, one touchdown (a 47-yard fourth-quarter strike to wide receiver Vance Johnson) and one interception. As Lawrence Taylor said, "I think their best offense is any time John has the ball in his hands." With the Giants keying on Elway by blitzing heavily, the Broncos gained only two net yards of offense in the second half.

Despite the loss, there was still plenty to cheer about in Denver after the 1986 season. There were 35 individual and team records established. Defensive end Rulon Jones was named the AFC Defensive Player of the Year by United Press International after recording 13.5 quarterback sacks, while linebacker Karl Mecklenburg's 9.5 sacks and productivity helped him earn AFC Player of the Year honors by the *Football News*. About 63,000 fans attended a send-off party for the Broncos before they left for the Super Bowl and another 100,000 attended a downtown parade after they lost.

While it was apparent that the Broncos needed a legitimate rushing threat to alleviate some of the pressure on Elway, Denver selected a wide receiver in the first round of the 1987 draft. Ricky Nattiel of the University of Florida joined Mark Jackson and Vance Johnson to form the Three Amigos, a spin-off of a popular comedy movie. The trio was no laughing matter on the field, as the Three Amigos became one of the NFL's more dangerous corps of wide receivers over the next few seasons.

By now, Elway's popularity was so great that the NFL wanted to use him to help promote the league internationally. The Broncos were sent to Wembley Stadium in London to play a 1987 preseason game against the Los Angeles Rams. In later years, Elway and the Broncos were sent to play in such locales as Tokyo (twice), Berlin, Barcelona and Mexico City.

Reeves, though, didn't have time for sightseeing in 1987. Rather, he was trying to keep his team together through some tumultuous times.

The problems started almost immediately following the Super Bowl loss to the Giants. Three key veteran defensive players—nose tackle Rubin Carter, linebacker Tom Jackson and free safety Steve Foley—retired. The exodus not only spelled the end of the "Orange Crush" era of Denver's defense but also left a huge leadership void that wasn't helped when cornerback Louis Wright retired just before the start of training camp.

The Broncos were then plagued by an injury bug that left the roster looking like a MASH unit. Players hit with major injuries were nose tackle Tony Colorito (knee), center Billy Bryan (knee), wide receiver Steve Watson (six broken ribs), running back Gerald Willhite (broken leg), Ricky Nattiel (fractured hand), running back

John Elway looks for a target in the 1987 opener, a 40-17 win over Seattle at Mile High Stadium. Despite missing four games due to the '87 players strike, Elway still threw for 3,198 yards and was named AFC Offensive Player of the Year by United Press International.

"If we hadn't struck in 1987 and demanded free agency and had not decided not to settle until we got it, we would not be talking about player freedom or about the ability of teams to rebuild their franchises."

Like most of his teammates, Gary Kubiak struggled mentally with the 1987 players strike. But he felt it ultimately benefitted the players, not only in '87, but in future years.

Steve Sewell (fractured jaw), safety Dennis Smith (broken arm) and Vance Johnson (dislocated shoulder).

The Broncos opened the 1987 season with an 1-0-1 record before facing yet another distraction. The NFL Players Association and franchise owners still could not reach an agreement regarding free-agency, so players walked out after the second game of the season.

"It became a real division between management and players," Pat Bowlen said. "It fueled a lot of animosity, especially because certain players did not want to be out, yet they felt they had to be in order to support the union. A lot of things went on that were sour."

Unlike in 1982, the owners had a plan ready to provide a television product. This way, teams wouldn't lose out on television-generated revenues, which is how teams make the bulk of their money. So franchises began assembling squads of replacement players who would wear the uniforms normally associated with the best football players in the world. Instead of watching Elway and Co., the Broncos were reduced to players such as Ken Karcher, Joe Dudek and Shane Swanson. Almost every regular player on the Broncos roster walked out on strike (only one of the 50 players dissented in a team vote), although some such as Elway did so more because they didn't want to alienate their teammates rather than a belief that the strike was right. Elway refused to walk the picket line with teammates and kept a low profile until the regular players returned to work.

"I never really got into it," Elway said. "I don't know if you ever get anything out of striking. We didn't get anything out of that strike, because we all went back in."

Said quarterback Gary Kubiak, who was Elway's backup in 1987: "It was extremely hard. I was a young player and I had a family and two kids. You only have that chance to make that kind of living and play for so long, so it was extremely hard to sit there. But it was for the betterment of the players down the road. In your life, sometimes you have to give up some things so that other people can benefit from them. Fortunately, the players are benefitting now."

The Broncos were one of the teams that benefitted—eventually. Although the NFL did not adopt a free-agency system until 1993, some players contend that the strike of '87 put the wheels in motion. Free-agency played a large role in the Broncos winning Super Bowl XXXII, as the system allowed Denver to add such key players as fullback Howard Griffith, linebacker Bill Romanowski, cornerback Ray Crockett, guards Mark Schlereth and Gary Zimmerman, and defensive linemen Keith Traylor, Alfred Williams and Neil Smith.

"If we hadn't struck in 1987 and demanded free agency and had not decided not to settle until we got it, we would not be talking about player freedom or about the ability of teams to rebuild their franchises," NFLPA president Gene Upshaw said. "Look at Denver. That's a good example. They go out on the free-agent market and it makes them competitive again real quick."

Said linebacker Ricky Hunley, who was Denver's union representative during the strike: "Look around now and see all the money guys make. That [the strike] was a start. It gave the league a taste of what free agency can really do. I think most of the goals the Players Association had set up to accomplish ultimately have been."

In 1987, though, it was hard to think about the future. Rather, it was easier to remember the past. After the players strike of 1982, the Broncos posted a 1-6 record and missed the playoffs.

Reeves deserves credit for assembling a fairly decent strike team in about a week's worth of time. After a loss to Houston, Denver's "replacement" players won games against the Raiders and Chiefs to give the Broncos a 3-1-1 overall record and second place in the AFC West. When the 24-day strike ended, the real Broncos returned with the comfort of knowing two key divisional opponents had already been defeated.

Only one replacement player (linebacker Tim Lucas) was on Denver's active roster during the Super Bowl. Yet even Hunley—who once branded two Broncos who crossed the picket line as "cowards"—acknowledges Denver may not have gotten as far without the fill-ins.

Vance Johnson emerged as a dangerous receiving threat during the strike-shortened '87 season. He led the Broncos in receptions (42) and receiving yardage (684) for the first time in his career.

"Without those two games, who knows what would have happened," said Hunley, who became the associate head football coach at the University of Missouri in the late 1990s. "Everybody had to play the hand they were dealt. Obviously, we were more prepared for the situation and had a better hand. But you have to tip your hat off more to management than anything else. Those players could have just as easily been somewhere else. In those games, there was not a lot of time to teach. You depended more on your athletic players."

As for the fans, more than 300,000 tickets were returned league-wide during the strike. But Denver weathered the situation better than just about any other NFL team. While the first replacement game drew only 38,494 fans—breaking the team's 130-game streak of consecutive sellouts at Mile High Stadium—the attendance was still more than double the NFL average for the weekend.

Then came what Bowlen said was the "game that broke the back of the strike"—a Monday night contest between Denver and the Raiders that drew 61,230 fans.

"We played it in the third week [of the strike] and [the regular players] were back in the fourth week," said Bowlen, whose team gave away 6,000 tickets for the

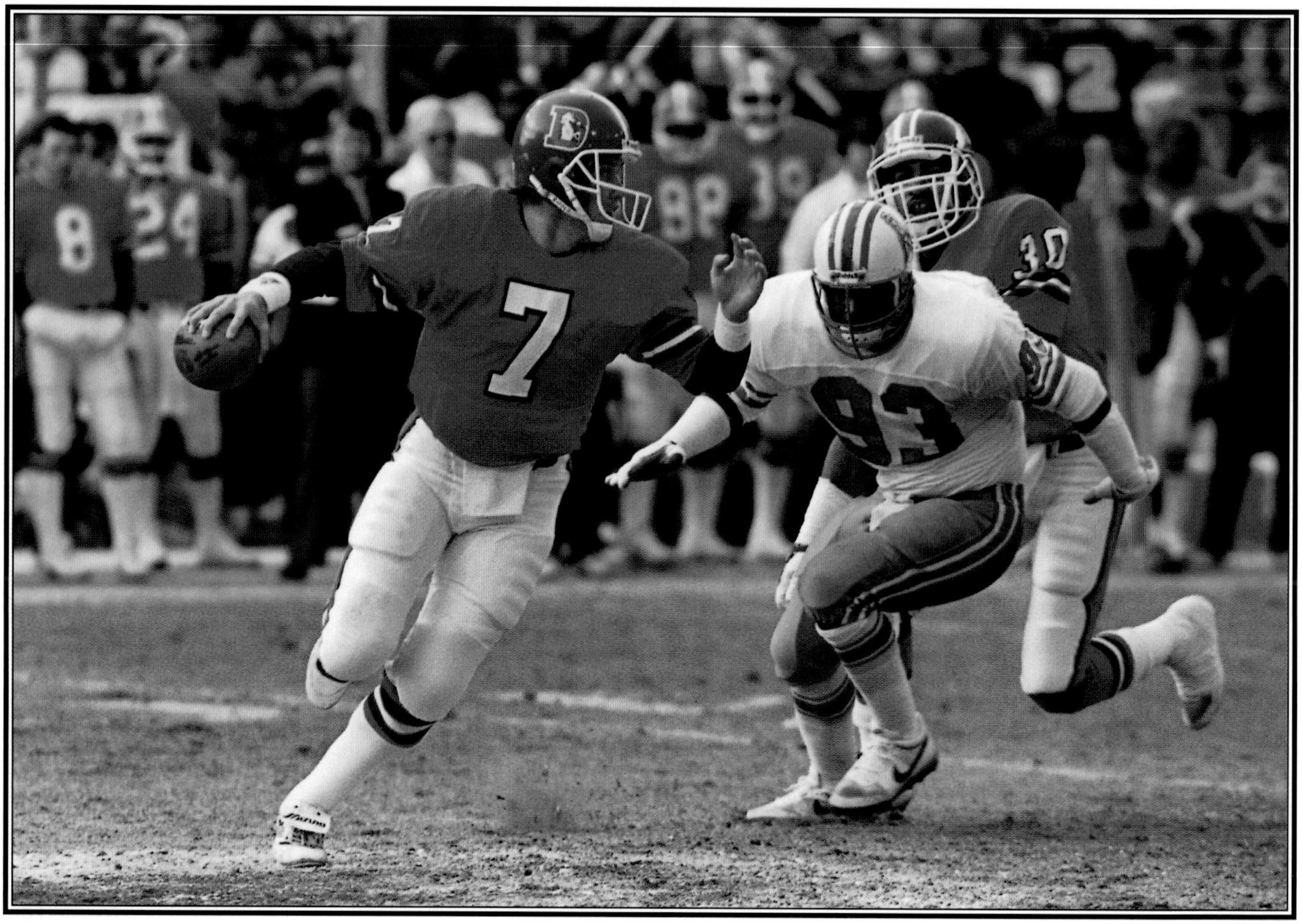

Elway scrambles against Houston in a 1987 AFC Divisional playoff game. Oilers coach Jerry Glanville boasted that Denver would be just one stop on his "four-game playoff schedule." But Elway threw two touchdown passes and scored on a 3-yard touchdown run as the Broncos won, 34-10, at Mile High Stadium.

Raiders game. "It was apparent that we weren't drawing 3,000 or 4,000; we were drawing 60,000-plus. And it was a pretty interesting game."

When the regular Broncos returned, some fans may have wished the replacement players were still around. That's because Denver lost two of its first three games after the strike and found itself three and a half games behind San Diego in the AFC West race. But then in a game that would probably dictate how the rest of the season would unfold, the Broncos hosted the 7-1 Chicago Bears on "Monday Night Football."

Both teams had earned their reputations through stingy defenses, but this game wasn't a highlight film for either unit as Denver and Chicago combined for 885 yards of total offense. Ironically, it was a replacement player who made the key play to lead Denver to a 31-29 win. Cornerback K.C. Clark intercepted a pass by Bears quarterback Jim McMahon and returned it 20 yards to Chicago's 39-yard line. Elway took advantage of the opportunity by leading the Broncos on a 61-yard drive capped by a 5-yard touchdown run by Steve Sewell, giving Denver its margin of victory.

Denver's defense saved face in the fourth quarter by sacking McMahon three times and forcing him out of the game with a leg injury. After that game, the Broncos would lose only one of their final six contests en route to a 10-4-1 record.

"It was a turning point," wide receiver Mark Jackson said of the Chicago game. "If we didn't make the turn, we knew we were going the wrong way."

The Broncos won the AFC West title by stopping San Diego, 24-0, in a blizzard on the final game of the season. That made Denver the NFL's only team to win at least 10 games eight times from 1977-87.

When asked about the possibility of inclement weather, Oilers coach Jerry Glanville said, "If it snows, tell [the Broncos] to wear snowshoes, 'cause we're going to run right around them."

Jeremiah Castille prepares to strip the ball from Cleveland's Earnest Byner on the Denver 3-yard line in the 1987 AFC Championship game at Mile High Stadium. The Browns were driving for the tying touchdown, but Castille recovered the fumble and the Broncos held on for a 38-33 victory.

The Broncos were obviously headed in the right direction entering the post-season, but Houston Oilers coach Jerry Glanville felt the same way about his club. In fact, Glanville's pre-game comments before an AFC Divisional playoff game at Mile High Stadium were bulletin-board material.

Glanville said the Broncos were "just the second stop on a four-game schedule. We're going to San Diego [for Super Bowl XXII]." When asked about the possibility of inclement weather, Glanville said, "If it snows, tell [the Broncos] to wear snowshoes, 'cause we're going to run right around them."

As it turned out, it was the Oilers who needed Mercury-like shoes. The Broncos converted two Houston turnovers to take a 14-0 lead in the first quarter. By halftime, it was 24-3 and the rout was on. Elway completed 14 of 25 passes for 259 yards and scored on a 3-yard run to help lead Denver to a 34-10 blowout of the Oilers.

Once again, the Broncos found themselves one game away from the Super Bowl. And once again, the opponent was the Cleveland Browns, although Mile High Stadium would be the site for the AFC Championship game.

Early in the third quarter, it appeared the Broncos would be coasting to a victory. An 80-yard completion from Elway to Mark Jackson extended the lead to 28-10. Bernie Kosar, though, didn't want Elway to believe he had cornered the market on comebacks. Kosar—whose lack of speed and grace made him the anti-Elway—answered with three touchdowns, including scoring passes to Earnest Byner and Webster Slaughter, as the Browns tied the score at 31-31 early in the fourth quarter.

The Broncos stormed back to take a seven-point lead on a 20-yard touchdown pass from Elway to Sammy Winder. But once again, Kosar led the Browns back. With 1:12 remaining and the ball on the Denver 8-yard line, Byner took a handoff and appeared headed for the game-tying touchdown. That's when cornerback Jeremiah Castille made a play that cemented his place in Denver Broncos history.

Castille forced Byner to fumble and recovered the ball on the 3-yard line. Cleveland eventually got the ball back after punter Mike Horan intentionally ran out of the end zone for a safety, but Kosar didn't have enough time to rally the Browns. Denver held on for a 38-33 victory to become the first AFC team in nine seasons to make back-to-back trips to the Super Bowl. The game was watched in 91 percent of Denver households, which was an all-time NFL record for local viewership.

Ricky Nattiel takes a serious jolt from Redskins defensive back Todd Bowles, but recovers to make the catch in the third quarter of Super Bowl XXII in San Diego. Nattiel scored Denver's only touchdown, a 56-yard pass from John Elway in the first quarter, as the Broncos were thrashed, 42-10.

"I just felt like [Byner] was in such a position that it wouldn't have done me any good to make the tackle," said Castille, who almost forced a Byner fumble on the previous play. "He was going to score. I had to try and strip it. That's all I had left."

Reaching the Super Bowl after such a turbulent season was a source of pride for Reeves, who received praise from around the NFL for the job he did coaching in 1987.

"No question we've had some adversity," said Reeves before Denver's Super Bowl XXII matchup against Washington. "The fact we had to survive all those things really makes you feel good. What it does is make you feel like, because you've been able to handle it, you're able to handle other things that might come up."

No team, though, could handle what Washington did to the Broncos on one of the darkest Sunday afternoons in Denver history. The Redskins posted the highest single-quarter scoring output in Super Bowl history, putting 35 points on the scoreboard in the second quarter. More Super Bowl records were set when the Redskins finished with 602 total yards of offense, including 204 yards by rookie running back Timmy Smith. Not only had he never scored a touchdown before the Super Bowl, but Smith never did anything noteworthy in the NFL again before retiring after the 1990 season and relocating to, of all places, Denver.

Smith actually was overshadowed by Washington quarterback Doug Williams, who was named the game's Most Valuable Player after completing 18 of 29 passes for a Super Bowl-record 340 yards and four touchdowns. Williams became the first black quarterback in NFL history to win the award.

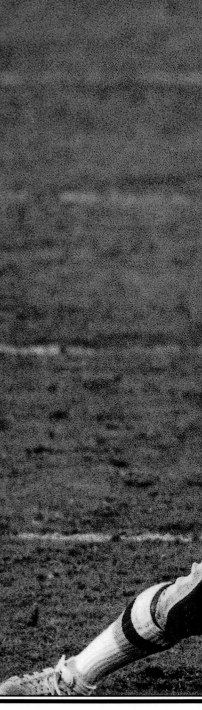

Making the 42-10 loss even more shocking was the fact Denver took a 10-0 lead into the second quarter. The Broncos only needed a Super Bowl-record one minute and 57 seconds to record their first score on a 56-yard touchdown pass from Elway to Ricky Nattiel. But that was about the only positive moment for the Broncos. Unable to adjust after the Redskins began using safety Alvin Walton as a "spy" against Elway, the NFL's Most Valuable Player in 1987 completed just 14 of 38 passes for 257 yards with one touchdown and three interceptions.

"Walton was just hanging there in the middle," said Elway, who completed only two of 11 passes in the second quarter. "If I would start to move [out of the pock-

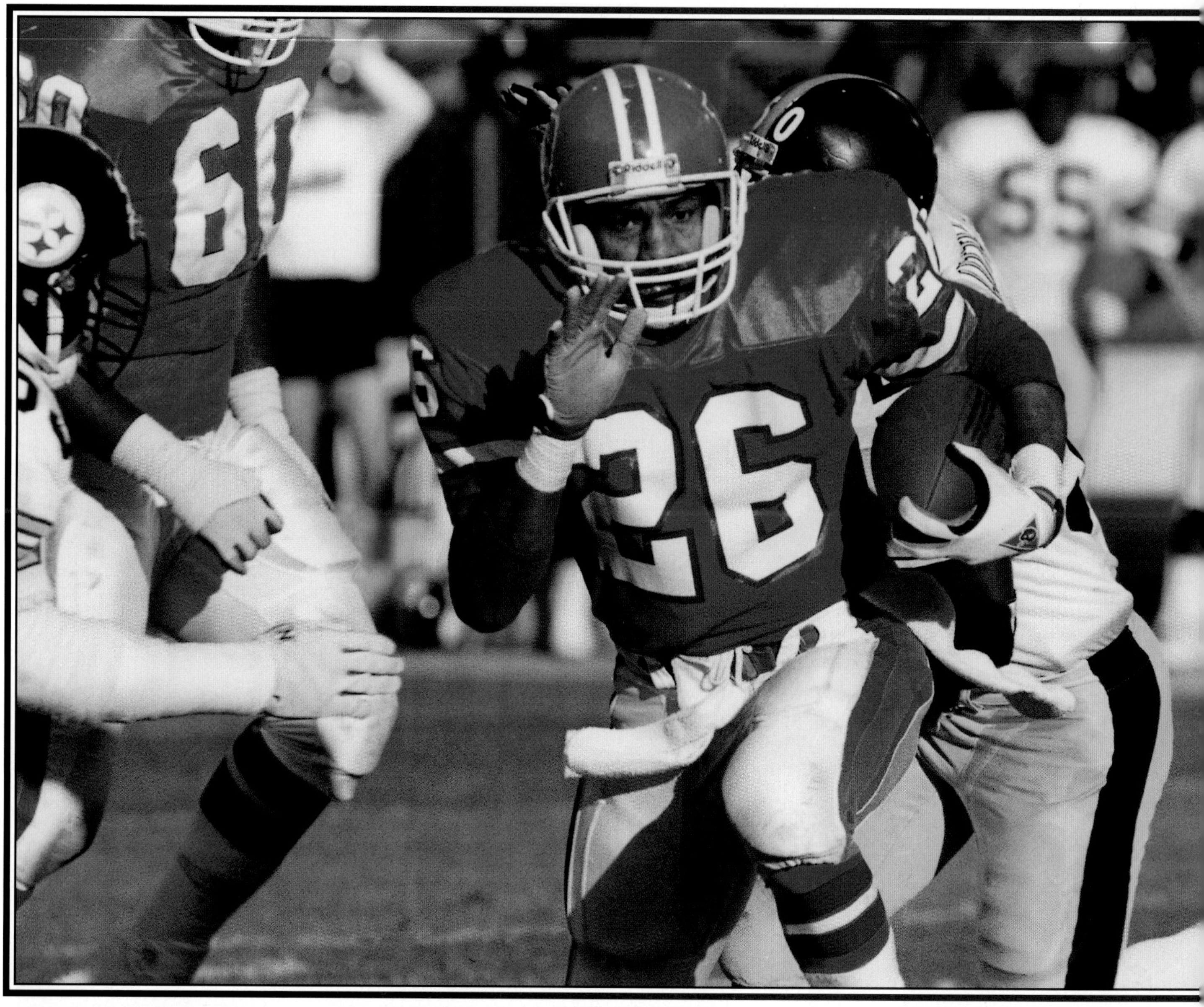

Bobby Humphrey escapes a defender in the Broncos' 24-23 victory over Pittsburgh in a 1989 AFC Divisional playoff game at Mile High Stadium. Humphrey led the Broncos in rushing in 1989 with 1,151 yards, fifth in the AFC.

et], he would come after me. If I looked like I was going to pass, he would drop back in coverage."

Unlike the loss to the Giants in the previous Super Bowl, the Broncos weren't able to bounce back from this Super Bowl defeat quite as easily. Tight end Clarence Kay seemed to set the tone for the 1988 season after the loss to Washington by saying, "This really sets us back, coming out here two years in a row and getting beat like that. Something has to be done somewhere."

The Broncos tried addressing their offense in the off-season by acquiring future Hall-of-Fame running back Tony Dorsett from the Dallas Cowboys. Clearly on the downside of his career at age 34, Dorsett finished the 1988 campaign with 703 yards rushing on 181 carries. It was his only season in Denver and last in pro football. The Broncos missed the playoffs altogether by finishing with an 8-8 record.

Still in search of a topflight running back, the Broncos finally found a player who could take some of the pressure off Elway. Bobby Humphrey of Alabama was taken in the first round of the 1989 supplemental draft by the Broncos and made an immediate impact, finishing his rookie season with 1,151 yards and seven touch-

Sammy Winder can't escape the clutches of Cleveland linebacker Clay Matthews in the 1989 AFC Championship game. Winder broke free at other times, however, scoring two TDs in the Broncos' 37-21 victory at Mile High Stadium.

downs. Vance Johnson also came into his own, becoming the first Broncos wide receiver since Steve Watson in 1984 to post a 1,000-yard season. Johnson finished the season with 76 receptions for 1,095 yards and seven touchdowns.

The Broncos also received an added boost early in the 1989 season. When the Los Angeles Raiders fired head coach Mike Shanahan after four games, he returned to assume the role of Denver's quarterbacks coach. He was a major factor in Elway's rebound from a sub-par 1988 campaign.

The Broncos lost three of their final four games in 1989, but still finished with an 11-5 mark and were able to play both playoff games at Mile High Stadium. That is significant because crowd noise played an important role in Denver's 24-23 victory over Pittsburgh in the first game.

A 1-yard touchdown run by rookie running back Melvin Bratton gave Denver its first lead of the game with just 2:27 remaining in the fourth quarter. The Steelers got the ball back, but rookie center Dermontti Dawson—a perennial Pro Bowl selection later in his career—couldn't hear the snap count on a third-down play. Steelers quarterback Bubby Brister bobbled an early snap and the ball was recovered by Denver's Randy Robbins, ensuring the Broncos'. victory.

A 37-21 victory over Cleveland in the AFC Championship game was much easier. The Broncos dominated the Browns from the outset, jumping to a 24-7 lead early in the third quarter. The Browns closed the gap to three points, 24-21, on two third-

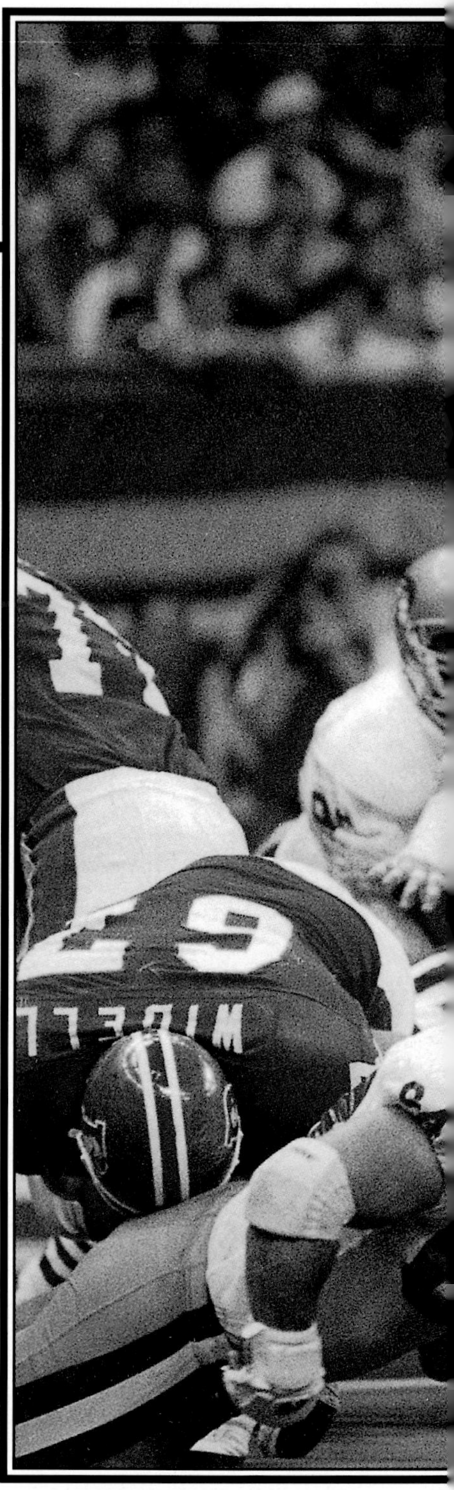

Bobby Humphrey ran into John Elway after taking this handoff in Super Bowl XXIV. The Broncos were nearly run out of the Louisiana Superdome by Joe Montana, Jerry Rice and the rest of the 49ers, who scored two touchdowns in each quarter to win, 55-10. The 45-point differential was the third highest in NFL championship history.

quarter touchdowns, but the Broncos took control in the fourth quarter on a 39-yard scoring pass from Elway to Sammy Winder and two field goals by David Treadwell.

Elway was brilliant in one of his all-time best performances, completing 20 of 36 passes for 385 yards, three touchdowns and no interceptions.

But even after the performance, Broncos fans feared the worst for their team in Super Bowl XXIV against San Francisco, a team that will be regarded as one of the greatest in NFL history.

A poll taken by a local television station asked fans whether they wanted the Broncos to play in the game. Those who voted "no" outnumbered those who said "yes" by a 1,500 to 1,300 margin.

Elway became infuriated by the negative reaction of some of the fans and local media. He also wasn't afraid to state how important this Super Bowl was to his career and to the Broncos organization. "For me to be the quarterback I want to be, we've got to win this game," he said.

But unfortunately for the Broncos and their quarterback, Elway was even worse against the 49ers than he was versus the Redskins in Super Bowl XXII. Played in New Orleans at the Louisiana Superdome, Elway completed only six of 20 passes in the first half as his team fell behind, 27-3. He finished 10-of-26 for 108 yards, no touchdowns and two interceptions.

The final score of 55-10 tied Detroit's 59-14 win over Cleveland in 1957 as the third-highest point differential (45) in NFL championship history. Only the Chicago Bears' 73-0 victory over the Redskins in 1940 and the Browns' 56-10 win over the Lions in 1954 were more lopsided.

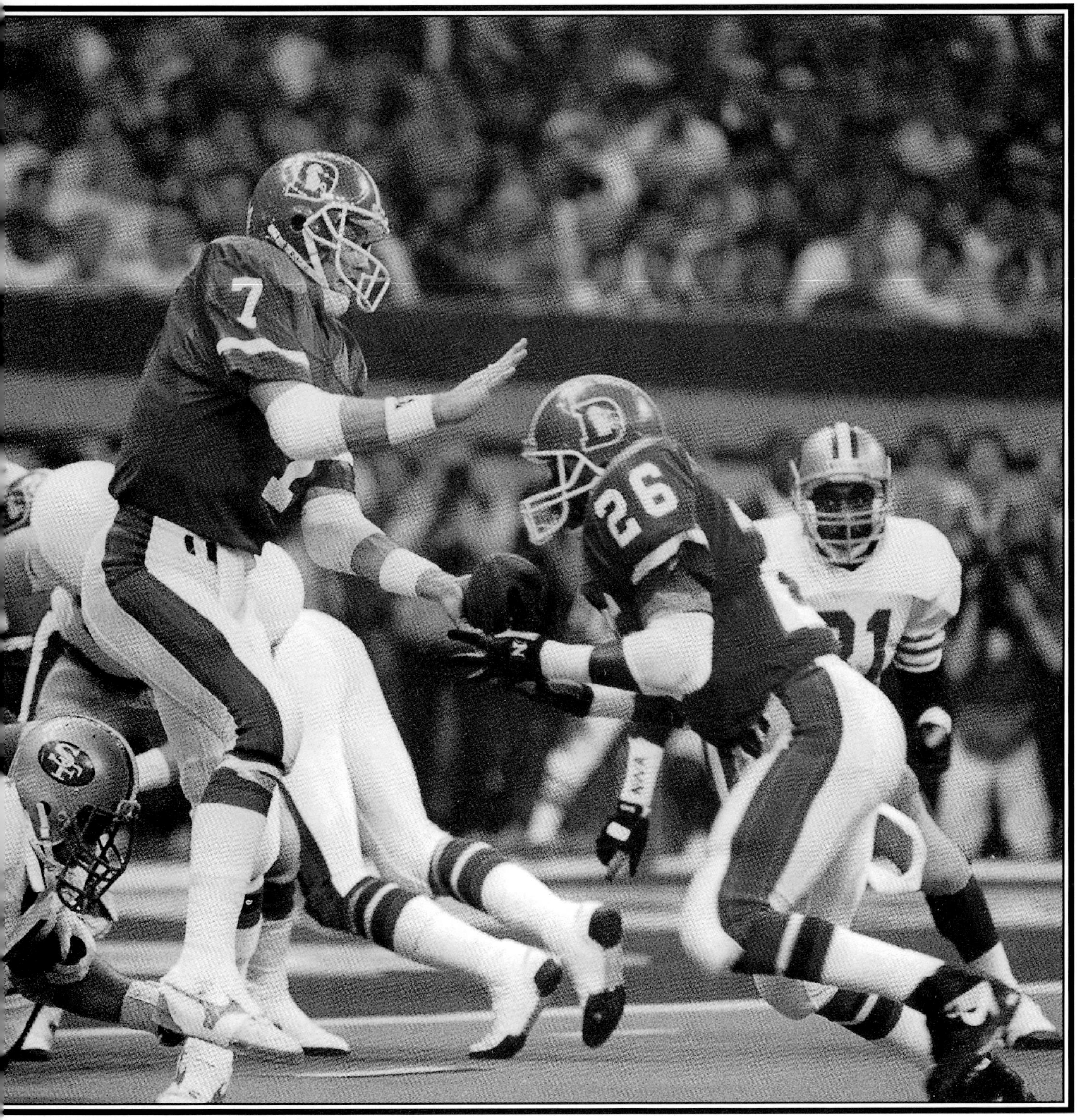

The Broncos' only scoring came on David Treadwell's 42-yard field goal in the first quarter and on Elway's 3-yard run in the third quarter. Making the defeat even more painful was the outstanding performance turned in by 49ers quarterback Joe Montana, who riddled Denver's defense for five touchdown passes—three to Jerry Rice—while completing 22 of 29 passes with no interceptions. Elway also was stung by comments from established NFL quarterbacks who claimed he simply was not good enough to win the NFL's biggest game.

"This is going to live with me," Elway said after the game. "I know that."

John Elway races for yardage in a 17-7 win over Cleveland in 1991. The Broncos finished the season at 12-4 and were racing toward the Super Bowl, but stumbled in a loss to Buffalo in the AFC Championship game.

Broncos owner Pat Bowlen was asked in December 1994 whether helping John Elway win a Super Bowl ring was his No. 1 priority. Bowlen responded by saying, "No, but it's close." Such steadfast loyalty to a player is admirable. But it also probably cost two head coaches their jobs. The firings of Dan Reeves and Wade Phillips were prompted largely by the fact that Bowlen felt neither coach was close to leading the Broncos to a Super Bowl title during Elway's career.

The situation with Reeves turned particularly ugly in the three seasons following Denver's 55-10 loss to San Francisco in Super Bowl XXIV. Elway believed Reeves was much too conservative on offense, which the Broncos' quarterback felt was a mistake because of the team's lack of a solid rushing attack and his own throwing ability. Elway even doubted that he would make the Hall of Fame because of his passing statistics.

"We rarely threw except on passing downs, and people knew when we were ready to throw," Elway said. "That was the style of the offense. We didn't have the quick game we have now. When people were coming at us,

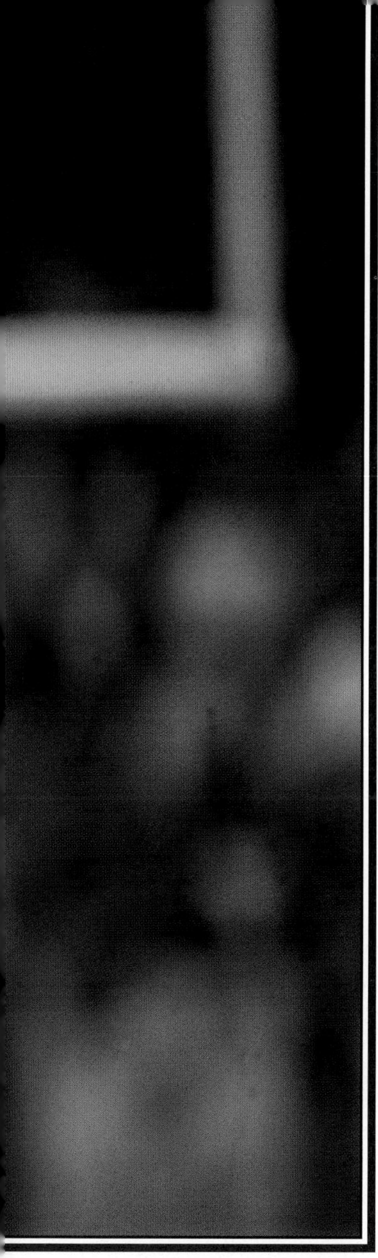

we weren't able to get out of there. If we had a tough time protecting on that day, it usually made for a long day. We had some good years. We had a good offensive team, but it seemed to go downhill."

As did the relationship between Elway and Reeves. Offensive coordinator Mike Shanahan had been fired by Reeves after the 1991 season because of what he felt was insubordination. Elway and Shanahan were accused of scripting plays without Reeves's knowledge. Also in 1991, Reeves and former Washington head coach Joe Gibbs had a discussion about the possibility of an Elway trade. Reeves then drafted UCLA quarterback Tommy Maddox in the first round of the 1992 draft, indicating that he was more concerned with planning for the future than immediately winning a Super Bowl. Maddox never came close to becoming a quality NFL starter and retired after four seasons, only two of which were spent in Denver.

Chapter 7

1990–1994

Rockier Roads

The Broncos become a team in transition as they adapt to the changing NFL of the '90s and look for new paths to the Super Bowl.

Even amid the turmoil, there was some success. After a 5-11 campaign in 1990, the Broncos rebounded with a 12-4 record in 1991. A 26-24 victory over Houston in an AFC Divisional playoff game featured an Elway fourth-quarter comeback that led to David Treadwell's 28-yard game-winning field goal with 16 seconds remaining.

But the Broncos ran out of magic in a 10-7 loss to Buffalo in the AFC Championship game. Despite a stellar performance by Denver's defense, which limited the host Bills to only 213 yards of offense and 12 first downs, the Broncos failed to take advantage of four scoring opportunities inside Buffalo territory. Elway was knocked out of the game late in the third quarter with a thigh injury.

This meant that backup quarterback Gary Kubiak would have to become the King of Comebacks. With the Broncos trailing 10-0, Kubiak scored on a 3-yard run at 13:17 of the fourth quarter. The Broncos recovered the subsequent onside kick with 1:43 remaining. But Denver's Super Bowl dreams died when Buffalo recovered a fumble by running back Steve Sewell and ran enough time off the clock so that Kubiak could only lead the Broncos to the 50 as time ran out.

It appeared that Elway and the Broncos would redeem themselves in 1992 when the team opened with a 7-3 record. But to no one's surprise, they went down as quickly as Elway did.

During a 27-13 win over the New York Giants on Nov. 15, Elway bruised a tendon in his right shoulder, an injury that sidelined him for the next four games. With Kubiak—the long-time dependable backup—having retired, Reeves was forced to turn to reserves Maddox and Shawn Moore. Neither quarterback could win one of the four games Elway missed, dropping Denver's record to 7-7. The Broncos still had a chance to make the playoffs after Elway returned, but a 42-20 loss at Kansas City in the season-finale left them at 8-8.

Seeing his quarterback suffer personally and his team apparently stuck in neutral, Bowlen felt a change was needed. After notching a 117-79-1 record (including 10 playoff games and three Super Bowls) in 12 seasons, Reeves was fired.

Reeves, though, doesn't harbor any animosity toward his former team. Now the head coach of Atlanta, Reeves hugged and shook hands with Bowlen and three of the four players who remained from his coaching era when the Falcons played the Broncos during the 1997 season.

The only player Reeves didn't shake hands with? Elway.

"I've never had a football team the whole time I was in Denver that I didn't feel were the right kind of people," said Reeves, who was hired by the New York Giants shortly after being fired in Den-

While offense was the controversial topic in the early '90s, defense remained a strength. It included linebacker Mike Croel (above) who recorded 10 quarterback sacks in 1991 to win AFC Rookie of the Year honors.

John Elway believed the Broncos weren't taking full advantage of their passing-game potential during the latter years of the Dan Reeves era. Elway failed to finish in the top five in AFC passing statistics every season from 1988-92.

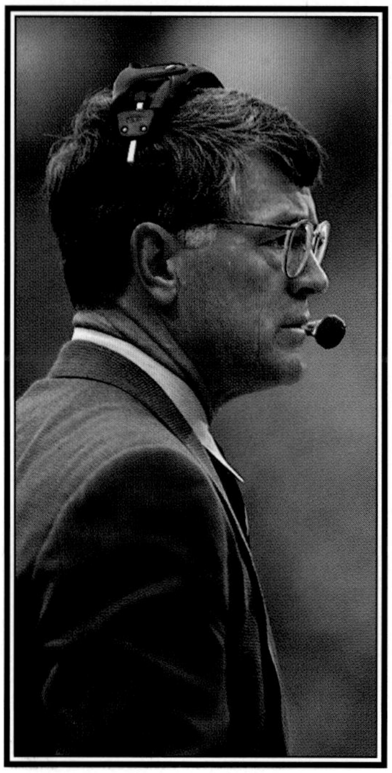

Dan Reeves was fired after the Broncos lost five of their last six in 1992 to finish at 8-8 and miss the playoffs for the second time in three seasons. His 12-year record (including playoffs) was 117-79-1.

ver. "We had the success we had because they were the right kind of people. We had a couple of years there where we weren't successful, but it wasn't because of the people.

"There were some circumstances of us losing some close ball games and having some injuries. There were some things that kept us from succeeding. But it wasn't because of the players' effort. I never felt it was because the players didn't play hard."

Bowlen now needed to select a new head coach. Among the candidates Bowlen expressed interest in were Dennis Erickson, Ray Rhodes, Steve Spurrier (who was waived as a quarterback in the Broncos' 1977 training camp) and Dave Wannstedt. But the obvious first choice was Mike Shanahan, whose innovative offense and relationship with Elway made him a perfect fit.

In retrospect, Bowlen would probably have hired Shanahan at any cost. But after Shanahan's bad head coaching experience with the Los Angeles Raiders—where he felt Raiders owner Al Davis meddled too much—he wanted control over personnel decisions. That was something Bowlen was unwilling to grant because he felt Reeves was wielding excessive power with such a privilege. Bowlen also wanted a bigger say in personnel moves in hopes of getting Elway a championship.

When the two sides became too far apart in salary negotiations, Bowlen and Shanahan graciously called off contract talks. Shanahan decided to remain as the San Francisco 49ers' offensive coordinator, where his unit enjoyed the most productive three-year run in NFL history.

"The situation wasn't right for me at the time," Shanahan said.

With Shanahan out of the picture, Bowlen turned to the son of a Bum.

Bum Phillips, that is.

Wade Phillips had spent the past four seasons as Denver's defensive coordinator, directing a unit that picked up the slack when Elway couldn't. Denver reached the Super Bowl in Phillips's first season in 1989, followed by a 1990 campaign where Denver's defense led the NFL in 12 categories. In 1991, the Broncos had the NFL's top-ranked defense. Phillips seemed destined for an NFL head coaching job since entering the NFL at the age of 27. His father, O.A. "Bum" Phillips, was a well-

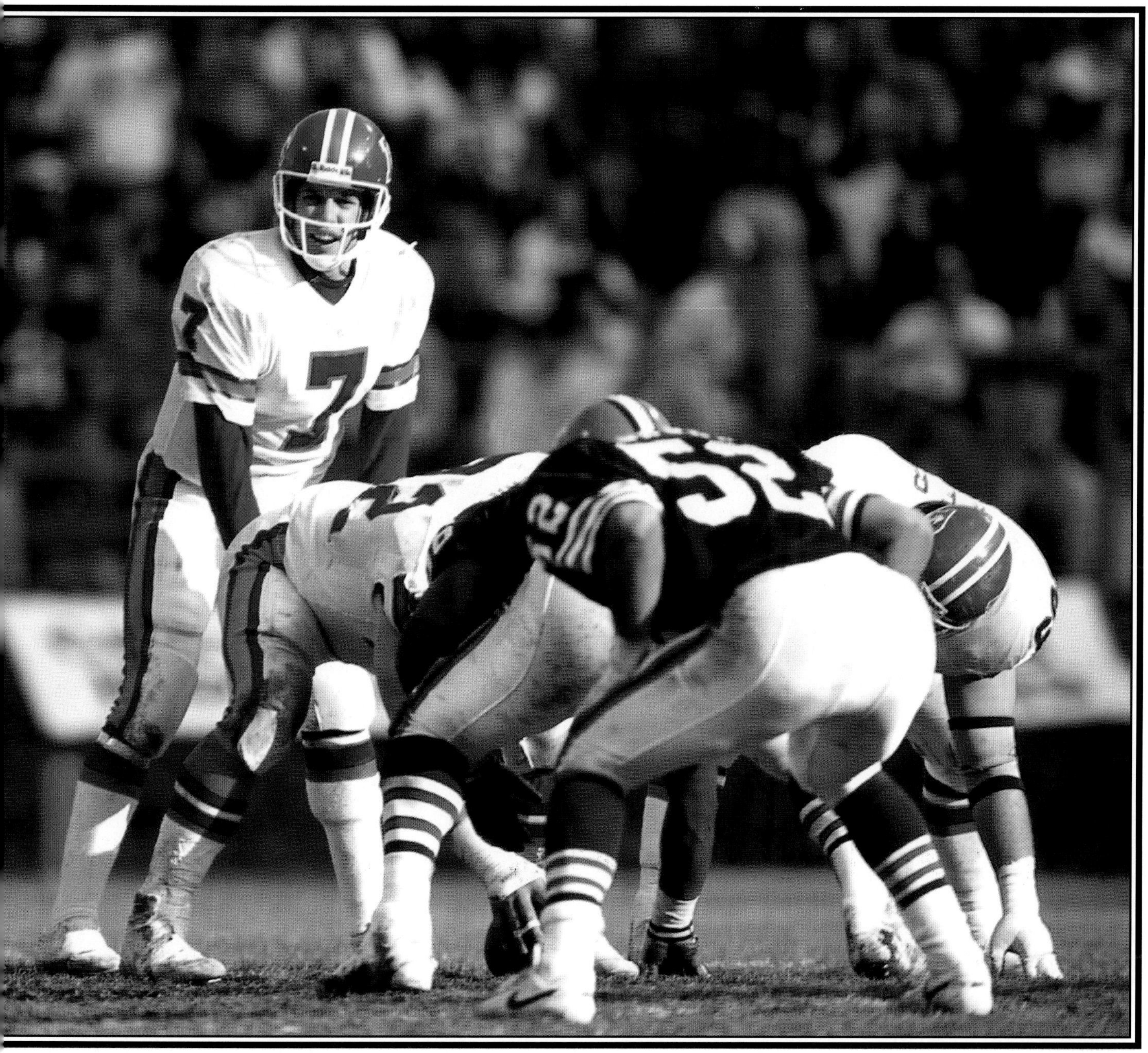

respected head coach with the Houston Oilers (1975-80) and New Orleans Saints (1981-85). His 11-year coaching record (including playoffs) was 86-80.

Phillips also was regarded as a player's coach, something Reeves was criticized for not being during his final years in Denver.

During his first news conference as head coach, Phillips said, "I'm going to try to be myself. I'm not Bum Phillips, and I'm not Dan Reeves. The reason I got this job was because of the way I am. Whatever way that is . . . that's what got me here."

Even though Elway would have loved having Shanahan as his head coach, he emphatically supported the hiring of Phillips.

"I think the best man got the job," Elway said. "I knew all along that Pat was going to get the guy [who] was going to be the best for the Denver Broncos, and that's Wade Phillips right now."

Phillips was just as eager to please Elway. Perhaps too eager.

The first order of business for new coach Wade Phillips was to improve the offense. John Elway welcomed the opportunity.

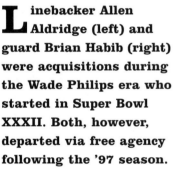

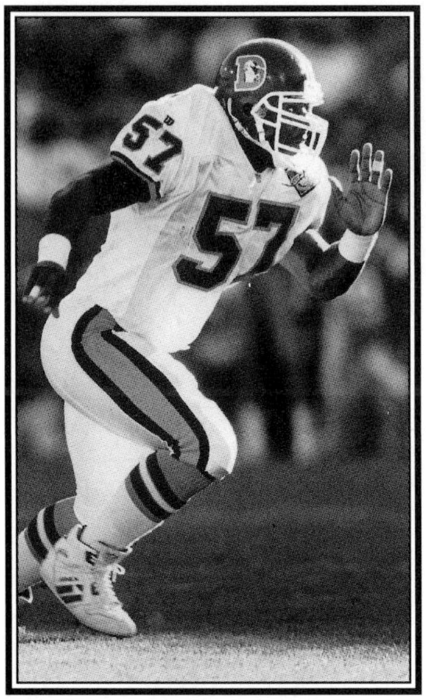

Linebacker Allen Aldridge (left) and guard Brian Habib (right) were acquisitions during the Wade Philips era who started in Super Bowl XXXII. Both, however, departed via free agency following the '97 season.

The first order of business in the off-season for Phillips was to improve an offense that some felt was ignored during the Reeves era. The Broncos had a golden opportunity to do that via the NFL's new free-agency system.

In 1993, the NFL and its players union came to terms on a new collective bargaining agreement that would give unrestricted free agency to players with four years of experience whose contracts had expired. Until then, players were basically restricted to the team that drafted them unless they were traded or released.

The Broncos became one of the more aggressive teams in free agency under the direction of Bowlen, Phillips and personnel director Bob Ferguson. Four of the five players signed in 1993 were on the offensive side of the football. Unfortunately for the Broncos, only guard Brian Habib became a productive player. Running back Rod Bernstine and tackle Don Maggs—two players Denver was counting on heavily—became epic busts.

There were some good-to-great players acquired via trade or the draft during Phillips's two seasons, notably tackle Gary Zimmerman, center Tom Nalen, linebacker Allen Aldridge, kicker Jason Elam and punter Tom Rouen. Cornerback Ray Crockett was another player from the Phillips era who was a starter on the Broncos team that won Super Bowl XXXII.

But because acquiring offensive talent was never a Reeves priority, Phillips tried to overcompensate. Only three marginal defensive players were signed via free agency during his two-year coaching tenure.

Place-kicker Jason Elam (left) was a third-round draft choice in 1993. Cornerback Ray Crockett (above) was signed as a free agent from Detroit in 1994.

"Wade was given a pretty short leash [by Bowlen]," said Ferguson, who is the Arizona Cardinals' player personel director in 1998. "We felt we had to go out and do some things quickly to give John Elway some weapons. We felt we had to go out and try to make some things happen. Some of the decisions worked out and some didn't."

Phillips also attempted to utilize Elway's skills better by installing a West Coast-style offense, a system that emphasizes short drops by the quarterback and quick routes by the wide receivers. Jim Fassel—Elway's offensive coordinator at Stanford who became head coach of the New York Giants in 1997—was given the position.

Phillips was embraced by the city of Denver upon his hiring. But the honeymoon ended before the 1993 season ended. While Reeves compiled a 9-3 record with the New York Giants, the Broncos were 7-5 and struggling, having lost four games by three points each. Fans and media complained that Phillips was too lenient on players, something that made Elway take umbrage.

"Why is it every time we lose a football game, someone has to question Wade's coaching ability and whether he's too light?" Elway asked. "We're not losing because

Under new offensive coordinator Jim Fassel (right), Denver installed a West Coast-style offense in 1993. Elway responded with a career-best 4,030 passing yards and was named AFC Offensive Player of the Year by United Press International.

of discipline. We're not losing because guys aren't playing hard."

The Broncos made the playoffs as a wild-card with a 9-7 record, but it was not pretty. Facing the Raiders for the first time in the playoffs since the 1977 AFC Championship game, the Broncos were punished, 42-24, in Los Angeles.

Phillips, though, was upbeat after the season. After all, the Broncos had fielded the league's youngest roster in 1993 with an average 3.1 years of NFL experience. In addition, there were 25 players who were spending their first season with Denver, which is a large turnover for any head coach to handle.

The Broncos' coach became so optimistic about his team's chances that he spoke about reaching the Super Bowl in 1994. Phillips now believes he goofed by speaking from the heart.

"I may have made a mistake by saying, 'Well, we're going to win now,'" Phillips said. "We got into the playoffs the first year and then everybody wanted more. Maybe I should have said like most coaches do to protect themselves, 'Well, we're going to try to bring it along and we don't have everything now' and that type of thing. In retrospect, that might have hurt me. Everybody wants instant gratification anyway. But I was taking over a team that wasn't a playoff team and had some weaknesses, [but] played hard.

"I look at things and say, I would have done this or that different, certainly. But once it's gone, I'm going on to the next thing."

Phillips was gone from Denver after the 1994 season—a losing campaign at 7-9. A sluggish beginning by Elway helped contribute to an 0-4 start. The Broncos lost their season-opener at home to San Diego, 37-34, when the ball slipped from Elway's hand on what probably would have been the game-winning drive in the fourth quarter. The same thing happened to Elway in a 27-20 loss at Buffalo when the ball slipped from his hand on an attempted pass into the end zone.

Elway also had interceptions returned for touchdowns in each of the first three games: the San Diego defeat, plus losses to the New York Jets (25-22 in overtime) and the Los Angeles Raiders (48-16).

"Defense was his specialty and it was kind of our downfall at the time. He went out and got us some free-agents offensively that made us better there. Maybe that hurt us a bit defensively."

Getting routed by the Raiders at Mile High Stadium prompted some fans in the south end zone to pelt Phillips with debris. A Denver radio station set up its morning show outside team headquarters with posters reading, "Wade must go."

Four consecutive losses tied the 1964 Broncos for the worst start in franchise history. Although Phillips was given a vote of confidence, Bowlen did urge him to become more involved in coaching the defense. Phillips had given that task to defensive coordinator Charlie Waters so he could focus on other matters. Denver's defense, though, ended the season with the worst ranking in team history.

"Defense was his specialty and it was kind of our downfall at the time," said Elway, who broke the 3,000 mark in passing yardage (3,490) for the ninth time in his career in 1994. "He went out and got us some free-agents offensively that made us better there. Maybe that hurt us a bit defensively."

Defensive coordinator Charlie Waters (left) and head coach Wade Phillips (right) were unable to get the Denver defense untracked in 1994. The Broncos gave up 396 points, the most since the 1968 season.

Said free safety Steve Atwater: "A lot of it has to do with the way you teach. You can try to teach and teach. But if it's not the correct way, you can teach all day and the person won't learn, whereas with another method you could teach for 15 minutes and it would sink in forever. I don't dwell on it, but it was that more than anything."

Phillips was also perceived as being too easy on his team—an image that wasn't helped when Bowlen raised concerns about the Broncos' discipline because of excess penalties during the '94 season.

"Things went on," said linebacker Keith Burns, who was a rookie in 1994. "We had guys hanging out and whatever off the field. You know, late nights out. I don't think that has anything to do with the coach himself. I think it's more of a personal thing. You have to know what you need to do at this level.

"That all hurt us in the end. Come Sunday, we weren't prepared mentally. He [Phillips] had the game plan put in, but mentally we weren't there."

Said Elway: "Wade was a player's coach. He was really a passionate guy, a soft-hearted guy—maybe too much to the point it got him in a little bit of trouble."

Transition in the Denver defense included the retirement of 12-year veteran linebacker Karl Mecklenburg after the 1994 season.

There were also outside forces ripping at the Phillips regime besides Elway's aging and a losing season in '94. The baseball Colorado Rockies had begun play in the National League in 1993 and were taking a chunk of the city's sports dollars. The Denver Nuggets of the National Basketball Association also had a following, while the Quebec Nordiques were making plans to move to Denver and become the Colorado Avalanche of the National Hockey League.

Bowlen—who has endured personal struggles with his finances—wasn't going to risk his team losing the top spot in the market.

"To stay competitive in this town, you can't be in the middle of the pack," Bowlen said. "You see that more than ever now. At that time, baseball was starting out and, in order to stay competitive, we had to win. The other consideration was John. I just felt that we weren't getting there. I certainly wouldn't put much of the blame on Wade. I felt he didn't have some of the support that he needed."

Until late in the season, Phillips felt he had a strong chance of returning for the final year of his contract. The Broncos enjoyed a 7-2 stretch in the middle of the '94 season in spite of losing starters for a combined 78 games due to injury.

The Broncos, though, lost their final three games and Phillips was fired during the week after the season ended. Ironically, the defeat that eliminated Denver from post-season contention came against Shanahan and the 49ers on Dec. 17. The Broncos were drummed, 42-19, at San Francisco.

"We had a lot of people injured that year and I knew we were going to come back and do well after that," Phillips said. "And I knew we had to improve defensively. That's my strength. We needed some players on defense, but we [had] spent some money on offensive players to get that started. Then we were going to go after defense. We had a plan."

But whatever Phillips had in mind, some players didn't completely buy it.

"I thought he was a great person," said Broncos tight end Shannon Sharpe. "There's no question about that. You look at the personnel and how he gets [it] to play. He's a great defensive coach. The thing was that if he had surrounded himself with better talent and the coaching staff, who knows what would have happened."

Said Elway: "It's kind of hard to say [whether Phillips was fired too soon], because we've been real successful with Mike [Shanahan] in here. But Wade's going to get another shot."

After three successful seasons as the defensive coordinator in Buffalo, Phillips did get another chance. When Marv Levy retired as the Bills' head coach following the 1997 season, Phillips was named his successor.

When the Broncos needed a head coach in 1995, Bowlen knew who he wanted. Mike Shanahan was given a lucrative seven-year contract to become Denver's head coach. He also was given control over all personnel moves, an extremely valuable commodity considering Bowlen would spend freely on free-agent players to make the team better.

It may have been Bowlen's wisest move to date.

Tight end Shannon Sharpe became an offensive force during the Wade Phillips era, averaging 84 receptions in 1993-94. He finished in the top five among AFC receivers each season and was named to the Pro Bowl twice.

Terrell Davis breaks away from a pack of Panthers at Mile High Stadium on Nov. 9, 1997. The Broncos won, 34-0, the ninth victory in the first 10 games of their Super Bowl season.

Mike Shanahan was no stranger to the Denver Broncos when he was appointed head coach in January 1995. Shanahan began his NFL career in Denver when he was named wide receivers coach by Dan Reeves in 1984. And after Shanahan was fired as head coach of the Los Angeles Raiders four games into the 1989 campaign, he returned to the Broncos as quarterbacks coach that same season.

But the Shanahan who became the 11th head coach in Broncos history wasn't the same person who left the franchise again after the 1991 season to become offensive coordinator of the San Francisco 49ers.

"I think every [coaching] situation I've been in I've learned a lot from," said Shanahan, who began his coaching career at age 21 as an assistant at Eastern Illinois University. "But the one I think that helped me the most at the pro level was my three years with San Francisco. Some of the reasons why are all the success they've had and how they've continued to be on top and run their organization in a first-class manner."

It was this experience that helped Shanahan convert the Broncos into what could be considered the Rocky Mountain version of the 49ers. The full-contact practices that were a staple of Reeves and Wade Phillips were abolished. Instead, Shanahan instituted a system that put less wear and tear on his player's bodies.

This philosophy is the major reason why the Broncos managed to avoid significant injuries during the 1996 and '97 seasons. Shanahan also was able to attract people from San Francisco to Denver. Neal Dahlen—considered one of the NFL's best assessors of talent—left the 49ers in March 1996 to become Shanahan's director of player personnel. The Broncos team that won Super Bowl XXXII had more of a San Francisco flavor than Rice-a-Roni, with seven ex-49ers on the roster. Starters included linebacker Bill Romanowski, defensive end Alfred Williams and wide receiver Ed McCaffrey. But emulating the 49ers was one thing. Having as much on-field success was another, as the Broncos learned during Shanahan's first season as head coach.

Chapter 8

1995–1997

Summit Salute!

Elway, Davis and Co. get it done! The wild ride to the mountaintop is over as the Broncos become Super Bowl champions!

The 1995 campaign was a roller coaster for Denver. The team never lost more than two consecutive games, but didn't win more than two straight either. Despite the familiarity between Shanahan and Elway, the Broncos weren't quick to grasp another West Coast-style offense that was installed. Elway had played in a similar system under ex-offensive coordinator Jim Fassel, but Shanahan's scheme was more sophisticated.

During the '95 training camp, Elway said "it's the hardest camp I've had since my first couple years [in the NFL]. It's not too bad physically, because I'm in pretty good shape. It's been more mental than anything."

Although the Broncos averaged 27 points in the first three games of the 1995 season, a 17-6 loss to the San Diego Chargers on Sept. 24 marked the first time in almost three years that Denver failed to score a touchdown.

The next six games were just as bumpy. Denver scored only one touchdown in a 27-10 loss to Seattle, but ripped New England, 37-3, when the Broncos shifted to a shotgun formation. A 27-0 shutout of Oakland was followed by a 21-7 defeat against the Kansas City Chiefs at Mile High Stadium. It marked the first time since the 1971 and '72 seasons that the Broncos lost two consecutive home games to the Chiefs.

The Broncos seemed to have righted themselves the following week with a 38-6 blowout of Arizona, only to have their momentum halted again after a 31-13 drubbing by Philadelphia. Elway suffered a concussion in the second quarter, basically ending Denver's chances of winning.

By this point in the season, the Broncos were 5-5 and clearly not headed for playoff glory. But it was quickly becoming obvious that the Broncos had found the rushing threat that Elway was missing for most of his career—albeit in a highly unusual manner.

After leaving the 49ers to coach the Broncos in 1995, Mike Shanahan gave Denver a San Francisco flavor, installing a new version of the West Coast-style offense and signing several former 49ers over the next two seasons.

In an era when television and technology have made college scouting a high-tech operation, Terrell Davis was one of the rare players who slipped through the cracks.

When he attended Lincoln High School in San Diego, Davis played six positions—including nose guard—but none spectacularly. The best scholarship offer Davis received was to Long Beach State, which was being coached by George Allen, who led the Washington Redskins to victory in Super Bowl VII.

After a respectable freshman year (Davis rushed for 262 yards and two touchdowns), Long Beach State discontinued its football program. Davis accepted an offer to transfer to Georgia, which has produced such acclaimed running backs as Herschel Walker, Rodney Hampton, Garrison Hearst and Tim Worley.

But although Georgia is considered a pipeline to the NFL for running backs, Davis was flushed down the drain by the Bulldogs' coaching staff. After Hearst joined the NFL, Davis was considered his heir apparent. But then-Georgia coach Ray Goff switched to a pass-oriented offense midway through Davis's junior season.

> ***"How was anyone supposed to know I'd be doing what I'm doing now? There was no way to measure whether I'd be successful at this level. All they had to go by was what I did in college, and I didn't do much."***

As a result, Davis only started 13 games during his final two seasons and finished with a paltry 317 carries. He was so disregarded as a senior by Goff that Davis was not even given a sideline pass for a game he missed against Louisiana Tech because of an injury. Davis watched from the stands.

When it came time for the 1995 NFL draft, Davis wasn't waiting anxiously by the telephone. Instead, he was at a street party in Atlanta when the Broncos called to say he was their sixth-round pick.

"I don't have any resentment," said Davis, who still wears Georgia paraphernalia but has no love remaining for Goff. "I look at it like this. How was anyone supposed to know I'd be doing what I'm doing now? There was no way to measure whether I'd be successful at this level. All they had to go by was what I did in college, and I didn't do much."

Mike Shanahan doesn't try to take praise for unearthing Davis. Not only was Davis drafted behind more than a dozen other running backs, but he wasn't even Denver's first pick in the sixth round. That honor went to Iowa guard Fritz Fequiere, who was later released by the Broncos.

Shanahan happened upon Davis during the team's scouting meetings. After watching Davis make a cut on film, Shanahan became so intrigued that he asked his staff to find more clips. Davis made his initial impact on special teams during training camp. By the final preseason game, injuries to other players gave Davis his first chance to start at running back. He has never looked back.

Davis almost singlehandedly ensured Denver's offense would not be stymied by San Diego again when the two teams met in a rematch at Mile High Stadium on Nov. 19. Davis plowed for 176 yards—which was the third-highest total in franchise history at the time—on 30 carries to help Denver post a 30-27 victory.

In the 13th game, Davis again made history by becoming the lowest drafted running back ever to gain 1,000 yards during his rookie season. Davis crossed that mark with an 84-yard performance in a 31-23 victory over Jacksonville.

Denver learned just how valuable Davis was to its offense after he suffered a season-ending hamstring injury in the 14th game against visiting Seattle. The Broncos lost that game, 31-27, and again the following week at Kansas City, 20-17, to end the team's playoff dreams. By finishing 8-8, the Broncos had posted two non-winning seasons for the first time since the 1971-72 campaigns. But it was obvious that the Broncos were making strides.

Shanahan's offense set team records in seven offensive categories: Points scored (388), total yards (6,040), average yards per play (5.7), average yards per rush (4.53), touchdown passes (27), passing yards (4,045) and first downs passing (205). Wide receiver Anthony Miller, tight end Shannon Sharpe and tackle Gary Zimmerman were voted to the Pro Bowl.

Significant progress was also made on defense. New coordinator Greg Robinson helped the NFL's 28th-ranked defense the previous season finish with a respectable

Anthony Miller became a valuable offensive weapon in coach Mike Shanahan's first campaign. A wide receiver, Miller was a 1995 Pro Bowl selection after leading the Broncos in receiving yardage (1,079) for the second straight season.

It became obvious in the season opener that Denver's defense would be greatly improved from previous years. The Broncos registered nine sacks to pace a 31-6 pounding of the New York Jets.

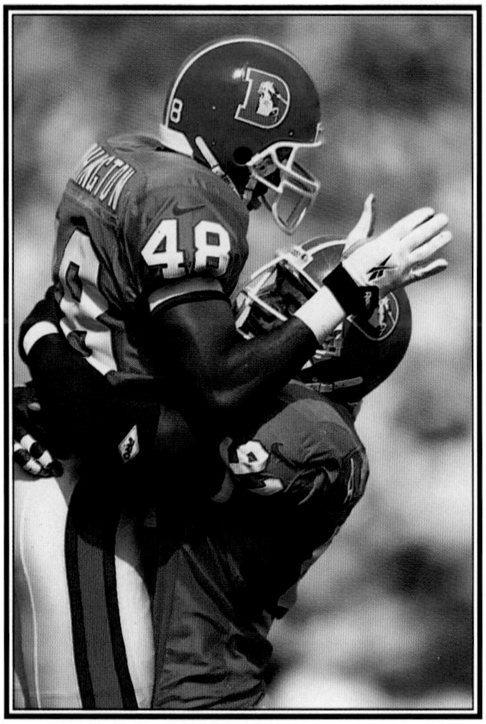

Mike Shanahan's defensive acquisitions in 1995-96 included cornerback Lionel Washington (left) and defensive end Alfred Williams (right). Both were signed via free agency.

No. 15 rating in 1995. The Broncos posted a shutout (27-0 against Oakland) and held three other opponents to under 10 points. Shanahan, though, was aware that personnel upgrades were needed on defense. This is where his prowess in judging talent became evident.

Ever since the free-agency system was adapted by the NFL in 1993, the Broncos were among the biggest spenders but had experienced only mixed success from the players they landed. Shanahan changed that while proving adept at maneuvering under the salary cap, which limits how much a team can spend on players.

Shanahan began his key acquisitions in 1995 by signing four players (strong safety Tyrone Braxton, left guard Mark Schlereth, wide receiver Ed McCaffrey and defensive tackle Maa Tanuvasa) who started for the Broncos team that won Super Bowl XXXII. He also landed defensive tackle Michael Dean Perry and cornerback Lionel Washington, two productive players during the 1995 and '96 seasons.

Shanahan's focus during the 1996 off-season was to improve his defense. So the Broncos inked linebacker Bill Romanowski and defensive end Alfred Williams to contracts that were each worth $9 million over five seasons. Shanahan was familiar with Romanowski and his hard-hitting style of play from the time they spent with the 49ers.

Williams was another ex-49er, but his tenure in San Francisco came in 1995 when Shanahan was already back coaching the Broncos. Still, Shanahan and the rest of the NFL were familiar with Williams after the ex-University of Colorado star notched 4.5 sacks as a situational pass-rusher for the 49ers.

The Broncos also filled another hole at linebacker when John Mobley was drafted in the first round. While Mobley played at Kutztown State in Pennsylvania, there was little doubt that he could make the transition from a Division II college football program to the NFL. Mobley did not miss a start during his first two NFL seasons.

But the biggest move of all may have been boosting Elway's confidence during the off-season. After the loss to Kansas City ended Denver's 1995 post-season hopes, Elway talked openly about the possibility of retirement even though his statistics were among the best of his career. He completed 316 of 542 passes for 3,970 yards with a career-high 26 touchdown passes and 14 interceptions.

"Everyone's talking about what I want to do," Elway said after the Chiefs loss. "I think the Broncos have to figure out what they want to do."

That became obvious shortly after the season ended: Keep Elway for as long as he wants to play in the NFL. Elway was re-signed to a five-year contract, ensuring he would end his career as a Bronco.

With the strong off-season moves and few free-agent losses, the 1996 Broncos seemed poised to contend for the AFC West title. But nobody could have envisioned just how good they became—and how quickly they fell.

It became obvious in the season opener that Denver's defense would be greatly improved from previous years. The Broncos registered nine sacks to pace a 31-6 pounding of the New York Jets.

And even though Elway began the season slowly, he no longer needed to singlehandedly carry the Broncos to victory. Davis rushed for 100 yards in five of Denver's first seven games, including a franchise-record 194 yards in a 45-34 victory over Baltimore.

Elway, however, demonstrated he was still the NFL's premier clutch quarterback during a Monday night game on Nov. 4 at Oakland. Despite being hampered by a sore hamstring, Elway rushed for a career-high 70 yards in leading his NFL-record 40th fourth-quarter comeback. His 49-yard touchdown pass to wide receiver Rod Smith gave Denver a 22-21 victory.

Terrell Davis finds a hole in the 1996 opener versus the New York Jets at Mile High Stadium. The Broncos won, 31-6, the first of three straight victories to begin the season.

"It was the scariest throw of my life, because Rod was so wide open," Elway said.

Any doubts that the Broncos were legitimate Super Bowl contenders were erased two games later when Denver destroyed the AFC-East leading New England Patriots, 34-8, at Foxboro Stadium. The Broncos took a 24-0 halftime lead and were winning so handily that tight end Shannon Sharpe screamed into a sideline headset, "Get the National Guard! The Broncos are killing the Patriots!"

But as strange as this sounds, so much early season success may have caused the Broncos' demise. After improving to 12-1 with a 34-7 pasting of Seattle, Denver learned it had not only clinched the AFC Western Division title but home-field advantage throughout the playoffs. The date was Dec. 1, meaning the Broncos had to wait more than a month before playing in another game of significance.

Although the hiatus permitted the Broncos to rest their key players, it also allowed rust to settle in. Plus, the Broncos learned something Pittsburgh and Kansas City were already well aware of: having home-field advantage throughout the playoffs does not ensure a Super Bowl berth.

In January 1995, the Steelers lost to San Diego in the AFC Championship game at Three Rivers Stadium. The Chiefs' demise the following season was even worse. Kansas City brought a 13-3 record into the playoffs, but lost in their first post-season game to the wild-card Indianapolis Colts at Arrowhead Stadium.

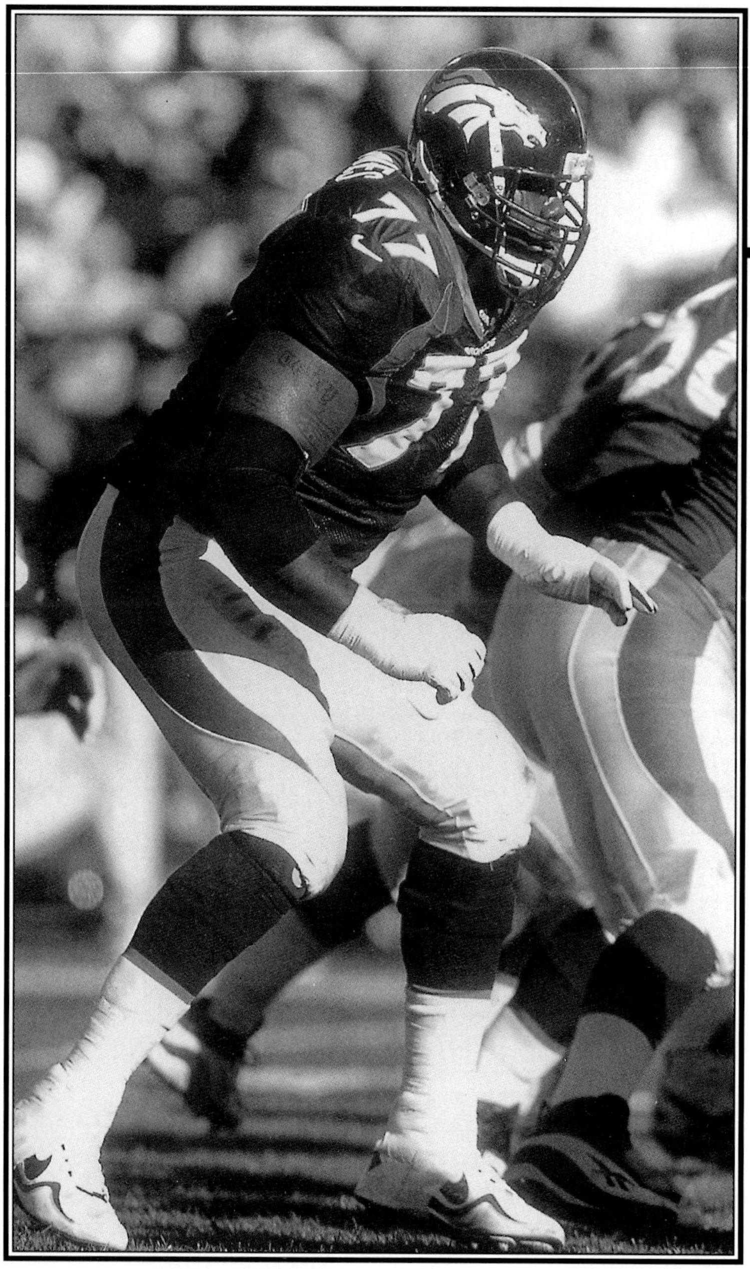

The Jacksonville Jaguars were considered an even bigger long shot than the Colts were the previous season. In only its second NFL season, Jacksonville opened the 1996 campaign with a 4-7 record. But six consecutive victories—including an upset of host Buffalo in an opening-round wild-card game—gave the Jaguars the "honor" of traveling to Denver to play the Broncos.

The Broncos were 18-point favorites, meaning a Jacksonville victory would become the NFL's biggest playoff upset since the New York Jets beat the Baltimore Colts, 16-7, in Super Bowl III.

Although no Jacksonville players were guaranteeing a victory a la Jets quarterback Joe Namath, Oakland Raiders safety Lorenzo Lynch had already made his prediction. During the season, Lynch said the Broncos had a "glass chin" and would not reach the Super Bowl.

Thanks to Jacksonville's Mark Brunell and Natrone Means, Lynch became the most accurate predictor of future events since Nostradamus.

With his strong arm and outstanding mobility, Brunell played like a young Elway while Means plowed through the Broncos' defense for 140 rushing yards and one touchdown on 21 carries.

The Jaguars took a 30-20 lead with 3:39 remaining and not even Elway had enough magic to bring the Broncos back. A touchdown pass to Ed McCaffrey closed the deficit to three, but the Jaguars recovered Denver's onside kick attempt and ran out the clock.

When reflecting upon the loss a year later, Elway said, "I believe this and I've said it for a year straight—[Jacksonville] played a great football game last year. They made all the plays and made everything happen. Sure, we didn't play as well as we can. But they played great and they beat us."

That didn't erase the sting of what many felt was the most devastating loss in Broncos history. Some of the older players like Elway and Michael Dean Perry contemplated retirement. Shannon Sharpe said the franchise may need years to recover. And Terrell Davis handled it like most other players by personally questioning whether he could have done more.

Davis sprained his knee shortly after ripping off a 47-yard run in the first quarter. Even though Davis quickly returned, the Broncos made a questionable decision by abandoning the NFL's top rushing attack.

Experience was added to the offensive line in 1997 when Denver acquired nine-year veteran left tackle Tony Jones from Baltimore for a second-round draft choice. With Gary Zimmerman a fixture on the left, Jones was moved to the right.

"I didn't want to answer my phone," said Davis, who had only six second-half carries. "I didn't want to do anything. . . . I can remember sitting on the bench when time expired wishing we had more time on the clock. I was thinking, 'How am I going to explain this?'

"I felt like I let a lot of people down. It's like, 'What could I have done to win this game? Was my effort there?' I always question that. I let a lot of people down. That was just my attitude. That was the way I was thinking after the game."

Shanahan didn't allow himself much time to reflect on the loss. Rather, he went about completing the most brilliant round of off-season maneuvers in team history.

The first transaction was acquiring offensive tackle Tony Jones in a trade with Baltimore for a second-round pick. Free-agent fullback Howard Griffith was the next player in the fold. Not only was Griffith regarded as one of the NFL's best fullbacks with Carolina, but he also was a locker room leader.

The defense was addressed by the free-agent signings of Keith Traylor, Darrien Gordon and Neil Smith. Traylor was drafted as a linebacker by the Broncos in 1991, but since then had grown into a 305-pound run-stuffing force with Kansas City. Gordon was one of the NFL's best punt returners who also had the ability to start at cornerback, something that became necessary when promising Tory James suffered a season-ending knee injury during a preseason game.

The Broncos strengthened their defensive line while weakening Kansas City's. Two ex-Chiefs, defensive tackle Keith Traylor (left) and defensive end Neil Smith (right), were signed as free agents prior to the 1997 season.

Smith was Elway's nemesis during his nine seasons with the Chiefs. The most career sacks Smith has against any NFL quarterback is the 15 he recorded against Elway. When the opportunity arose to sign Smith, Elway was so supportive that he restructured his contract to give the Broncos enough room under the salary cap to complete the deal.

The Broncos also managed to escape free-agency without losing any significant players. When training camp finally began in mid-July, the Broncos were picked by many as the AFC's top Super Bowl contender. In fact, the feeling was that anything short of a Super Bowl title would be a failure.

But the expectations almost ended on a football field south of the border, in Mexico City. Elway ruptured the biceps tendon in his right arm during the second preseason game against the Miami Dolphins. After hearing a "pop" in his arm, Elway and the Broncos feared that his playing career was in jeopardy.

Remember, however, that this is John Elway. Not only did he return to start the preseason finale, he also said the injury was a blessing because it alleviated much of the pain he was feeling in his shoulder. Of course, having Davis in your backfield would make any quarterback feel better. Davis began the regular season by rushing for more than 100 yards in five of the first six games, including a franchise-record 215-yard performance in a 38-20 victory over Cincinnati. He ended the season with 1,750 yards, the best performance in the AFC and in team history.

John Elway runs for yardage against Seattle on Nov. 2, 1997. He passed the 50,000-yard career mark in total offense in the 30-27 win. It was the Broncos' 13th straight regular-season victory at home, setting a new franchise record.

Davis also unveiled what would become a trademark symbol of the Broncos—the Mile High Salute. Every time he scored, Davis would give a military-style salute to his teammates. The gesture became so catchy that defensive players, fans and even Shanahan began performing the salute.

Davis said the salute indicated a "job well done." So it's understandable why the Broncos might have tired arms after opening the season with a 6-0 record.

Ed McCaffrey (left) and Terrell Davis demonstrate the Mile High Salute during the 1997 AFC Championship game in Pittsburgh.

But any dreams of an undefeated season ended against an old nemesis. The Oakland Raiders upset the visiting Broncos, 28-25, with running back Napoleon Kaufman rushing for a franchise-record 227 yards. No running back had ever torched the Broncos so badly in one game, leading to concerns that Denver's run defense may be the weakness that prevents the team from reaching the Super Bowl.

That wasn't the only problem the Broncos faced the following week against Buffalo. A blizzard dumped 24 inches of snow in Denver just before the team was scheduled to leave for the game. Some players, such as place-kicker Jason Elam, found themselves stranded on roads and in need of assistance to reach team headquarters. Television reports gave as many updates on the team getting assembled at its Dove Valley headquarters in Englewood as other blizzard-related topics.

The Broncos were finally able to leave Saturday night, getting clearance to become only the second airplane to leave Denver International Airport since the blizzard hit. Still, an exhausted Broncos squad squeaked past Buffalo with a 23-20 overtime victory that was decided by a 33-yard Elam field goal.

"I think we were destined to win this one after all it took to get here," said Elam, who needed eight hours to reach the team's headquarters. "I couldn't imagine if we would have lost this game."

The Broncos wouldn't lose again for another three weeks. But this defeat was a big one. Denver had a chance to basically wrap up the AFC West title by defeating

Mark Schlereth called a team meeting to clear the air after consecutive late-season losses to Pittsburgh and San Francisco. The Broncos' guard gave an inspirational speech that helped the team get back on track. They never lost again, all the way through Super Bowl XXXII.

Kansas City. A victory would have given the Broncos a three-game lead over every AFC Western Division rival with five games remaining.

Instead, the Broncos suffered a 24-22 defeat that was even more painful than the loss to the hated Raiders. Taking advantage of holes in Denver's prevent defense, the Chiefs penetrated Broncos territory with enough time remaining to allow Pete Stoyanovich to kick a game-winning 54-yard field goal on the final play. It was the second-longest game-winning kick in NFL history.

At this point, the Broncos knew their road to the Super Bowl had gotten much bumpier. Kansas City only trailed Denver by one game and the Broncos had yet to play the toughest part of their schedule. Denver had three consecutive road games ahead, and skeptics felt the Broncos would probably win just one of them.

They were correct. After beating the Raiders, 31-3, on Nov. 24 at Mile High, the Broncos beat the Chargers in the first of the three road games a week later, 38-28, in San Diego. But Denver was then bowled over by Pittsburgh and bruising running back Jerome Bettis (125 yards) in a 35-24 loss at Three Rivers Stadium.

It got even worse the following week during a 34-17 loss at San Francisco. The Broncos were eliminated from the AFC West title race as Kansas City clinched the division and home-field advantage throughout the playoffs. Davis injured his shoulder in the second quarter, raising questions about his health for the post-season. And Bill Romanowski spit into the face of San Francisco wide receiver J.J. Stokes, prompting a $7,500 fine from the NFL and tension in the Denver locker room. Some Broncos felt that Romanowski, who is white, would have been fined more if he was a black player spitting into a white man's face.

The Broncos were falling apart, so left guard Mark Schlereth decided to call a team meeting to clear the air. Schlereth, a team leader who held weekly bible studies at his house, even brought his Super Bowl ring from the 1991 Washington Redskins to the meeting to show players as inspiration.

"I saw our team slipping," Schlereth said. "I just felt I couldn't allow it. I felt it was my responsibility as a guy who's been here and understood what it takes to win championships to call that team meeting. I held [the ring] in front of the team and said, 'This ring is just a piece of jewelry. It entitles me to nothing.' But it does mean

"You become a great team not because you have talent, but when you get 60 guys that forget about individual goals and accolades [and] when they start playing hard for the guy that lines up next to them."

Terrell Davis scores on a 1-yard run in the second quarter of the AFC Divisional playoff game on Jan. 4, 1998, against the Chiefs at Arrowhead Stadium. Davis scored again in the fourth quarter of Denver's 14-10 victory.

something to me. And what it means to me is very spiritual.

"You become a great team not because you have talent, but when you get 60 guys that forget about individual goals and accolades [and] when they start playing hard for the guy that lines up next to them," he said.

"Mentally, guys had been abused by the fans and media. Everyone was coming down saying we were going to choke again and not fulfill our destiny. If you tell somebody something about themselves long enough, eventually they start to believe it.

"My idea was to say, 'This is our team. We're going to do what we're going to do with it. We need to take control of it. We've had some bad things happen. Let's wipe the slate clean, start playing for each other and let's make a run at this thing.' From the day of that meeting, we were undefeated."

Denver not only never lost again, but was able to extract revenge upon its worst enemies in the process. After a 38-3 pasting of San Diego in the regular-season finale, the "Rocky Mountain Revenge Tour" began when Jacksonville returned to Denver for a wild-card game. The Broncos were already hungry to punish the Jaguars, but became incensed even further upon learning that Jacksonville players had cheered when they were told Denver was their first playoff opponent.

The Broncos pulverized Jacksonville's defense in a 42-17 victory by rushing for a club playoff-record 310 yards. Davis led the way with 184 yards and two touchdowns, while Denver's defense made amends for its 1997 playoff performance by limiting Natrone Means to 40 yards rushing and holding Jacksonville to just 237 yards of total offense, the second lowest total in Broncos playoff history.

"Now [that] they got us, what have they got to cheer for?" a jubilant defensive end Neil Smith said.

Broncos fans, though, weren't celebrating for long. A game against the Chiefs loomed, which was scary for two reasons. First, the Chiefs entered the playoffs as the NFL's hottest team. Even more importantly, the Broncos had lost five of their last six games inside Arrowhead Stadium. But any time Elway plays against a team coached by Marty Schottenheimer, the Broncos have a chance. And what followed was a loss that may have been even more devastating to Schottenheimer than when Elway led "The Drive" against Cleveland in 1987. The Broncos escaped Kansas City with a 14-10 victory and a trip to Pittsburgh for the AFC Championship game.

WATER
27
82

By this point, it became apparent that the Denver defense wasn't going to be nicknamed Orange Crush. Defensive coordinator Greg Robinson had wisely decided to adopt a more gambling, blitzing style after the loss to San Francisco.

"We came together as a defense after we lost to Pittsburgh and San Francisco," cornerback Ray Crockett said. "We didn't think we were aggressive enough. We thought we did some things trying to hold back. But in a situation like this on the road, we knew what it was going to take. We had to be the aggressor. So we said, 'If we're going to lose, we're going to lose bringing everybody.'"

That's exactly what the Broncos did the following week in a 24-21 victory over Pittsburgh in the AFC Championship game. Denver blitzed Steelers quarterback Kordell Stewart silly, forcing him to throw three interceptions, including two in the Broncos' end zone.

When the Broncos' team flight landed at Denver International Airport, more than 20,000 fans had gathered to greet the team and celebrate the first Super Bowl appearance since the 1989 season.

But after a private victory party for the team that night, there was no more celebrating in the Broncos' locker room. The Green Bay Packers—who had won the Super Bowl the previous season—were already installed as a double-digit favorite. When the Broncos arrived in San Diego for a week's worth of preparation, the team was forced to constantly answer questions about its underdog status.

After all, Denver had lost four previous Super Bowls and an AFC representative had not won since the L.A. Raiders defeated the Redskins in Super Bowl XVIII after the 1983 season. The same Raiders also were the only wild-card entry ever to win a Super Bowl.

Shanahan asked his players to bite their tongues when it came to answering the media's questions. About the only statement that could even be con-

Cornerback Ray Crockett said the Broncos' defense learned to become the aggressor after consecutive losses to Pittsburgh and San Francisco late in the 1997 season.

Steve Atwater and Ray Crockett (hidden) get between Yancey Thigpen and Kordell Stewart's end zone bomb in the second quarter of the 1997 AFC Championship game. Crockett intercepted the pass in the 24-21 victory over Pittsburgh.

Darren Perry lands on his head while Shannon Sharpe lands with the ball on this pass play in the 1997 AFC Championship game at Pittsburgh. Sharpe caught three passes in the 24-21 win. He later guaranteed a Broncos victory over the Green Bay Packers in Super Bowl XXXII.

sidered controversial came when tight end Shannon Sharpe guaranteed a Broncos victory.

But on the inside, many Broncos were steaming from what they considered a lack of respect by the Packers. When Neil Smith appeared at a local night club the Tuesday before the game, he wondered aloud why so many Green Bay players were out socializing compared to Denver players.

"We heard some rumors that a lot [of the Packers] were talking about, 'What's Mike Holmgren going to say after the game after he gets that second [Super Bowl] trophy,'" guard Brian Habib said. "It makes you a little angry about that."

So there was no better place for the Broncos to take out their frustrations than at Qualcomm Stadium. But the aggravation occurred again in the first quarter when the Packers—installed as 12-point favorites—did nothing to prove the odds-makers wrong by slicing through the Broncos' defense for a touchdown. A 22-yard touchdown pass from quarterback Brett Favre to wide receiver Antonio Freeman gave Green Bay a 7-0 lead just four minutes into the game.

Such a quick strike may have caused a lesser team to begin doubting itself, especially one with as many prior Super Bowl woes as Denver. But this Broncos team was different. Any thought that the game was going to be lopsided in favor of the Packers was dismissed after the Broncos responded with 17 unanswered points.

The Broncos proceeded to march for a touchdown on their opening series. As he did all season, running back Terrell Davis was the focal point of Denver's attack. Playing in the same city where he attended high school, Davis accounted for 47 of his team's first 58 yards. Davis capped the drive with a 1-yard touchdown run that tied the score at 7-7 with 5:39 remaining in the first quarter.

Broncos owner Pat Bowlen said that such a quick response to Green Bay's score may have been the key to winning the game.

"I look back at that game and that was the turning point," said Bowlen, whose team had lost three previous Super Bowls during his ownership. "I think it sent a big message to Green Bay. Hey, you score on us. Now, we score on you. Now, you've got a ball game on your hands."

That score also seemed to serve as a wake-up call to Denver's defense. A unit that was under fire by fans and the media for much of the season came through by forcing two consecutive Green Bay turnovers.

Riddell
30

Broncos strong safety Tyrone Braxton intercepted a Favre pass, giving Denver possession at Green Bay's 45-yard line. Eight plays later, quarterback John Elway scored on a 1-yard bootleg to give the Broncos a 14-7 lead on the first play of the second quarter.

Denver's offense barely had time to catch its breath when it was given the ball again. Favre fumbled after being clobbered on a blitz by Broncos free safety Steve Atwater. Defensive end Neil Smith recovered, giving Denver possession on Green Bay's 33-yard line.

Broncos strong safety Tyrone Braxton makes a tackle in Super Bowl XXXII. Defensive end Alfred Williams (91) and linebacker Allen Aldridge (57) provide reinforcement.

The Broncos, though, were forced to take the field without their biggest weapon. Davis began experiencing the onset of a migraine headache on Denver's previous series, forcing him to stay on the sideline for attention from the team's medical staff. Migraines had plagued Davis during his first two NFL seasons. He thought he had corrected the problem through steps he had taken during the off-season, such as getting fitted with braces and eliminating caffeine from his diet.

For the first time, Denver's offense was held without a first down. But kicker Jason Elam came through with a 51-yard field goal, extending the lead to 17-7.

Denver's defense continued its stellar play by forcing the Packers to punt on their next series. But without Davis, Denver couldn't gain a first down either. That gave Green Bay a chance to regroup. Favre—who had won or shared the NFL's Most Valuable Player award for three consecutive seasons—orchestrated a 17-play drive that basically kept Denver's offense on the sideline for the rest of the first half. Favre connected with tight end Mark Chmura on a 6-yard touchdown pass to pull Green Bay within three points at halftime.

Could the Broncos have won the Super Bowl without Davis in the backfield? We'll never know—and the Broncos are fine with that. After being treated with migraine medication during a lengthy halftime, Davis was able to take the field again. But at first, his return was hardly heroic. Davis fumbled on his first carry, giving Green Bay the ball at Denver's 26-yard line.

Terrell Davis battled a migraine headache and the Broncos battled the ghosts of Super Bowls past on Jan. 25, 1998, in San Diego. Davis won the MVP award with 157 yards and three TDs. His Broncos won Super Bowl XXXII, 31-24.

The Broncos' defense, however, once again rose to the occasion. The Packers settled for a 27-yard field goal by Ryan Longwell to tied the score, 17-17.

John Elway spent 15 seasons in pursuit of a championship, then finally raised the Vince Lombardi Trophy after the Broncos' victory in Super Bowl XXXII.

Any questions about Davis's health were answered on a series later in the quarter. Davis rushed for 31 yards on eight carries, scoring on another 1-yard run to give Denver a 24-17 lead.

The Broncos then blew a chance to bust the game open. Broncos cornerback Tim McKyer—one of the few players on Denver's roster who already had a Super Bowl ring—recovered a fumble by Freeman on the ensuing kickoff at Green Bay's 22-yard line. But on the first play from scrimmage, Elway's pass to wide receiver Rod Smith was intercepted in the end zone by Packers safety Eugene Robinson.

The Packers capitalized on that second chance, with Favre leading Green Bay to another touchdown on a 13-yard scoring pass to Freeman.

At this point, the suspense was so great that Elway's father, Jack, appeared physically ill while watching the game from the press box. That tension continued to grow as both teams exchanged punts on four consecutive series.

But the Broncos finally got the break they needed when Darrien Gordon made a fair catch of a Green Bay punt at the Packers' 49-yard line. Suddenly, Green Bay's defense seemed to melt into the grass at Qualcomm Stadium.

First, Packers defensive end Darrius Holland was whistled for a 15-yard face mask penalty. One play later, Broncos fullback Howard Griffith turned a short pass from Elway into a 23-yard gain before being tackled at Green Bay's 8-yard line.

Even a 10-yard holding penalty on Denver wasn't enough to keep the Broncos down. Davis scampered for 17 more yards on another carry to Green Bay's 1-yard line. With the Packers' defense wilting, head coach Mike Holmgren told the unit to let Davis score on his third 1-yard touchdown run so Green Bay's offense would have sufficient time to tie the score. The plan didn't work out like Holmgren had hoped. The Packers made it to Denver's 31-yard line with 42 seconds remaining, but three consecutive Favre incompletions gave Denver the ball back.

As Elway kneeled down to run out the clock before the 68,912 fans who stayed until the very end, the cheers of Broncomaniacs watching in Denver echoed

Elway was hit so hard by Packers safety LeRoy Butler that he spun in the air like a ceiling fan. The play left a welt on Elway's ribs that still had not gone away three weeks after the game.

throughout the Rocky Mountains. The Broncos would not become the first five-time loser in Super Bowl history.

"Nobody thought we could do it," right guard Brian Habib said. "It's just the sweetest victory because of that."

Davis became the first player to ever win the Super Bowl's Most Valuable Player honor in his hometown, finishing with 157 yards and three touchdowns on 30 carries.

Elway, though, was the real story of this game. The sentimental favorite to finally win a Super Bowl after a storied 15-year career, Elway only threw 22 passes, completing 12 for a paltry 123 yards with no touchdowns.

But what the statistics don't capture is the passion with which Elway played. Late in the third quarter, Elway broke into a scramble and ran toward the Green Bay end zone. Rather than tuck into a baseball slide before getting hit, he decided to dive for more yardage.

Elway was hit so hard by Packers safety LeRoy Butler that he spun in the air like a ceiling fan. The play left a welt on Elway's ribs that still had not gone away three weeks after the game.

The moment of glory. Ed McCaffrey is the first to congratulate the triumphant Elway as the clock ran out in Super Bowl XXXII.

But players on Denver's sideline were sent into a frenzy by Elway's determination. And it was no surprise when Pat Bowlen uttered the following four words after Denver's 31-24 victory: "This one's for John."

"You could just see his eyes were so big," Broncos wide receiver Rod Smith said. "He was like a little kid who just got a brand new bike for Christmas."

"We hung in there and made some plays when it counted," said Broncos coach Mike Shanahan, whose team became the second in NFL history to win a Super Bowl as a wild-card. "I'm happy for John that he will finally get a Super Bowl ring. I'm proud not only for John, but for the city of Denver."

Said Elway, who had lost in his three previous Super Bowl appearances: "Other than my wife and my four kids, there's nothing better than this. I can't believe it. It's been a lot of work."

The same can be said for the entire Broncos organization. From the vertically-striped socks to the Lombardi Trophy, the 38-year road to the mountaintop was never easy for the Denver Broncos. And that was reflected in the team's most successful season ever.

It has become the one word that is synonymous with the Denver Broncos: Elway. As in John Elway, the golden-armed quarterback who has become the most popular athlete in the history of the Rocky Mountain region and one of the NFL's greatest players ever. After winning Super Bowl XXXII, there is just about nothing Elway has not accomplished. He has thrown 278 touchdown passes, rushed for 32 others and even caught a touchdown pass during his 15-year career. Elway has punted and could even handle extra-point duties as a kicker—if the Broncos would let him.

Chapter 9

The Offense

In 1997, Elway moved into second place all-time in passing yards (48,669), attempts (6,894), completions (3,913) and total offense (51,982) behind the Miami Dolphins' Dan Marino. But the statistics don't do justice to how much Elway has meant to the Broncos.

Elway and Company

Quarterbacks

Running Backs

Receivers

Linemen

Often surrounded by inferior offensive talent during his 10 years playing under head coach Dan Reeves, Elway almost always found a way to win games singlehandedly. He has more regular-season victories (138) than any starting quarterback in NFL history, many of them coming at crunch time. That's because Elway also holds the record for the most game-winning or game-saving drives in the fourth quarter (45) of any NFL quarterback. Four of that total came during the 1997 campaign. Elway led regular-season victories over Buffalo and Seattle, and post-season wins over Kansas City and Green Bay.

John Elway sets up and spots a receiver in a 38-3 victory over San Diego on Dec. 21, 1997.

Elway was sacked 494 times during his first 15 seasons, yet missed a total of only 10 games.

"There's probably 15 or 20 in there that he should have missed, but he didn't because he's John," said Bubby Brister, who became Elway's backup late in the 1997 season. "That's just the way he is."

Riddell

After winning his first Super Bowl at age 37, Elway debated his return for the 1998 season. In anticipation of his decision, Denver drafted Michigan quarterback Brian Griese in the third round of the '98 draft. Finally on June 1, Elway announced he would return for a 16th season to help the Broncos defend their title.

Despite the beatings he took early in his career, Elway showed no signs of decline in 1997. He was voted a starter to the Pro Bowl (he declined the invitation after the Super Bowl because he needed minor shoulder surgery) and threw for a franchise-record 27 touchdown passes with only 11 interceptions. Elway also passed for more than 3,000 yards for the 12th time in 15 seasons.

Because of his on-field heroics, Elway is able to enjoy an off-field lifestyle that would make anyone envious. He opened a car dealership in Denver that he sold in 1997 for $82.5 million. The deal made him financially set for life even though he has always been among the NFL's highest-paid players. Elway is so popular in Colorado that he may have political aspirations following his playing career. He also has established The Elway Foundation to raise money for charity.

But of all the things he has achieved, Elway is most thankful for his wife, Janet, and their four children, Jessica, Jordan, Juliana and Jack.

"I'm happy with my life, I'm happy with my kids and I'm really happy with my wife," Elway said. "I think as you get older, things get into perspective and priorities get into line. I just feel very fortunate to be where I am and that I have a healthy family. Those are the types of things you take for granted. I have for a long time, so I just want to make sure at this point in time that I'm thankful for what I do have and appreciate how good it really is."

Entering the '98 season, John Elway was in second place all time in passing yards (48,669), attempts (6,894), completions (3,913) and total offense (51,982). His 138 victories are the most by a starting quarterback in NFL history.

Elway's fourth-quarter comebacks are legendary. Through 1997, he has engineered 45 game-saving or game-winning drives, the most in NFL history.

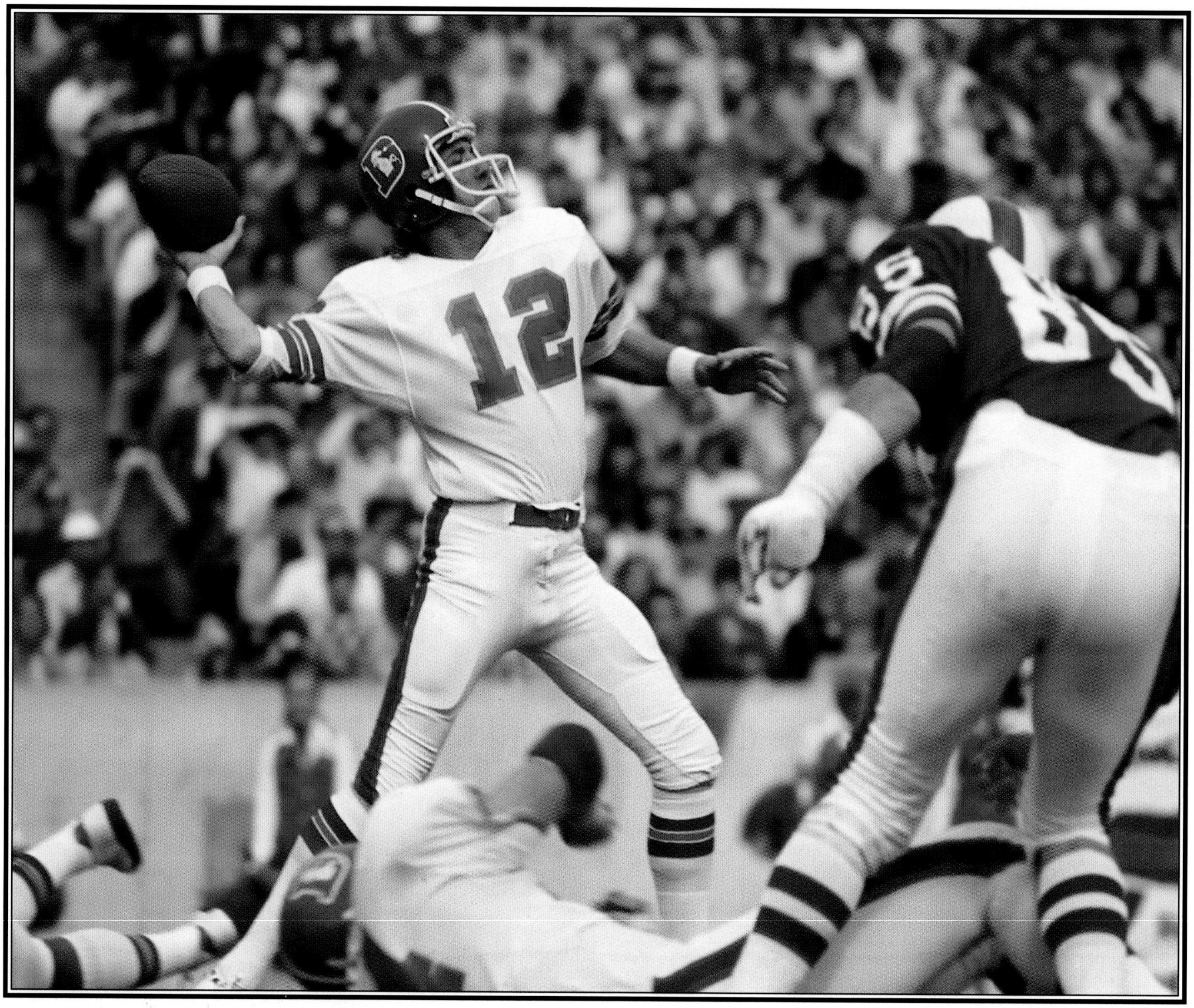

Charley Johnson had the brains and the experience to direct the Broncos' offense to the first winning seasons in franchise history.

Elway has led Denver to 10 winning seasons in his 15-year career, but the Broncos never finished above .500 until one season after veteran Charley Johnson took over at quarterback. Obtained from the Houston Oilers in 1972 for a third-round draft choice, Johnson was one of the most intelligent players in the game, earning a doctorate degree during his playing career. The subject was chemical engineering with a specialization in polymer plastics.

"Despite the school I've had, I still consider myself a professional football player first," Johnson explained. "Through all of it, I looked forward to the day when I could play football full-time. As a player, I never considered myself an intellectual. I don't know if there is room for an intellectual on a football team. Any help I've gained in football from the education I've had is from the discipline of learning and remembering."

Compared to chemical engineering, understanding formations and defenses was easy for Johnson. He passed for 24,410 yards during his 15-year NFL career, including back-to-back 3,000-yard seasons in 1963 (3,280) and 1964 (3,045) for the St. Louis Cardinals. But as smart as Johnson was, NFL success didn't come easy. He underwent 10 surgeries during his professional career, missing portions of the 1965 and '66 seasons with the Cardinals because of injuries. At the same time, Johnson was pursuing his master's degree from nearby Washington University. Johnson would attend classes at 7:30 a.m., rush to practice from 11 a.m. to 3 p.m., then attend more classes at night. The routine went on for five years, with Johnson finally earning his master's degree in 1971, a decade after beginning the program.

Johnson missed more than half of the 1967 and '68 seasons because of an army commitment. He was given a budget and a laboratory at the Langley Research Center in Houston, where he discovered a way to melt and mold plastic. The research was so impressive that NASA patented the work.

Johnson was traded to Houston in 1969. After being sent to the Broncos in '72, he provided veteran stability at quarterback. Following a 5-9 record in his first season as a starter, Johnson led the Broncos to their first winning mark in franchise history (7-5-2) in 1973. He set a team record for completion percentage in 1972 (55.5) and bettered it by .1 in 1974. Johnson also led the Broncos to a 30-23 victory over Oakland in 1972, marking the first time Denver had won on the road against the Raiders since 1962.

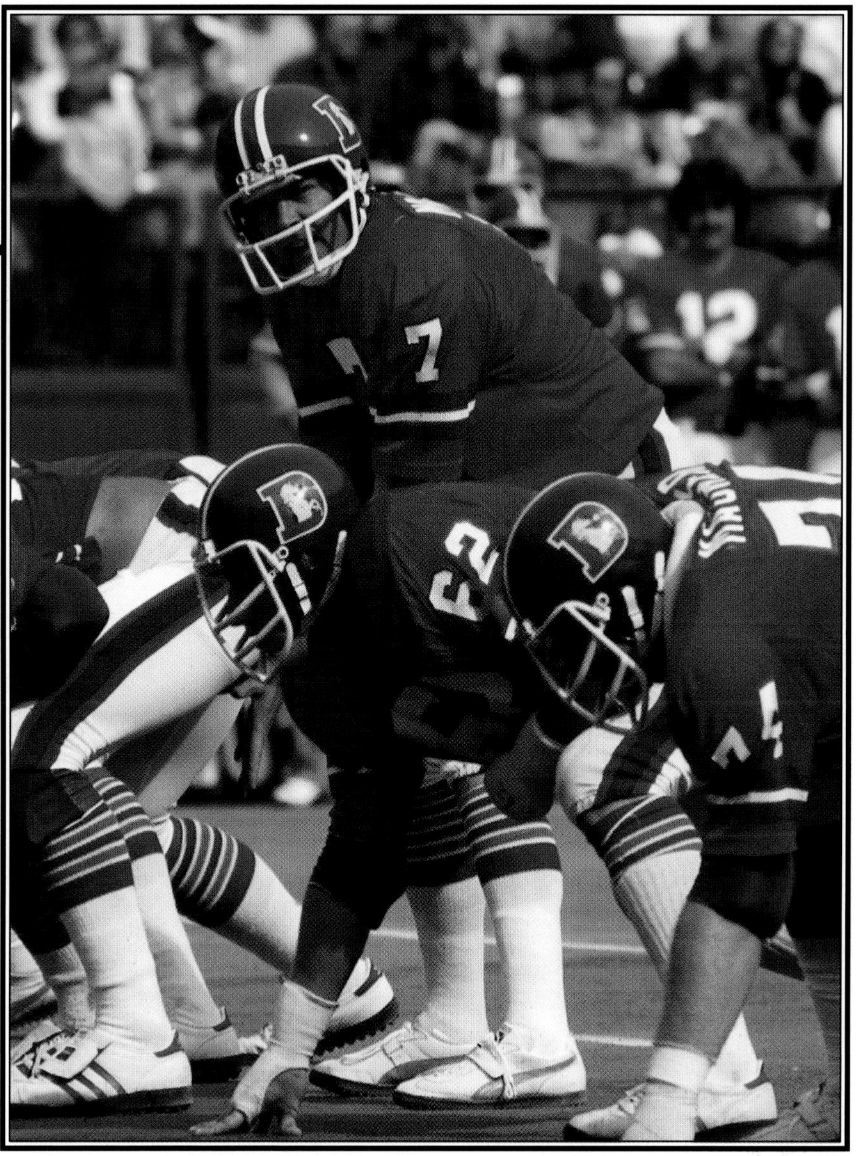

Craig Morton came from the Giants to lead the Broncos to their first-ever Super Bowl appearance.

Johnson, who was inducted into the Broncos Ring of Fame in 1986, was one of the many "recycled" quarterbacks in Denver history—those acquired in hopes of finding a winning formula. The most successful of all was Craig Morton, who led the Broncos to Super Bowl XII after a turbulent career with the Dallas Cowboys and New York Giants. Until joining the Broncos, some regarded Morton as a quarterback who would fold under pressure. As the Cowboys' quarterback in Super Bowl V, Morton threw an interception in the final two minutes that led to Baltimore's game-winning field goal in a 16-13 defeat.

Morton, however, enjoyed six quality seasons with the Broncos before retiring in 1982. He was named the AFC's Most Valuable Player in 1977 and ranks second in Broncos history behind John Elway in total offense (12,155 yards), most passes attempted (1,594), most completions (907), most passing yards (11,895) and most touchdown passes (74). He was inducted into the Broncos Ring of Fame in 1988.

Frank Tripucka consistently connected with Lionel Taylor (87) to form the most productive quarterback-receiver combination in the AFL.

"What I remember most about him was his leadership," former Broncos wide receiver Rick Upchurch said. "He was a fun-loving guy, but when he stepped on the field, he exhibited total confidence.

"The most memorable game I had with Craig was when we came from behind and beat Seattle [in 1979] after we were trailing, 34-17. Norris Weese had started and had a horrible game. Craig came in [during] the middle of the third quarter and said we were going to win the game. I was just hoping we were going to make [the score] look good. But with Craig, and thanks to some turnovers, we got into the end zone and won the game, 37-34. I thought, 'Oh my goodness. What kind of magic potion did he have in his pocket?'"

Frank Tripucka, a 1986 Broncos Ring of Fame inductee, was the first quarterback to enjoy success in Denver during the latter years of his career. He was brought in by the Broncos from the Canadian Football League as an assistant for the team's first season of 1960, but became the starting quarterback at age 32 when he played better than anyone else in training camp.

Tripucka's best season came that first year when he completed 51.9 percent of his passes for 3,038 yards and 24 touchdowns, combining with Lionel Taylor to become one of the AFL's most productive quarterback-wide receiver combinations. Tripucka led the Broncos to their first non-losing season (7-7) in 1962 and earned a trip to the AFL All-Star game in the process. But he then retired after two games of the 1963 season.

"The only regret I have is that I didn't get to play for Denver sooner," said Tripucka, whose son, Kelly, had a successful career in the National Basketball Association. "I was an old man by the time that team started and I got there."

Tripucka's pro career began with the Detroit Lions in 1949. He moved on to the Bears in 1950 where he became part of a quarterback logjam that included Johnny Lujack and Hall-of-Famers Sid Luckman and George Blanda.

Blanda also later joined the AFL and led the Houston Oilers to the league's first two championships in 1960 and '61.

Tripucka divided the 1952 season between the Bears and the Dallas Texans (the forerunners of the Baltimore Colts), then played in the CFL through 1959.

Steve Tensi played four seasons with the Broncos and ranks sixth all-time in completions (348) and passing yards (5,153). In 1969, he completed 11 straight in a game against the San Diego Chargers.

Tripucka's 662 completions still ranks third on the Broncos' all-time list behind Elway (3,913) and Morton (907). Next comes Charley Johnson (517) followed by a trio of Steves—Steve Ramsey (456), Steve Tensi (348) and Steve DeBerg (314).

The most scrutinized of the Steves was Steve Tensi, obtained from San Diego in 1967 for two first-round draft choices. As the Broncos floundered in the late 1960s, Tensi became a scapegoat for public criticism. Tensi was battered behind a weak offensive line, breaking his left collarbone twice during the 1968 season. He retired after the 1970 campaign, citing his lack of enthusiasm for football.

Next came Steve Ramsey, who was obtained from New Orleans for a fourth-round draft choice in 1971. Ramsey and Don Horn both struggled that season, combining for 27 interceptions and just eight touchdowns. Thus, it was no surprise when the Broncos traded for Charley Johnson before the 1972 season.

The third Steve was Steve DeBerg, who was acquired in a trade with San Francisco before the 1981 season. He enjoyed a lengthy NFL career, but had the misfortune of playing on the same teams as some of the best quarterbacks in NFL history. The 49ers traded him to Denver because they had Joe Montana in the fold. The Broncos moved him after the 1983 season because of the promise shown by a rookie named John Elway. DeBerg finished his career in 1993 with Miami where he filled in for yet another all-time great who was injured at the time—Dan Marino.

Floyd Little is the Broncos' all-time leading rusher with 6,323 yards from 1967 through 1975.

The early Broncos struggled to find a topflight running back until Floyd Little came aboard in 1967. Before Little, Denver had six leading rushers—David Rolle (1960), Don Stone (1961-62), Billy Joe (1963), Charlie Mitchell (1964), Cookie Gilchrist (1965) and Wendell Hayes (1966)—in the team's first seven seasons. Little then led for the next seven.

One of the classiest and most successful players in Broncos history, Little set Denver's all-time rushing records for yardage (6,323) and attempts (1,641). He was inducted into the Broncos Ring of Fame in 1984.

Little, though, was much more than just a topnotch player. In 1967, he became the first opening-round draft choice to sign with Denver. Little wanted to play in New York, but changed his mind shortly after signing his contract. That was good news for the Broncos, who usually lost most of their players to the rival NFL.

"I thought there were still coyotes running around the streets out there and cowboys and so forth," Little said. "Every Western [movie] they made, people were heading for Denver. I was really upset until I had a chance to visit the town. Then, I kind of fell in love with it."

Just like the city fell in love with him. As his career skyrocketed, so did Little's involvement with Denver charities. Little became involved with fund raising with the YMCA, March of Dimes and the Epilepsy Foundation. He toured Vietnam with a group of NFL players in 1970. He also served two years as a minority affairs adviser to Colorado governor John Love.

In his prime, Little led the AFC in rushing in 1970 (901 yards). He then won the overall NFL title in 1971 with 1,133 yards—the first Bronco to break the 1,000-yard barrier. In 1972, he enjoyed one of his most memorable performances against Minnesota and its "Purple People Eaters" defense. Little rushed for 100 yards and two touchdowns in a 23-20 loss, a performance that prompted the Broncos Quarterback Club to celebrate "Floyd Little Day" before a game against Cleveland.

Little also was an effective kickoff returner. He is the Broncos' all-time leader in kickoff yardage (2,523) and is tied with Ken Bell for the most returns (104). The numbers are impressive because he was the primary returner only two seasons.

During the apex of his career, Little said he was hoping to finish as a backup because "it would be easier for me to retire after a season of playing only part time

Little is Denver's all-time leader in touchdowns with 54. He was named to two AFL All-Star games and three Pro Bowls.

Little retired after the 1975 season (above) with 324 career points, sixth on the Broncos' all-time list. His No. 44 jersey is one of only two to be retired in team history. The other is No. 18 worn by Frank Tripucka.

than it would be if I played regularly and had a big year. I'll have a chance to get out more gradually if I play behind someone else."

That's exactly what happened. The Broncos chose running back Otis Armstrong in the first-round of the 1973 draft and Little soon found himself slowing down because of the constant beating given his 5-10, 196-pound body. Little, though, couldn't have ended his playing days in better fashion than in a 25-10 Broncos victory over Philadelphia at Mile High Stadium in December 1975.

Little had 163 yards of total offense and two touchdowns against the Eagles before making a tear-filled exit to the sidelines. Several fans broke through security after the game to carry him off the field on their shoulders.

"It was super, like somebody wrote it into the script," Little said.

Sadly, Armstrong didn't end his prolific career in the same happy fashion.

Armstrong made an impact during his rookie season, but didn't assume a starting role until replacing a banged-up Little in the 10th week of the 1974 campaign. He finished with a team-record 1,407 yards, including a franchise-record 183-yard outing against Houston.

Hampered by a hamstring injury in 1975, Armstrong rebounded with 1,008 yards rushing the following season.

Otis Armstrong played eight seasons in Denver (1973-80) and ranked third on the all-time rushing list with 4,453 yards entering the 1998 season. He led the NFL in 1974 with 1,407 yards and, after an injury in 1975, gained 1,008 in '76.

24

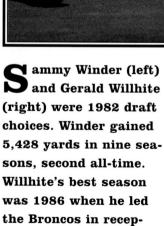

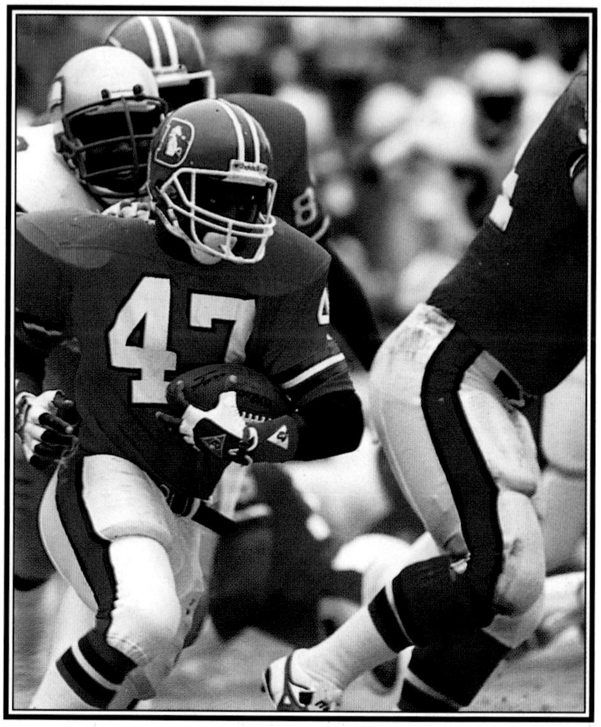

Armstrong remained one of Denver's top rushers from 1977-79, but was forced to retire in 1980 after being diagnosed with a congenital spinal condition. He went numb after being tackled in the first quarter of a game against Houston. If Armstrong would have been involved in another head-on collision, doctors told him he could have been paralyzed or killed.

"I remember my legs felt like I'd run a thousand miles," said Armstrong, who has battled back pain ever since. "I was numb. I said to myself then, 'If I ever get up and make it to the sidelines, I won't go out there again until I find out what's wrong.'"

Sammy Winder (left) and Gerald Willhite (right) were 1982 draft choices. Winder gained 5,428 yards in nine seasons, second all-time. Willhite's best season was 1986 when he led the Broncos in receptions with 64.

The Broncos were unhappy with their rushing attack in 1981, which prompted them to draft two running backs—Gerald Willhite (first round) and Sammy Winder (fifth)—the next spring. Willhite led the Broncos in rushing during his rookie season, but started only seven games in his first five years in Denver. Willhite battled injuries throughout his career before getting released before the 1989 season.

Another player whose career was cut short by injuries was Steve Sewell, Denver's first-round draft choice in 1985. Sewell thought he was going to be used as a traditional running back, but he only rushed for 917 yards during his eight-year career.

Dave Preston (left) and Steve Sewell (above) played six and eight years, respectively. Preston joined Rick Parros in a revamped backfield in 1981, gaining a career-high 640 yards. Sewell was mostly a backup from 1985-92, but became an effective pass catcher, averaging 27 receptions a season.

Sewell, though, contributed as a pass-receiver out of the backfield, with his average of 12.6 yards per catch the highest ever for a Broncos running back.

Sewell also will be remembered for throwing a 23-yard touchdown pass to Elway in 1986, the longest scoring reception by a quarterback in NFL history. After retirement, Sewell became the Broncos' community relations youth coordinator.

Sammy Winder enjoyed a more successful career than Willhite or Sewell, leading the Broncos in rushing from 1983-87. Winder never averaged as much as four yards per carry, but his relentless style of running helped him finish as the second-leading rusher in Broncos history with 5,428 yards. Winder was also a fan favorite for his "Mississippi Mud Walk" which celebrated the touchdowns he scored.

Like Little, Winder was one of the most respected players to wear a Broncos uniform. To reward his loyalty to the organization, Broncos coach Dan Reeves made him a surprise starter for the final game of his career in 1990.

"I thought I was just being announced one last time," said Winder, who rushed for a team-high 80 yards in a 22-13 victory over Green Bay. "I didn't know I was actually going to start. That's what really shocked me."

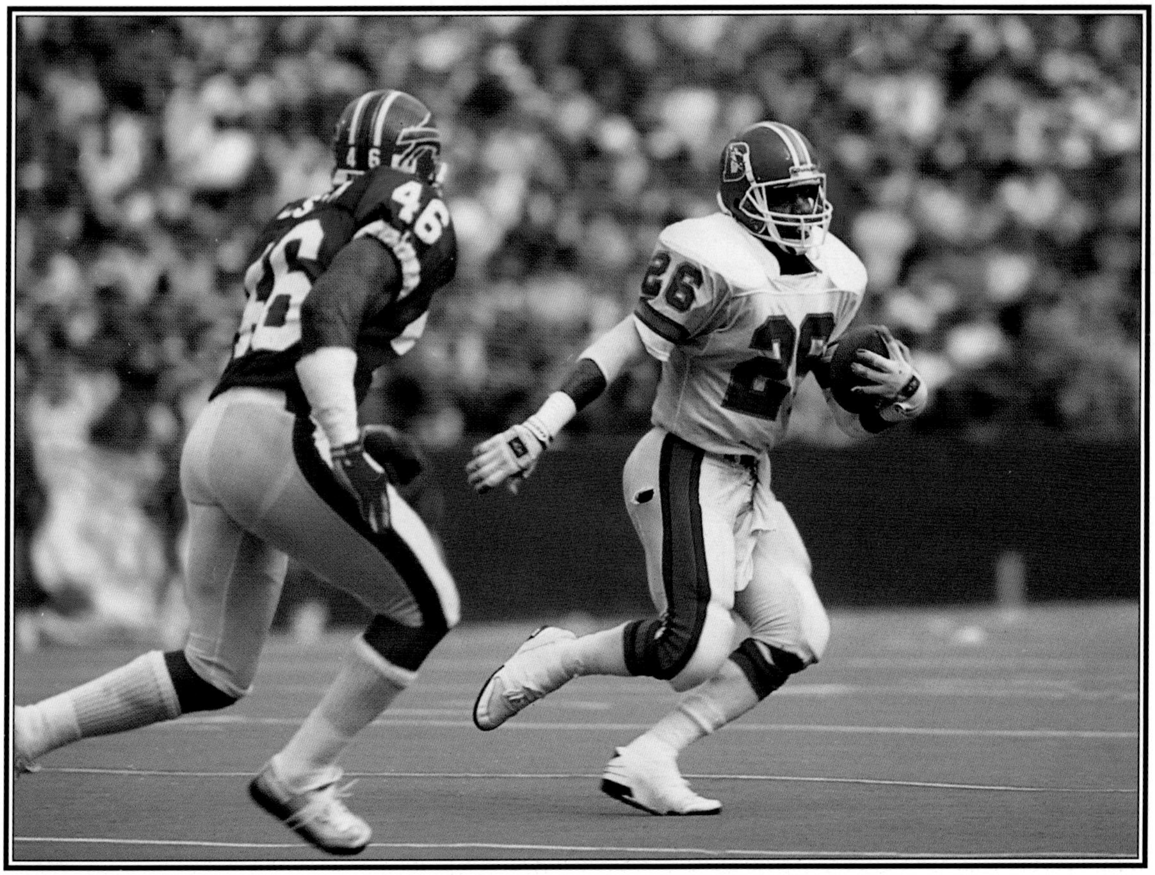

Bobby Humphrey blazed through two 1,000-yard seasons, the first in Broncos history to do it back-to-back. He gained 1,151 as a rookie in 1989 and followed with 1,202 in 1990.

Winder's departure didn't leave a hole in Denver's backfield because the Broncos had acquired a player in 1989 who had all the earmarks of a superstar. The Broncos drafted Alabama running back Bobby Humphrey in the first round of a supplemental draft for players who weren't entered into the traditional spring draft. He quickly made the 16 teams who passed on him in that draft regret doing so by becoming a major factor in the Broncos reaching Super Bowl XXIV—1,151 rushing yards and seven touchdowns on 294 carries.

Humphrey was even better in 1990 by rushing for 1,202 yards. But as quickly as he gained praise as one of the NFL's top young running backs, Humphrey's career plummeted. Humphrey missed half of the 1991 season in a contractual holdout, then returned to the Broncos out of shape. He only carried the football 11 times and was traded to Miami after the season.

In the time Humphrey was away, the Broncos found a new workhorse in Gaston Green, who was obtained in a trade with the Los Angeles Rams. Green didn't possess the field vision that Humphrey had, but earned a Pro Bowl berth with 1,037 rushing yards in 1991.

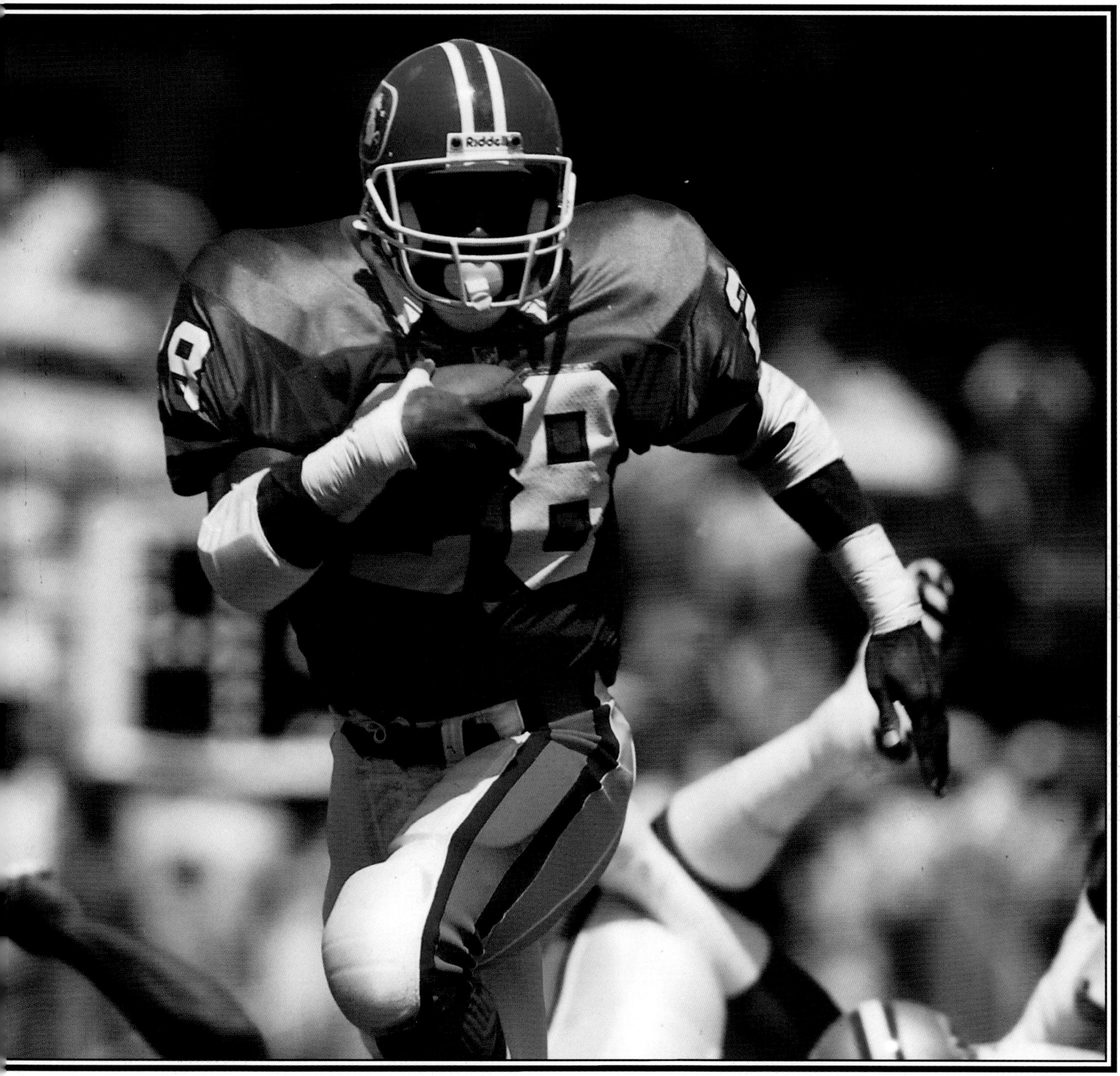

Green was a one-season wonder, as he wasn't physical enough to repeat his 1991 success the following season. After gaining 648 yards in 1992, he was traded to the Los Angeles Raiders for a third-round draft choice. He became expendable because the Broncos thought they had signed a marquee running back in Rod Bernstine, who left San Diego via free agency for Denver. But the injury problems that haunted Bernstine throughout his NFL career continued in Denver and he carried the football only 40 times from 1994 through '95. Leonard Russell led the Broncos in rushing in 1994 with 620 yards, but averaged only 3.3 on 190 carries.

In defense of these running backs, the Broncos were lacking the punishing fullback that had become a team strength in the mid-1970s when Jon Keyworth was obtained in a trade with Washington. Keyworth was a steady force in the Denver

Gaston Green came from the Rams in 1991 for one season of glory. He gained 1,037 yards for the '91 AFC West champion Broncos.

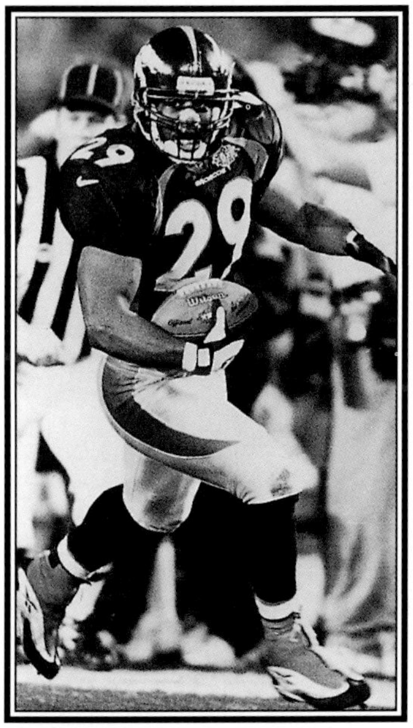

Howard Griffith (above) became the blocking fullback for Terrell Davis (right) in 1997 after being signed as a free agent from Carolina. Behind Griffith and one of the best offensive lines in team history, Davis gained 1,750 yards in '97, a new Broncos single-season record.

attack for seven seasons (1974-80), ranking sixth all-time in rushing yardage with 2,653. After Keyworth, the Broncos auditioned a number of successors in the 1980s including Jim Jensen, Dave Preston, Rick Parros, Larry Canada and Nathan Poole.

In 1997, the Broncos signed fullback Howard Griffith away from the Carolina Panthers. Griffith immediately established himself as a dominating blocker for one of the NFL's most dominating running backs—Terrell Davis. In 1995, Davis became the running back who could actually upstage John Elway as the focus of Denver's offense. An unheralded sixth-round draft choice in '95, Davis has opened his career on pace to shatter every rushing record in Broncos history.

After only three seasons, Davis already has 4,405 rushing yards and two AFC rushing titles to his credit. Only three running backs have ever reached 4,000 yards more quickly than Davis—Eric Dickerson, Jim Brown and Earl Campbell.

Davis was at his best in Denver's run to Super Bowl XXXII, rushing for more than 100 yards in each of the Broncos' four playoff games.

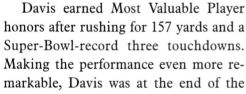

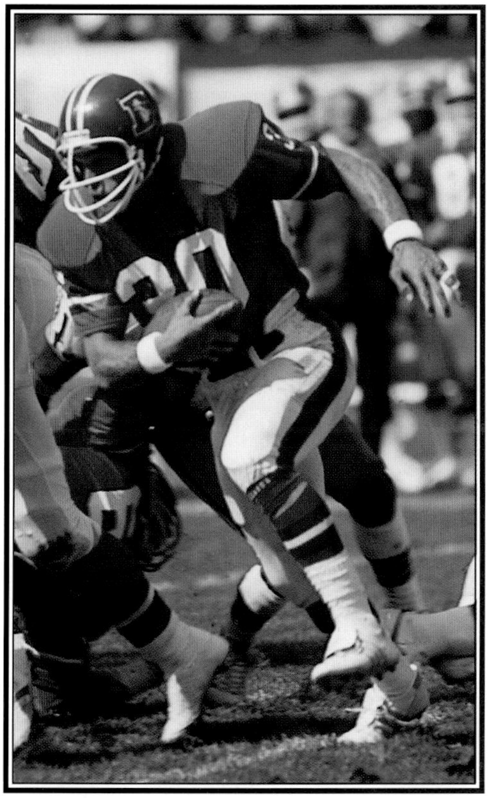

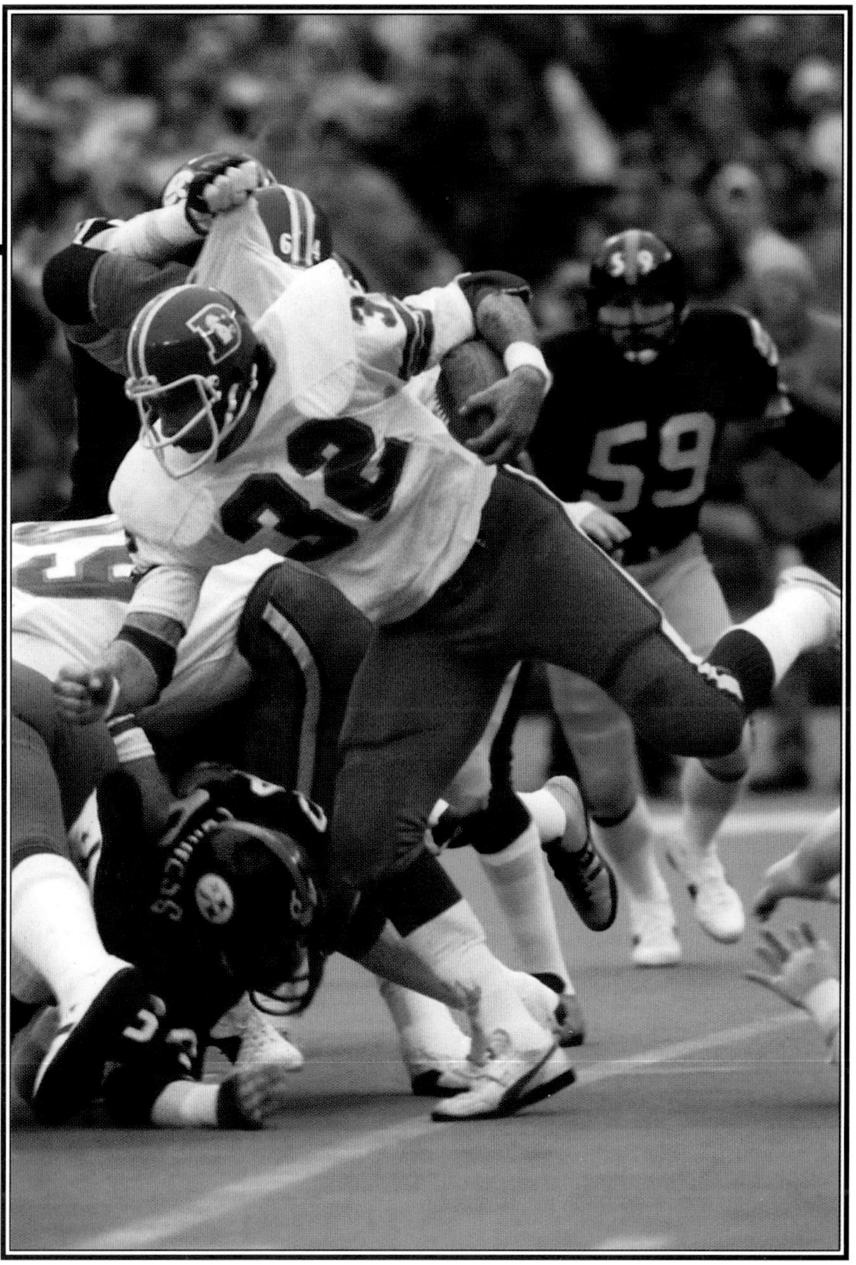

Davis earned Most Valuable Player honors after rushing for 157 yards and a Super-Bowl-record three touchdowns. Making the performance even more remarkable, Davis was at the end of the busiest season for running backs in NFL history. He gained 2,231 yards between the regular and post-season combined on a whopping 481 carries.

Davis credits his durability to his off-field workout schedule: "I think a lot of it has to do with [what happens] after the game and how you prepare yourself," Davis said. "I get a lot of massages and I rest my body. I use a hot tub. You have to pamper yourself as a running back, because you take such a beating on Sundays. During the course of the week, I try to do things so I can feel my best when it comes to Sunday."

Davis quickly earned the respect of Broncos head coach Mike Shanahan, who ripped up Davis's rookie contract after the 1995 season and rewarded him with a new five-year deal that ensures Davis will play with the Broncos through at least the 2000 season.

"Terrell Davis, to me, is a very special human being," Shanahan said. "He's very mature, even though he's only been in the NFL for a couple of years. He knows how to handle himself."

Jim Jensen (left) and Jon Keyworth (right) were a pair of fullbacks, each standing at 6-3, 230 pounds. Keyworth played seven seasons (1974-80) as Otis Armstrong's backfield mate. Jensen came from the Cowboys in '77 and played through 1980.

Tripucka-to-Taylor meant trouble for AFL secondaries in the early 1960s. Frank Tripucka (left) averaged 218 completions in the league's first three seasons. Lionel Taylor (right) averaged nearly 90 receptions.

The only bona fide superstar when the Broncos began play in 1960 didn't have the credentials one would expect for someone in that role. Wide receiver Lionel Taylor's first experience with football was quite unpleasant. Taylor played as a tackle during his freshman year of high school and disliked it so much that he quit the team. Taylor returned only when told that he wouldn't be able to play basketball if he didn't play football.

Taylor was then switched to wide receiver and played well enough to earn scholarship offers from Ohio State and Michigan. Taylor, though, opted for tiny Highlands University in New Mexico.

After college, it took Taylor three years to make his mark. He spent the 1957 season coaching offense for a high school team, then was given a tryout with the Chicago Bears as a linebacker. He didn't make the team, but was brought back in 1959 and given a spot on Chicago's taxi squad.

The Bears wanted him to stay on the taxi squad in 1960, but he instead accepted an invitation to join the Broncos before the third game of the exhibition season against New York. It was one of the best decisions Taylor ever made. With his ability to catch almost every football thrown in his direction, Taylor made an immediate impact by catching six passes for 125 yards and one touchdown against the Titans.

The Broncos weren't very organized on offense but that didn't prevent Taylor from becoming the most prolific wide receiver in franchise history. Denver quarterback Frank Tripucka always found a way to connect with Taylor.

Said Taylor: "A lot of times, [Tripucka] made up plays in the huddle and said, 'Taylor, we need 10 [yards]. You're on your own.' He gives me a certain portion of the field and I run whatever pattern I like. He reads my fakes. Sometimes, he'll throw the ball before I've completed the pattern. He'll yell, 'Left.' I turn left and there's the ball."

Taylor was the AFL's most productive receiver from 1960-65. He became the first player in pro football history to catch 100 passes in a season in 1961.

In 1963, Taylor was voted the Broncos' most valuable player by his teammates after catching 78 passes for 1,101 yards and 10 touchdowns. He posted those numbers despite having to play with four different quarterbacks.

"I've seen 'em all, but Lionel has got to be the best," said Mac Speedie, who was promoted from Denver's wide receivers coach to head coach four games into the

1964 season. "All of Taylor's 78 receptions came tough. Many were on third-down passing situations where the other teams know what we're going to do. Still, he makes the catches.

"He works so hard in practice that in the game he does everything right, because he has figured out what he's going to do in any given situation. And he never stops trying to improve. . . . Pass receivers are made, not born. And Lionel has made himself one of the very best."

Taylor finished his Broncos career with 543 receptions for 6,872 yards and 44 touchdowns—all team records. In 1967, he was dealt to Oakland in one of the Broncos' more memorable trades. Taylor and center/guard Jerry Sturm were sent to the Raiders for guard Dick Tyson, linebacker Ray Schmautz and a defensive end who would play a major role in years to come—Rich Jackson.

Taylor, however, never played in silver and black—moving on to Houston where he spent his final two seasons as an Oiler, retiring in 1968. Overall, he caught 567 passes in nine AFL seasons for 7,195 yards and 45 touchdowns. He was inducted into the Broncos Ring of Fame in 1984.

After Taylor departed, Al Denson became the top target for Denver's quarterbacks over the next five seasons. He caught 250 passes for 4,150 yards and 32 touchdowns during his seven-year Broncos career (1964-70), then finished with the Minnesota Vikings in 1971. One season later, there began the slow emergence of a player whom the Buffalo Bills had given up on.

Lionel Taylor (right) was the first receiver in pro football history to catch 100 passes in a season (1961). After he departed in 1967, Al Denson (left) became a primary target for the Broncos' quarterbacks.

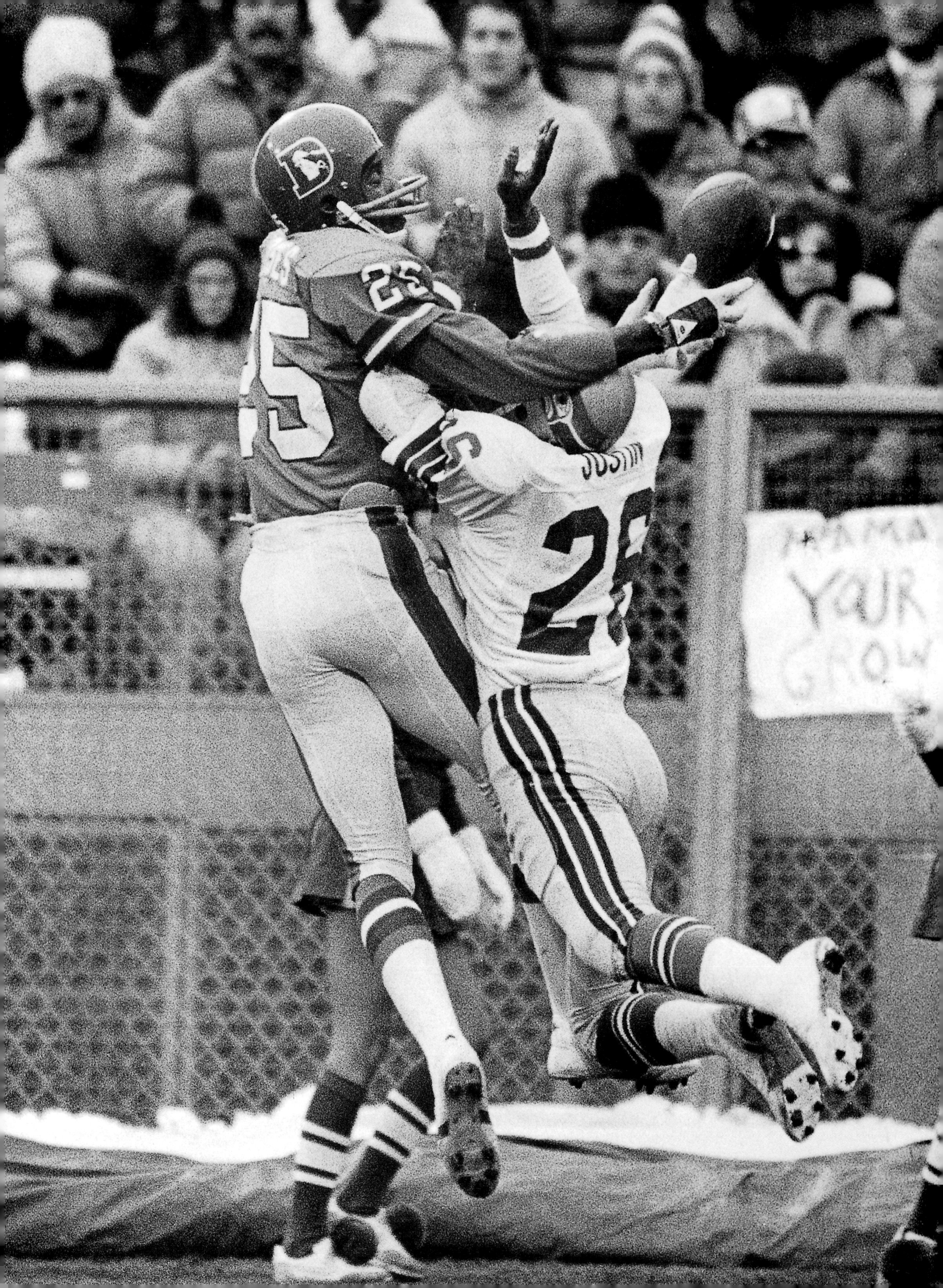
25
YOUR

Haven Moses was obtained in a trade during the 1972 season for wide receiver Dwight Harrison, who had fallen out of favor with Broncos management after a locker room incident. Moses quickly exhibited his big-play potential by scoring a team-high five touchdowns on only 15 receptions in the remaining eight games of the season.

Moses, who was inducted into the Broncos Ring of Fame in 1988, never posted a 1,000-yard season in his 10-year Denver career, but few players during that span (1972-81) commanded as much respect from their teammates.

"He was like a big brother," ex-Broncos receiver Rick Upchurch said. "He worked with me and schooled me and talked with me. He was just there for us. Haven had the desire to play the game, and he was very crafty. He'd do things out on the field that would make defensive backs say, 'Gee whiz, how do we stop this guy?' Haven was so crafty that he had more ways to do things to set up a cornerback. That's what made him so unique."

At one point, Moses and Craig Morton were labeled the "M&M Connection." Moses wanted to retire after the 1980 season, but felt a commitment to new coach Dan Reeves and played one more year. He retired with 302 receptions as a Bronco (sixth on the all-time list), 5,450 yards (fifth) and 44 touchdowns (tied with Lionel Taylor's all-time mark). Overall, he caught 448 passes for 8,091 yards and 56 touchdowns in his 14-year pro career.

"My career wasn't overly exciting, but it was a good one," Moses said upon his retirement. "Football was good to me, but there's a lot more to Haven Moses than just athletics."

Moses proved that in January 1997, quitting a corporate job with Coors Brewing Company to work with underprivileged children through the Archdiocese of Denver.

A wide receiver who faced even longer odds than Moses was Steve Watson, who joined the Broncos in 1979 as a college free-agent after not being drafted out of Temple University because of questions about his speed.

Steve Watson led the Broncos in receptions four times from 1981-85. His best season was '81 with a team-record 1,244 yards on 60 receptions for a 20.73 yards-per-catch average.

Haven Moses caught 302 passes from 1972-81, sixth on the Broncos' all-time list. His 44 touchdown catches is tied with Lionel Taylor for first in Denver history. Moses averaged 18 yards per catch, best among Broncos full-time starters.

The Three Amigos arrive in the end zone to celebrate Ricky Nattiel's 56-yard first-quarter touchdown catch to open the scoring in Super Bowl XXII. From left to right are Nattiel (84), Mark Jackson (80) and Vance Johnson (82).

"I've always had these crazy labels that everybody always gave me, which I guess is why I was a free agent," Watson said. "They doubted my speed and a few other things, so I always felt I had to work a little bit harder than the other guy."

Watson did just that during his nine seasons in Denver. After catching only 12 passes during his first two seasons, Watson made a huge splash in 1981 with a team-record 1,244 receiving yards and 13 touchdowns on 60 receptions. Watson then became John Elway's favorite target during the quarterback's first three seasons, catching 189 passes for 3,218 yards and 17 touchdowns from 1983-85.

"He doesn't have the great speed, but I think his speed is underrated," Elway said. "I think he's got better speed than people think he does. . . . There's no doubt in my mind he's got the best hands in the league, and he does a great job running routes. And he's tough. When you need the big catch, he's going to make it."

As Watson began to slow later in his career, the Broncos didn't find just one replacement. Rather, three receivers combined to give Denver one of the NFL's most dangerous receiving corps. Vance Johnson, Mark Jackson and Ricky Nattiel were known as the Three Amigos, a nickname that became so popular that the trio was featured on a poster garbed in Mexican gunfighter attire.

"Speed is the thing that scares you to death," Broncos coach Dan Reeves said of the Amigos. "It's what scares you when you have receivers who can really fly. Any

Vance Johnson (above) led the Broncos in receptions just three times in 10 seasons, but ranks third behind Lionel Taylor and Shannon Sharpe on the all-time list with 415 catches. Mark Jackson (left) caught 276 passes in seven seasons, seventh on the all-time list, including a team-leading 57 in 1990.

time they touch the football, they've got the ability to go all the way. It puts pressure on the defense, particularly when you've got a guy like John who can scramble around and find extra time. Those receivers never quit working, because they know John can find them and hit them."

Johnson was the Amigo who exhibited the most flare, admitting during his playing career that he "liked the fame." In 1991, "The Vance" reported to training camp with a pompadour that hung over one eye. The haircut shocked Reeves so much that he said it was "not possibly the worst—it is the worst haircut I've ever seen. You'd definitely need a big headgear to cover that thing up."

However, Johnson backed up his outrageous attire and haircuts with blazing speed and productivity. Johnson led the Broncos in receiving from 1987-89 (including a career-high 1,095 yards in '89) and helped create opportunities for his teammates by stretching opposing defenses.

As Broncos senior director of media relations Jim Saccomano has said, "Vance is like nine Porsches in the garage."

Johnson suffered a fractured ankle in 1993, but recovered to play one final season for the Broncos in 1995. During that time, Johnson wrote a book with teammate Reggie Rivers about Johnson's problems with domestic abuse that caused him to spend time in prison.

Shannon Sharpe became pro football's premier tight end in the 1990s. With 5,991 receiving yards, Sharpe was first among active tight ends entering the '98 season. He led the Broncos in receptions from 1992-97, resulting in six straight Pro Bowl selections.

Ricky Nattiel seemed destined for greatness after being selected in the first round of the 1987 draft. But after two solid seasons, he suffered a cracked kneecap that led to tendinitis and eventually a screw being inserted into his leg. Nattiel only caught 44 passes over the next three seasons and ended the 1991 campaign as Denver's fifth wide receiver. Nattiel was traded to Tampa Bay in '92, but was released. He is best remembered for his rookie season when he averaged 20.3 yards a reception, the third-highest average in Broncos team history.

Mark Jackson was primed to become Denver's primary wide receiver in 1992 and did a nice job with eight touchdown catches, the most by any player in the Elway era to that point. But when Dan Reeves was fired and became the New York Giants' head coach during the 1993 off-season, Jackson followed as a free agent to New York.

Jackson's departure was made less painful by the emergence of Shannon Sharpe as the best pass-catching tight end of the 1990s. Sharpe began to blossom in 1992 with a team-high 53 receptions and proceeded to better that total each of the next two seasons. Sharpe finished the 1997 season on pace to surpass Todd Christensen as the

most prolific pass-catching tight end in NFL history. Sharpe leads all tight ends in the 1990s in receptions (465) and yardage (5,991) after his 72-catch, 1,107-yard campaign in 1997.

Sharpe has become such a threat that many teams opt to either double-team him on pass routes or assign a cornerback to cover him. That may not be possible in future years, because the Broncos have two wide receivers with superstar potential on the horizon.

Ed McCaffrey (left) and Rod Smith (right) were Denver's wide receiver duo in Super Bowl XXXII. McCaffrey caught 45 passes in 1997, while Smith caught 70.

After starting only two games in his first two seasons, Rod Smith became a big-play threat in Denver's 1997 offense. Smith enjoyed one of the best seasons for a receiver in franchise history, catching 70 passes for 1,180 yards and 12 touchdowns. Smith and fellow starter Ed McCaffrey—considered one of the NFL's best blocking wide receivers—now have some company in Marcus Nash, Denver's first-round draft choice in 1998. Nash was one of the most productive wide receivers in school history at the University of Tennessee and has the speed to make the NFL's top-ranked offense in 1997 even more dangerous.

Before Sharpe, the most notable tight end in Broncos history was Riley Odoms. Denver's first-round draft choice in 1972, the 6-4 Odoms was one of the NFL's first tight ends to possess a combination of size, quickness and athletic ability (he was a high school champion in the high jump after clearing six feet, nine inches). He

Riley Odoms was one of the best tight ends in pro football during the 1970s. He was named to four Pro Bowls in his 12-year Broncos career, retiring in 1983 with 396 catches, fourth on Denver's all-time list.

reached the Pro Bowl four times during his 12 seasons in Denver and finished his career with 396 catches for 5,755 yards.

Odoms was a reliable receiver for Broncos quarterbacks throughout the 1970s, catching at least one pass in 33 consecutive games from 1973-76 and in 41 straight from 1976-79. He caught the first touchdown pass in Broncos playoff history against the Steelers in 1977, but the play he will most be remembered for came in a 21-17 loss to Oakland in the final game of the '73 season.

"We had a chance to win the division, but we needed to beat Oakland," Broncos linebacker Tom Jackson said. "Riley was thrown a pass over the middle. [Oakland safety] Jack Tatum literally knocked him unconscious just as the ball got there, but Riley came down with it. I'll never forget it, Riley stretched out on the field on his back with the ball on his chest. Tatum said in his book [*They Call Me Assassin*] that he actually thought he'd killed Riley with that hit. That game was characteristic of how Riley played. He was a guy who always had the big game in a big game."

When one reflects upon the biggest game in Broncos history—the 31-24 upset of Green Bay in Super Bowl XXXII—the unit that deserved much of the credit was Denver's offensive line. Left tackle Gary Zimmerman, left guard Mark Schlereth, center Tom Nalen, right guard Brian Habib and right tackle Tony Jones helped pave the way for Terrell Davis's 157-yard rushing performance and did not allow John Elway to get sacked.

If you didn't hear much about the Broncos' offensive line before the Super Bowl, that was by design. The unit refused to speak with the media from training camp until the week before the Super Bowl. The linemen would have remained silent throughout the entire year, but didn't want to face a steep fine from the NFL by not talking.

Most linemen say the code of silence was the brainchild of Alex Gibbs, one of the NFL's best offensive line coaches. Gibbs likes talking to the media as much as one likes undergoing root canal, an attitude some of his players also share.

Broncos left tackle Gary Zimmerman joined the team in 1993 after a trade with the Vikings. He has provided critical pass protection for John Elway all the way to the Super Bowl.

In what has become an annual ritual, linemen initiated a series of fines for such things as being quoted in a newspaper or having their name in print. The kangaroo court even fined two players for missing practice when their children were born.

When Zimmerman returned from retirement, he was fined $8,000, although that penalty was later reduced to $6,000. There were three reasons Zimmerman received such a steep fine: garnering front-page attention for his comeback, missing all of training camp and getting tackle Scott Adams cut because the Broncos needed to open a roster space.

"It's been fun, because it lightens up the day," Nalen said. "There's something new and something different in the meeting room. If it wasn't for that, it would be pretty monotonous every week doing the same thing."

After winning a Super Bowl, Zimmerman will be given serious consideration for the Hall of Fame. He has earned seven Pro Bowl berths during his first 12 NFL seasons after spending his first two campaigns in the United States Football League.

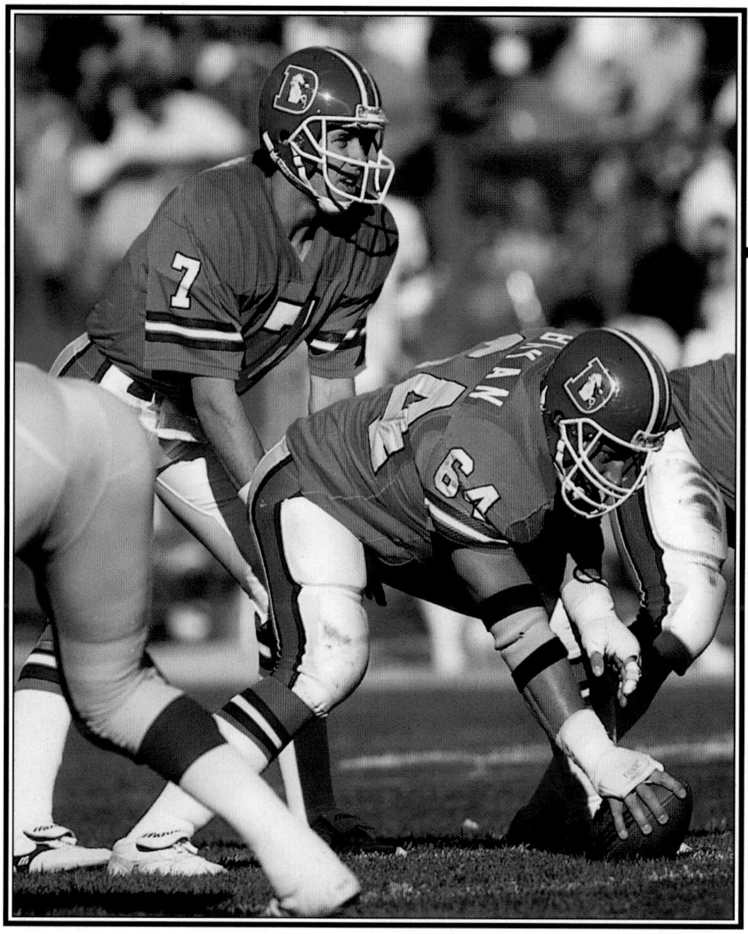

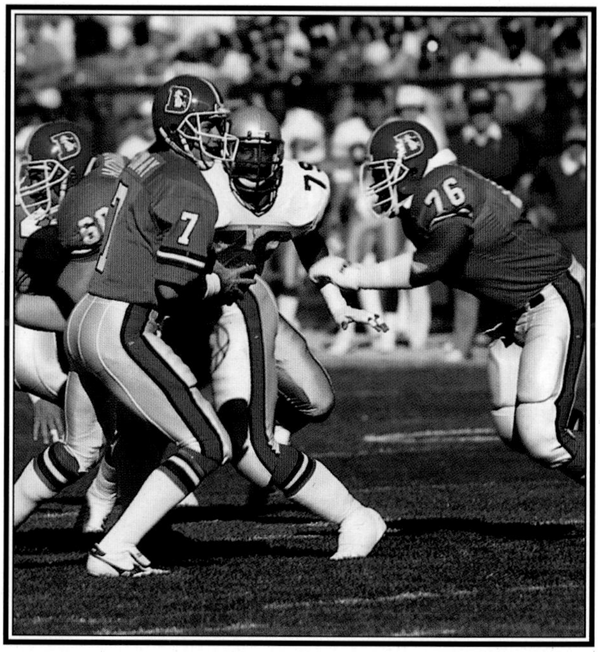

Center Billy Bryan (No. 64, left) and right tackle Ken Lanier (No. 76, right) provided experience on the line during John Elway's early career. Bryan and Lanier played 12 and 13 years, respectively, in Broncos uniforms.

"He has all the qualities of a great offensive tackle," said Buffalo Bills defensive end Bruce Smith, a lock for the Hall of Fame after his NFL career ends. "He's got great balance, he never seems to let his feet get out of position, he's pretty strong—although he's had some shoulder problems—and his knowledge of the game is one of the things that propels him to the next level and separates him from the ordinary offensive tackles."

Zimmerman wasn't the first standout offensive lineman to don a Broncos uniform. Right tackle Eldon Danenhauer was the first to go to the AFL All-Star game (1962 and '65). Four others—center/guard Jerry Sturm (1964 and '66), center Larry Kaminski (1967), right tackle Mike Current (1969) and left guard George Goeddeke (1969)—were also selected for the game during the 1960s.

Tackles Claudie Minor and Ken Lanier, guard Paul Howard and center Billy Bryan never earned Pro Bowl recognition during their tenures with the Broncos, but all four were quality starters whose longevity help them rank among the best linemen in franchise history.

Minor became an immediate starter at right tackle after being drafted in the third round in 1974. Minor proceeded to start 103 of 104 games during his first seven years with the Broncos, a streak

Paul Howard played more years than any guard in Broncos history. In 13 seasons, he played 187 games, started 146 and protected Charley Johnson, Craig Morton and John Elway. His career spanned Super Bowls XII (1977) and XXI (1986).

RSON
60
90

Keith Bishop (54), Paul Howard (60) and Ken Lanier (76) open daylight for Sammy Winder in 1985. Bishop was a Pro Bowl selection at left guard for the Super Bowl Broncos of 1986 and '87.

that helped make him the NFL's highest paid tackle in 1980. Minor remained a starter the next two seasons but retired because of his involvement in oil companies he had formed.

Lanier was just as dependable during his 13 seasons with the Broncos, starting at right tackle from 1982-92. Lanier played in 166 straight games from 1981-92 and considered himself fortunate to remain injury free through most of his career.

Paul Howard wasn't as lucky. A serious knee injury caused him to retire after the 1986 season—his 13th with the Broncos. It marked the end of an era: Howard was the last remaining active Bronco from the team that reached Super Bowl XII. Howard played in 187 games in Denver, including 146 starts at right guard.

The Broncos have been fortunate to also enjoy stability at left guard. After Tom Glassic started from 1976-83, Keith Bishop was able to fill the void from 1984-89. Bishop started 86 games for the Broncos, earning Pro Bowl honors in 1986 and '87 for the back-to-back AFC champions.

Billy Bryan is generally regarded as the best center to have played for the Broncos. Bryan started all but two games for the Broncos from 1978 until injuring his knee early in the 1987 season. Bryan returned to start the next season before retiring. Should he continue playing at a high level, Tom Nalen will someday be mentioned in the same breath as Bryan. Nalen, who was released as a rookie during the 1994 training camp and later re-signed, earned his first Pro Bowl berth in 1997.

Claudie Minor played nine seasons at both left and right tackle. He started 103 of 104 regular-season games from 1974-80.

51
BENGALS

Chapter 10

The Defense

A Crushing Experience

Linebackers

Defensive Backs

Linemen

One game into the 1977 season, Broncos assistant coach Stan Jones asked David Frei, an assistant in the team's media relations department, to help coin a phrase to describe one of the NFL's most dominating defenses. Frei's response? "Orange Crush," a nickname based upon a soda that was originally used a year earlier by a local newspaper writer.

Not only did the moniker stick—prompting a huge increase in people drinking orange soda in the Denver area—but it was quite appropriate. The Broncos crushed almost every opposing offense in 1977, allowing more than 14 points in just one of 14 regular-season games.

Injuries forced the Broncos to switch from a 4-3 defensive scheme to a 3-4 alignment in 1976, but that proved to be a blessing in disguise. The new three-man front allowed Denver to play four linebackers, which became the strength of the defense. Ironically, three of the four linebackers weren't supposed to become superstars. Only Randy Gradishar was taken in the first round of the NFL draft, and he lived up to all expectations and then some. The other three linebackers were either considered too small or too slow to excel in a 4-3 scheme, but they were at home in defensive coordinator Joe Collier's 3-4. Gradishar and Joe Rizzo played on the inside, while Bob Swenson and Tom Jackson became the outside linebackers.

Rizzo was the longest of long shots to make it to the NFL. The former Merchant Marine was working at the shipyards in San Diego when he was unearthed by the Broncos in 1974. Rizzo lasted seven seasons in Denver before a knee injury ended his career after playing just four games of the 1980 season His greatest game occurred on Oct. 16, 1977, when he intercepted Oakland quarterback Ken "The Snake" Stabler three times in a 30-7 rout of the host Raiders.

Broncos linebacker Bob Swenson crushes a Cincinnati Bengal in 1976.

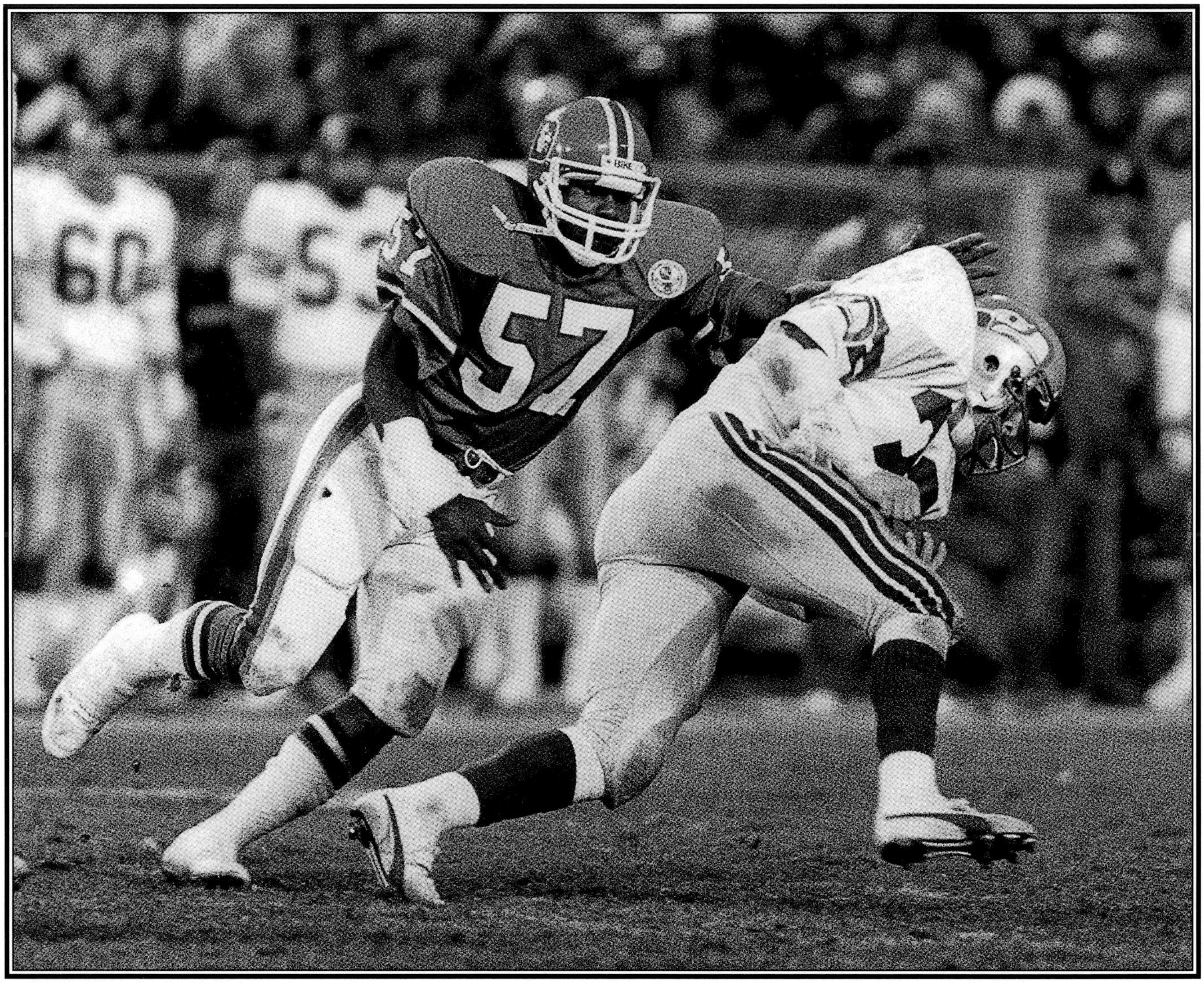

Outside linebacker Tom Jackson played 14 seasons in Denver, second all-time behind John Elway's 15. He started 177 of the 191 games he played from 1973-86 and was named to three Pro Bowls.

The victory was especially important to the confidence of the Broncos, who had lost six of their previous seven to Oakland.

"Rizzo was a real man's man," Gradishar said. "He would never back down to anyone. He would fight you. [He was] very studious and knew his football."

Bob Swenson was another long shot to make the Broncos roster, signing with the team as a free agent in 1975. Swenson spent nine years with the Broncos, but only enjoyed five full seasons. He missed the 1980 campaign with a broken arm, sat out most of 1982 in a contract dispute and spent his final two seasons hobbled by a knee injury that eventually led to his retirement.

When healthy, Swenson may have been the best linebacker in football, as exemplified during Denver's run to Super Bowl XII in 1977. Swenson and Tom Jackson combined for a goal-line stand in a 14-7 win over Kansas City for the Broncos' ninth victory, part of the team's second six-game winning streak that resulted in a 12-2 record. Swenson then helped ensure Denver's Super Bowl appearance by intercepting a Ken Stabler pass in the fourth quarter, halting a potential Raiders comeback, as the Broncos defeated Oakland in the AFC Championship game, 20-17.

Swenson was voted to the Pro Bowl in 1981, but his best season statistically came in 1979 when he recorded 17 turnovers, three of which went for touchdowns.

"I couldn't have written the script any better. I achieved everything I could in the game of football. I was here 10 years and played every game. Even though that may not mean much, it does to me."

"The ball's the most important thing in the game," Swenson said. "The ball is everything."

Billy Thompson (36) and Joe Rizzo (59) move in on Minnesota's Sammy White in 1978. Rizzo teamed with Randy Gradishar as the inside linebackers of the legendary Orange Crush defense from 1975-79.

Randy Gradishar's injury history stands in contrast to that of Rizzo and Swenson. Instead of getting hurt while playing in the NFL, Gradishar scared away most NFL teams because of a knee injury he sustained as a senior at Ohio State. Still, that didn't deter head coach John Ralston from making Gradishar a first-round draft choice in 1974.

"I remember when I got the phone call from Coach Ralston telling me I had been drafted by the Broncos," said Gradishar, who was labeled "the best linebacker I ever coached at Ohio State" by the legendary Woody Hayes. "People were asking why the Broncos would draft me and saying that they were wasting a choice on a guy who could be questionable. I was glad to have the chance to prove them wrong."

Did he ever. Gradishar never missed a game in his 10 NFL seasons, playing in 145 consecutive contests. He was heralded as the best linebacker in football during that stretch, reaching the Pro Bowl seven times and setting a team record with 1,985 tackles. Gradishar could have continued to play after the 1983 season, but wanted to leave the game while still healthy and playing on a high level.

"I couldn't have written the script any better," said Gradishar, who was inducted into the Broncos Ring of Fame in 1989. "I achieved everything I could in the game of football. I was here 10 years and played every game. Even though that may not mean much, it does to me."

Tom Jackson, a Ring of Fame inductee in 1992, was the heart and soul of the Broncos for 14 seasons and 191 games, both of which were franchise records for longevity until surpassed by John Elway. When he was drafted in 1973, most teams considered Jackson too small at 5-11, 220 pounds, to play in the NFL. Jackson proved them wrong by reaching the Pro Bowl three times from 1977-79 and registering 44 sacks and 20 interceptions during his career.

Statistics, though, can't measure how much Jackson meant to the defense. A franchise that had posted only one non-losing season before his arrival would have only two sub-.500 seasons with Jackson in uniform. Jackson was selected three times by his teammates as Broncos defensive MVP and he is a six-time recipient of the team's Bob Peck Memorial Award given to the most inspirational player. Jackson remains an avid Broncos fan even though he serves as an analyst for ESPN.

53

"I think the thing that impressed me the most is that I never saw Tom Jackson loaf," former Broncos coach Dan Reeves said. "Usually, if you have a guy that plays as hard as Tom did, he's going to take a break here and there. But I can never remember seeing Tom take a break, and that was true in practice. He had that unbelievable effort to never let up."

Like Jackson, Karl Mecklenburg was another player who seemed like he wouldn't find a suitable role in the NFL. He was a 237-pound nose tackle, which was much too light for the position. And because he ran the 40-yard dash in 4.9 seconds coming out of college, Mecklenburg seemed too slow to play linebacker.

But this 12th-round draft choice was such a good football player that Joe Collier adjusted his scheme. Mecklenburg became one of the first linebackers to play in a three-point stance near the line of scrimmage, using the quickness he had to blow past opposing tackles and get the quarterback. Mecklenburg played for 12 seasons to finish with the second-highest sack total (79) in franchise history. His best season came in 1986, when he was voted the AFC Player of the Year by the *Football News*.

Karl Mecklenburg played 12 seasons at inside linebacker (1983-94) and was named to six Pro Bowl teams. His 79 career sacks is second on the Broncos' all-time list.

"It was a big advantage for me coming into pro football as a 12th-round draft choice," Mecklenburg told *Sports Illustrated*. "A lot of people were the best guys on their team. They never had to work. Then when they got beat, when they got knocked down, it was a whole foreign thing. They didn't know how to react to it."

Inside linebacker Randy Gradishar was a first-round draft choice in 1974 from Ohio State. He never missed a game in 10 seasons (1974-83) and was named to seven Pro Bowls. Gradishar is the Broncos' all-time leader in tackles (1,958).

While Mecklenburg was a low draft choice who performed far above original projections, Mike Croel was a high-profile player who didn't fulfill high expectations. The fourth player taken in the 1991 draft, Croel became the NFL's Defensive Rookie of the Year after recording 10 sacks. But Croel flopped after Wade Phillips replaced Dan Reeves as Denver's

Outside linebacker Simon Fletcher is Denver's all-time sack leader with 97.5 from 1985-95. He led the Broncos in sacks seven consecutive seasons, including a team record 16.0 in 1992.

head coach in 1993. Croel is still trying to regain the form of his rookie year. He spent the spring of 1998 playing as a defensive end in NFL Europe.

One first-round pick who has lived up to expectations is linebacker John Mobley. Although he played college football at Division II Kutztown (Pa.) State, Mobley immediately became a starter at weakside linebacker during his rookie season in 1996. In his second season, he recorded a team-high 162 tackles and continued to build his reputation for making big plays.

Mobley's omission from the 1997 Pro Bowl team caused a minor furor in the Broncos' locker room.

"I know there will be a lot more opportunities for me," he said. "You really have to down play the situation and expect more in the years to come."

Mobley is not the first Broncos linebacker to find himself inexplicably snubbed by the Pro Bowl. Simon Fletcher led Denver in sacks for seven consecutive seasons and logged a franchise-record 97.5 in his 11 seasons (1985-95). His single-season sack totals of 16 (1992), 13.5 (1993) and 13.5 (1991) are also the top three marks in Broncos history.

Fletcher, though, always handled the disappointment of not making the Pro Bowl with grace. "That was just something I didn't get," Fletcher said. "But I didn't come into this to make the Pro Bowl. I came in to be accountable for Sunday afternoons."

Ricky Hunley only played in Denver for four seasons, but the talented linebacker will never be forgotten for several reasons. First, Hunley followed in the footsteps of John Elway by refusing to play for the team that drafted him in the first round. After reaching a contract impasse with Cincinnati in 1984, Hunley was dealt to the Broncos for first- and third-round picks in 1986 and a fifth-rounder in 1987.

At first, Hunley didn't live up to expectations and was unable to supplant Steve Busick as a starting inside linebacker. But Hunley blossomed in 1986 with more than 150 tackles on a team that reached Super Bowl XXI.

Just when Hunley was about to become a fixture on Denver's defense, the NFL players went on strike after two games of the 1987 season. As the NFL Players Association representative in Denver, Hunley was in the spotlight during a walk-out that split the allegiances of players, coaches and fans. When the strike ended, Hunley

didn't play well in his first few games and was threatened with benching by head coach Dan Reeves.

Even though Hunley rebounded before season's end, rumors abounded that he would be traded after the season because there was too much bad blood remaining from the strike. Sure enough, Hunley was dealt to the Phoenix Cardinals during the 1988 training camp for center Mike Ruether, who didn't become a starter during two seasons in Denver.

"Would you challenge Dan Reeves?" an angry Hunley asked after the trade. "Would you go head-to-head with him? Go ahead and try it. See what happens. No one can go head-to-head with Dan Reeves. If you're God, you're God."

John Mobley (left) became a starter at weakside linebacker as a rookie in 1996. Inside linebacker Ricky Hunley (right) had more than 150 tackles for the 1986 Super Bowl Broncos.

36

Goose Gonsoulin wraps up Buffalo's Ed Rutkowski in 1963. Gonsoulin was Denver's first defensive superstar, intercepting 43 passes in a seven-year career. His 11 interceptions in 1960 remains a team record.

Even though the Broncos have fielded plenty of talented linebackers, safety is the one position on defense that has remained a constant strength since the franchise's first season in 1960.

Denver's first star safety was Austin "Goose" Gonsoulin. A rookie from Baylor in 1960, he had been drafted by the Dallas Texans and traded to the Broncos for fullback Jack Spikes. The trade soon became one of Denver's all-time best as Gonsoulin recorded a team-record 11 interceptions in 1960—a mark that still hasn't been broken. Four pick-offs came in a 27-21 victory over Buffalo on Sept. 18.

Gonsoulin was known for his toughness and durability. He played seven seasons with the Broncos, never missing a game the first six. His career not only includes a string of 61 straight starts, but he played the final eight games of the 1963 campaign with a separated shoulder. Gonsoulin recorded 43 interceptions with Denver, a team record that would stand for 20 years until broken by Steve Foley's 44.

Gonsoulin was the last of the original Broncos to leave the franchise, jumping to San Francisco for his final season in 1967. For his on-field performance and loyalty during a time when the Broncos were an AFL laughingstock, Gonsoulin was one of the four original members elected to the Broncos Ring of Fame.

Two years after Gonsoulin's departure, the Broncos found one of the greatest defensive players in franchise history. Billy Thompson made an immediate impact as a rookie in 1969, starting at right cornerback and becoming the first player in AFL-NFL history to lead the league in both punt and kick returns.

Thompson remained a dangerous returner while honing his pass-coverage skills at cornerback, where he started until switching to strong safety in 1973. The move fit Thompson like a glove. He recorded 40 interceptions during his 13-year Broncos career, third all-time. He had such a nose for the football that he became one of only two players in NFL history to return four fumbles for touchdowns.

Billy Thompson started 178 of 179 games at cornerback or safety in his 13-year career (1969-81). He intercepted 40 passes (third all-time) for 784 yards (first) and recorded a team-record 61 turnovers. He was voted to three Pro Bowls.

Thompson's athletic ability was just as impressive. Not only was he able to remain injury free and start 178 games, but Thompson actually began earning league recognition later in his career with Pro Bowl berths in 1977, '78 and '81.

Bernard Jackson (29) teamed with Billy Thompson (36) to form a solid set of safeties on the 1977 Orange Crush defense.

After he retired, the Broncos still wanted Thompson to be part of their family. He served as a Broncos college scout for two seasons before moving into his current position as director of player relations and alumni coordinator. He was inducted into the Broncos Ring of Fame in 1987.

When asked what made him such a good player, Thompson said, "I think it was desire. I always wanted to win and I worked hard at it. I studied a lot of film. Another coach who taught me more about the game than I'd ever been around was [assistant] Richie McCabe. When I went from corner to safety, it was a change for me. He told me I would have to understand a lot more about what was happening because I was going to be in the middle of it.

"He got me watching film. Most of the time I went into the game, I was so confident in knowing what the team was going to do according to the formation they were in. I think that made me a good player. And with the desire on top of that, it just increased it."

One of Thompson's teammates in the Broncos' secondary during Denver's 1977 Super Bowl run was free safety Bernard Jackson, who was acquired in a preseason trade with Cincinnati. Jackson started all three playoff games that season and led Denver with six interceptions the following year.

"Once he got in there, we had a secondary that really didn't have any weaknesses," said defensive end Barney Chavous, who also played on Denver's Orange Crush defense. "He could cover man and he could cover zone. To play free safety, you have to be very intelligent because you have to be able to direct traffic. To be able to step right in says a lot about him. First, he became part of the team, and then he became part of the community."

Sadly, Jackson passed away from liver cancer in May 1997. He was 46.

The first big "hitter" in Denver's secondary was Dennis Smith, the team's first-round draft choice in 1981. In the mid-1980s, Smith rendered Cincinnati running back Billy Johnson unconscious while destroying his own face mask in the process. Seattle running back Randall Morris and San Diego wide receiver Nate Lewis are two of the other players who were KO'd by Smith.

That style of play shouldn't be a surprise from a safety who modeled his play after Oakland's Jack Tatum and was close friends with fellow punisher Ronnie Lott at Southern Cal.

Hard-hitting strong safety Dennis Smith attempts to put Warren Moon in orbit. Smith's shots were felt around the NFL for 14 seasons (1981-94). He was named to six Pro Bowl teams.

"Usually, I pick the area that will cause the most damage," Smith said two weeks after flooring Lewis in 1991. "And I hit that area so that the receiver will not forget me."

Smith's last great hit came in 1993 when he plowed into 260-pound Indianapolis running back Roosevelt Potts at full speed. *USA Today* writer Bryan Burwell said Potts "staggered off the field like some skid row bum in a dark alley. He wobbled. He weaved." Smith was hurting as well, but said, "I wouldn't allow myself to come out of the game. My thing is this: Take out the baddest and the biggest guy and the rest will follow. I was dazed, but no more than I've been before."

Smith was known to play with pain, but what he did during the 1987 season bordered on superhuman. In the final preseason game against Minnesota, Smith's left ring finger snapped when caught in a player's face mask. Smith, though, played in the Broncos' season opener. Smith then broke his finger again during the second game of the season, but was given some time to mend because of the four-week NFL players strike.

Upon his return, Smith tore cartilage in his knee but only missed one game. Against the Los Angeles Raiders in late November, Smith broke his right forearm. Smith, though, wouldn't miss starting in the AFC Championship game against

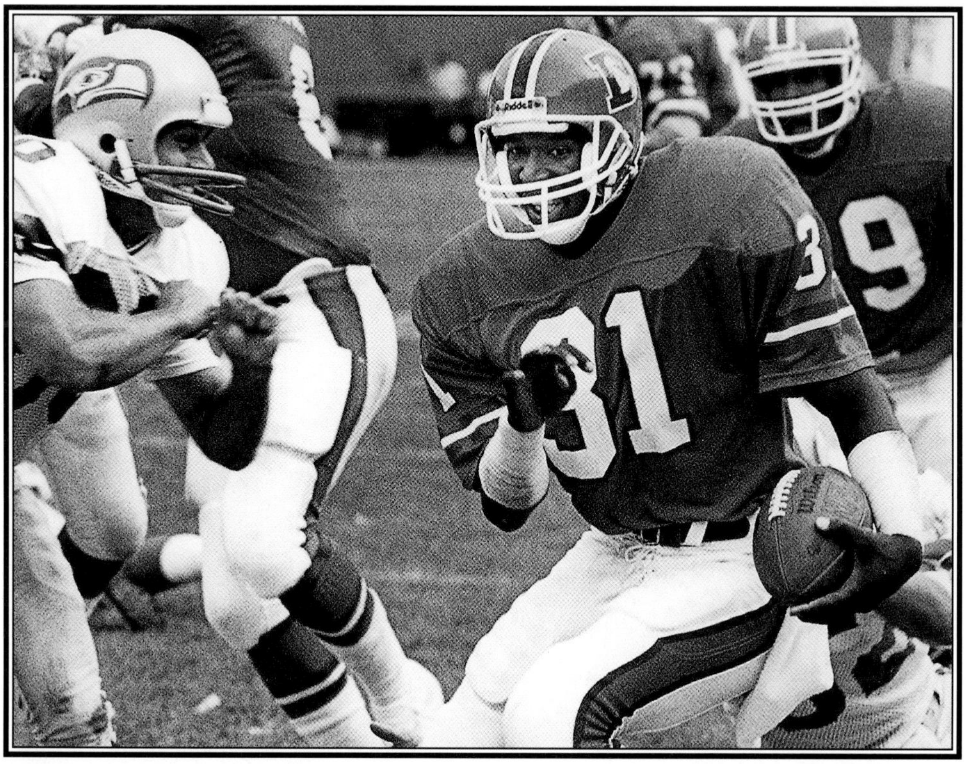

Mike Harden started at cornerback or safety through most of the 1980s. His 33 interceptions in a nine-year Denver career (1980-88) is tied with Tyrone Braxton for fourth on the Broncos' all-time list.

Cleveland. Smith wore a forearm pad and splint for his finger, but mangled his digit anyway. Not only was the tip of his finger purple from the cold at halftime, but one of the pins keeping his bone in place had shot through the skin.

So how did Smith respond to such excruciating pain? "The doctor just pulled it all the way out, taped it back up and I went out there and played," Smith said.

No member of the Broncos was happy after Denver lost to Washington, 42-10, in Super Bowl XXII. But Smith could take personal pride in leading the Broncos with nine tackles despite all his injuries.

Smith also was the focal point in one of the most bizarre finishes in Broncos history. In November 1985, a game between Denver and San Diego went into overtime with the score tied at 24-24. Smith blocked a 41-yard field goal attempt, only to have the play nullified because safety Mike Harden had called a time-out.

That didn't faze Smith, who proceeded to block Bob Thomas's next attempt as well. Cornerback Louis Wright scooped up the ball and ran 60 yards for the game-winning touchdown.

Harden and Steve Foley were two other outstanding defensive backs who played alongside Smith during the 1980s. Harden, who fluctuated between cornerback and

Steve Foley intercepted a team-record 44 passes in his 11-year career (1976-86). He converted from cornerback to safety in 1980.

safety during his nine seasons in Denver, returned four of his 33 interceptions for touchdowns. He also played in 128 games before finishing his career with the Los Angeles Raiders from 1989-90.

Foley was another Bronco who made the conversion from cornerback to safety later in his career. At either position, Foley made life bad for opposing quarterbacks. Foley finished his 11-year career with a team-record 44 interceptions, eclipsing the mark set by Goose Gonsoulin. The Goose was at the 1986 game when Foley intercepted a halfback pass by New England's Craig James to break the record.

"I met him for the first time before the game," Foley said. "I wanted him to sign the ball for me."

The latest in a long line of standout safeties is Steve Atwater, who lived up to the expectations that came with being Denver's first-round pick in 1989. As a rookie starting at free safety, Atwater tallied a team-high 86 solo tackles while playing in the same secondary as Dennis Smith. Atwater then proved he was as devastating a

Free safety Steve Atwater was named to seven straight Pro Bowls from 1990-96. A shoulder injury limited his play in 1997, but he still made critical defensive plays for Denver in Super Bowl XXXII.

hitter as Smith by leveling 260-pound Kansas City Chiefs running back Christian Okoye in a 1990 contest. Making the play even more memorable was the fact Atwater was wired with a live microphone by NFL Films.

"I think everybody who watched football or played football at the time remembers that hit," Denver safety Tyrone Braxton said. "Steve's had a lot of big hits since then, but that's kind of the one that let people know to expect that from [him]."

Said Atwater: "I was shocked by all the attention. It's weird. My kids love that tape. They know all the words. When the [narrator] says, 'Hi, I'm Steve Sabol,' they say, 'Hi, I'm Steve Sabol.'"

At 6-3 and 215 pounds, Atwater has the size of a linebacker but the speed to play safety. Combine that athleticism with football savvy and it's no surprise that Atwater set a team record in 1996 with his seventh straight Pro Bowl appearance. The string ended in 1997 largely because he battled a shoulder injury throughout the season. But he recovered in time to shine in the post-season. In Super Bowl XXXII, Atwater forced a fumble by Green Bay quarterback Brett Favre on a blitz and broke up a Favre pass in the game's final minute. Atwater underwent off-season shoulder surgery in 1998 in hopes of regaining his Pro Bowl form.

Tyrone Braxton wasn't supposed to play for more than a decade in the NFL. In fact, Braxton wasn't expected to stick around long after being the next-to-last player selected in the 1987 draft.

"Yeah, a 12th-round draft pick is definitely not supposed to stay around this long," said Braxton, who played in college at tiny North Dakota State. "Maybe one or two years. It's definitely been—I don't want to say Cinderella—but it's been good."

Good for everyone but the opposition. Braxton blossomed into a topnotch cornerback in 1989, registering six interceptions and 111 tackles. After missing most of 1990 with a knee injury, Braxton rebounded by averaging 100 tackles over the next three seasons. Braxton, though, was made a scapegoat after Denver's defense struggled in 1993. He spent the next season as a reserve in Miami before returning to Denver in 1995—as a strong safety.

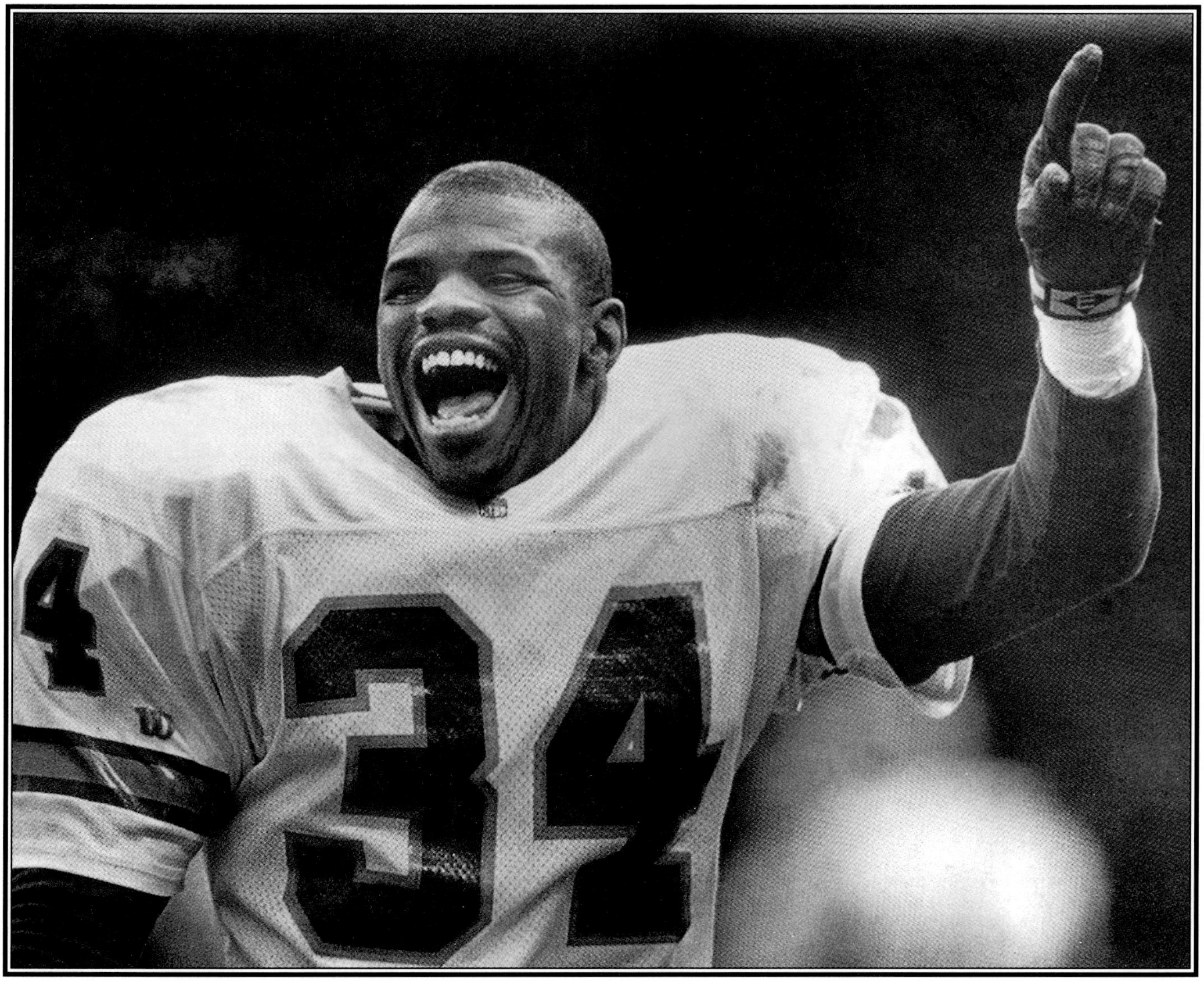

"I hate to admit it, but I didn't want him," Broncos defensive coordinator Greg Robinson said. "When this guy walked in, I thought, 'Are you kidding me? We're going to play this guy at safety?' But the people in the organization knew what he was all about."

Braxton is undersized for an NFL safety (5-11, 185 pounds), but few players have a better nose for the football. Braxton earned Pro Bowl honors in 1996 with 102 tackles and nine interceptions, which tied him for the NFL lead. Although Braxton's 1997 campaign wasn't as productive, he did intercept Green Bay quarterback Brett Favre in Super Bowl XXXII, leading to a Denver touchdown. Braxton now has three interceptions in the post-season, tying him for the most in franchise history.

As talented as Atwater and Braxton are, the strength of Denver's secondary in 1997 was the play of cornerback Ray Crockett. A free-agent signing from Detroit in 1994, Crockett enjoyed his best season in Denver with four interceptions, his highest total since the 1992 season. Crockett's best game came in Denver's 24-21 victory over Pittsburgh in the AFC Championship game when he recorded a team-high eight solo tackles, a sack and an interception in the end zone.

Crockett is arguably Denver's best cornerback since Louie Wright, who was inducted into the Broncos Ring of Fame after a stellar 12-year career. Wright start-

Strong safety Tyrone Braxton has made two stops in Denver, (1987-93 and 1995-97), separated by a one-year stint in Miami. He intercepted a pass in Super Bowl XXXII and is tied with Mike Harden for third on the Broncos' all-time interceptions list with 33.

"I don't try to get physical. I try to finesse them and beat them. If you beat them that way, there's nothing left at all for them. It's a confidence builder. They know that they can't do anything against you."

Cornerback Louis Wright started 163 of 166 games played in his 12-year career from 1975-86. He intercepted 26 passes, was named Most Valuable Defensive Player by his teammates twice and was named to five Pro Bowl teams.

ed 163 games during that span, intercepting 26 passes and earning five Pro Bowl berths. Wright also had the respect of his teammates, being voted Denver's Most Valuable Defensive Player on two separate occasions.

"You've got to know the receivers," Wright said. "It's like a weekly routine. You study the receivers, you know their best moves, their best patterns—all that stuff. But I really think that the most important factor is the quarterback. The receiver is really only as good as his quarterback. I've seen some great receivers and they've made some great moves, but the quarterback couldn't get the ball to them. No matter how good the receiver is, if you don't have the quarterback, you don't have to worry about the guy. He's never going to catch a pass."

Wright was such a good athlete—he once ran the 100-yard dash in 9.6 seconds—that he didn't need to employ the physical bump-and-run style used by all cornerbacks in the 1990s.

"I don't try to get physical," Wright said during his playing career. "I try to finesse them and beat them. If you beat them that way, there's nothing left at all for them. It's a confidence builder. They know that they can't do anything against you. I don't try to intimidate. I don't try to psych or talk or anything like it. I think that would just take away from my effort. If you can finesse them without saying a word, without touching them, without doing anything other than covering them perfectly, then that's it. They'll know they can't do anything against you."

Wright unexpectedly retired before the 1987 season, a decision that stunned his coaches and teammates. At the time, Wright was the last active member of Denver's Orange Crush defense.

Another cornerback who possessed as much ability as Wright was Willie Brown. But the Broncos didn't fully exploit Brown's talent. In fact, the Broncos traded Brown—who was signed as a college free agent out of Grambling in 1963—to the Oakland Raiders after four seasons in Denver.

Brown, who tied Goose Gonsoulin's single-game Broncos record with four interceptions in a 20-16 victory over the New York Jets in 1964, was elected to seven consecutive post-season All-Star games from 1967-73 and played with the Raiders until 1978. He was inducted into the Pro Football Hall of Fame in 1984.

The defensive line was a Broncos strength during the late 1960s. The '69 quartet included (left to right) Pete Duranko, Dave Costa, Jerry Inman and Rich Jackson.

Some defensive linemen sack quarterbacks. Rich Jackson buried them, which explains why his nickname was "Tombstone." During his six seasons with Denver from 1967-72, Jackson was considered by many as the NFL's best defensive end. Jackson's favorite pass-rushing maneuver was slapping the ear hole of an offensive linemen's helmet, which would cause excruciating pain. (The head slap was later banned by the NFL.)

Acquired from Oakland in a five-player trade in 1967 that sent wide receiver Lionel Taylor to the Raiders, Jackson anchored a solid defensive line that was one of the Broncos' strengths during the otherwise mediocre Lou Saban era. Jackson's line mates included end Pete Duranko and tackles Paul Smith, Jerry Inman and Dave Costa. Jackson (1968-69) and Costa (1967-69) became All-AFL selections.

After playing his first two seasons in Denver as a right end, Jackson moved to the left side—switching with Duranko—in 1969. From 1968-70, Jackson crushed opposing signal-callers 31 times. In 1970, he became the first Broncos player since the AFL-NFL merger to make the Pro Bowl. Jackson suffered a knee injury in 1971 that eventually forced him to retire, but he was still voted to the Pro Bowl that season. Jackson was one of the original four members inducted into the Broncos Ring of Fame in 1984.

An even more productive pass-rusher during his nine seasons in Denver was defensive end Rulon Jones, whose 73.5 sacks ranks fourth on the Broncos' all-time

Rubin Carter corrals a Green Bay Packer in the snow at Mile High Stadium. Carter started a record 151 games at nose tackle in his 12-year career (1975-86).

list behind Simon Fletcher (97.5), Karl Mecklenburg (79) and Barney Chavous (75). Jones set a Broncos single-season sack record of 13.5 in 1986 (surpassed by Fletcher's 16 in 1992) to earn his second consecutive Pro Bowl berth and be honored as the AFC Defensive Player of the Year by United Press International.

"I was kind of tabbed to have the potential to be All-Pro and reach the Pro Bowl," said Jones, who opted to retire in 1988 after suffering a serious knee injury. "I think I was really driven after that to accomplish that. I remember when workouts got tough, that's what I'd focus on. I had to work a little bit harder than the next guy to accomplish that goal. I think if I had to [retire] without accomplishing those goals, it would be a lot harder for me. I'd really feel let down. I'm just really glad I did."

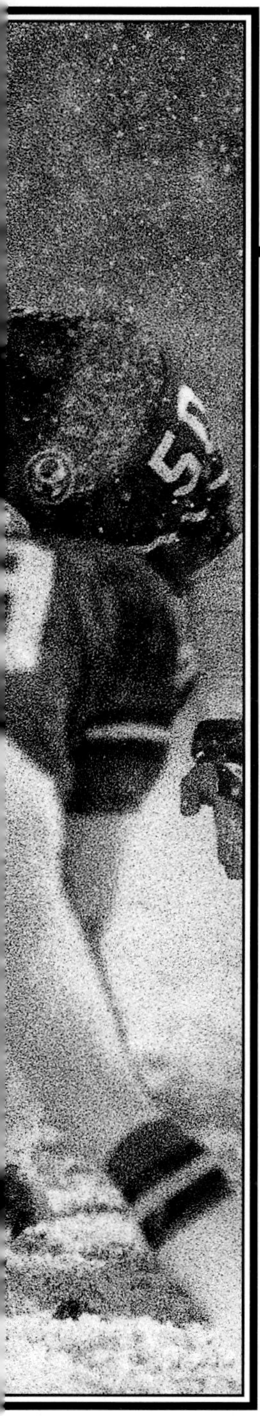

The most memorable play in Jones's career came in the 1986 AFC Divisional playoff game against New England in which he recorded a fourth-quarter sack of Patriots quarterback Tony Eason for a safety to help preserve a 22-17 Broncos victory. "He won a lot of games for us," Broncos linebacker Rick Dennison said.

The success of the linebackers in the Orange Crush defense wouldn't have happened without nose tackle Rubin Carter, who would frequently draw double-teams from opponents. Despite standing only six feet tall, Carter could bench press 525 pounds and showed amazing constitution for a player who regularly took an enormous beating. He started 151 games at nose tackle in a 12-year Broncos career (1975-86), the most for any player at that position in NFL history.

"I'm not as tall as many guys, but I've got a leverage advantage," Carter said. "In some ways, I'm like the guy in the middle with his finger in the hole in the dam. If I can't control the center, it's like a dam busting loose."

Another sack artist was Barney Chavous, who had 75 during his 13 years in Denver as a defensive end. When he retired during training camp in 1986, Chavous had

Rulon Jones unloads on Browns quarterback Brian Sipe before he can unload this pass in 1980. Jones played nine seasons at defensive end (1980-88) and was named AFC Defensive Player of theYear in 1986 by United Press International.

Iron men Paul Smith (70) and Barney Chavous (79) played 11 and 13 seasons, respectively, on the Broncos' defensive line.

played in 182 games and was in the starting lineup for all but five of them. Chavous returned to the Broncos in 1988 as a coaching intern and has remained with the club ever since.

Before Chavous, the Broncos had another iron man along their defensive line. Paul Smith was the first player to log more than 10 seasons in Denver, registering 55 sacks in 134 games from 1968-78 to earn a spot in the Broncos Ring of Fame. Smith began his pro career as a linebacker after being drafted in the ninth round out of New Mexico.

Following the 1972 season, Smith made the first of two straight Pro Bowl appearances after recording 47 tackles and 11 sacks. He was so dominating that Oakland offered quarterback Ken Stabler—who would lead the Raiders to victory in Super Bowl XI—for Smith in a straight-up trade. Smith ruptured his Achilles tendon in 1974, but returned from that career-threatening injury to play in 13 games and record 58 tackles in 1975. He then recovered from a serious knee injury to complete a decade's worth of service for the Broncos.

Another important defensive lineman for the Orange Crush was defensive end Lyle Alzado, who was one of the most popular players in franchise history during his time in Denver. Alzado was a fearsome pass rusher who recorded 64.5 sacks from

1971-78 despite missing almost the entire '76 campaign with a knee injury.

Alzado experienced a rough upbringing in New York. At age 15, he served as a bouncer in the bar his father owned. His brawling often got him into trouble with the law, although he later turned his skills toward Golden Gloves boxing.

But this angry young man also had a big heart. After joining the Broncos in 1971, Alzado became involved in charities benefitting such causes as cystic fibrosis, multiple sclerosis and the deaf. For his service, he was given the Whizzer White Award in 1977. Unfortunately, Alzado will be remembered more for his admitted problems with steroid abuse that he believed led to a rare form of brain cancer. Alzado died in 1992.

The Broncos' first stalwart defensive lineman was tackle Bud McFadin. He might have reached the same statistical heights as his successors had he joined Denver in his prime. At age 32, McFadin was an eight-year veteran, including five seasons with the Rams, in the Broncos' 1960 inaugural season. Yet he still made the AFL All-Star game from 1961-63.

In addition to McFadin, Rich Jackson and Goose Gonsoulin, other Denver defenders who achieved the same honor during the 1960s were defensive backs Bob Zeman (1962), Willie Brown (1964) and Nemiah Wilson (1967), linebacker John Bramlett (1966) and defensive tackle Dave Costa (1967-69).

Before the NFL adopted a free-agency system in 1993, the Broncos had acquired most of their talent through the draft. But several key defensive linemen who helped the Broncos win Super Bowl XXXII arrived in Denver after stints with other teams. One of the most intriguing acquisitions was Neil Smith, who signed a one-year contract with Denver in April 1997. Over the previous nine seasons with Kansas City, Smith had made life miserable for the Broncos—and John Elway in particular. Smith has sacked Elway more times (15) than any other NFL quarterback.

The Chiefs, however, thought Smith had finally worn down from the constant double-teaming a player of his caliber usually receives. Smith registered only six

Lyle Alzado once held up a baseball bat in a television commercial and said, "I gotta get me one of these." Alzado, however, required no accoutrements beyond talent and street-gang toughness to become AFC Defensive Player of the Year with the 1977 Super Bowl Broncos.

Alfred Williams found his heart in San Francisco, then brought a new sense of determination to Denver where he became a starter at defensive end for the Super Bowl champions.

sacks in 1996, his lowest total since his rookie campaign. When the Chiefs had a choice of signing either Smith or linebacker Derrick Thomas to a lucrative contract extension, Kansas City coach Marty Schottenheimer chose the younger Thomas.

"He [Schottenheimer] said to me I was on the decline," Smith said. "I'm not on the decline."

While Smith didn't post great sack figures in 1996, he did pressure opposing quarterbacks a team-high 77 times. Broncos coach Mike Shanahan wanted to sign Smith, but he needed to find room under the salary cap to do so. So who volunteered to restructure his contract? Elway, who was obviously tired of getting bashed by Smith for two games each season.

The move paid dividends for the Broncos. Despite playing half of the 1997 season with a partially torn triceps, Smith reached the Pro Bowl while registering 8.5 sacks to raise his career total to 95. Smith's performance helped earn him a significant raise, as the Broncos signed him to a four-year, $13.2 million deal in the 1998 off-season.

"As a lineman, he's the best athlete I've ever coached," Nebraska defensive coordinator Charlie McBride said. "He's a diligent worker both on and off the field, and he has always concentrated on improving. Neil has a lot of qualities and athletic ability that not a lot of linemen possess, especially his quickness and speed."

Those qualities are what has helped Denver's other defensive end—Alfred Williams—gain respect among the elite at his position. Williams reached the Pro Bowl in 1996 after registering 13 sacks and 65 tackles.

Having spent his college career at the University of Colorado, Williams had wanted to play in Denver long before he signed a five-year, $9 million contract as a free-agent in 1996. But the road that Williams took to reach the Broncos was filled with obstacles. In 1992, Williams was diagnosed with a hereditary heart ailment called Wolfe-Parkinson-White syndrome. He underwent eight hours of surgery hoping to correct the problem, but the procedure was unsuccessful. Williams wasn't even sure if he was going to live, let alone play football.

"I woke up on the operating table and looked around," Williams said. "I was there by myself, and I just broke down crying. I was scared, real scared. I was even more scared going into the second operation."

The next surgery was successful, which allowed Williams to return to the gridiron. But he was then forced to answer questions about whether he had any heart on the football field. Williams was considered an underachiever on a miserable defensive unit in Cincinnati, but he began to rebuild his reputation after joining San Francisco in 1995.

"I've taken many routes to get where I am now," Williams said after becoming a Bronco. "I'm home now. . . . My heart is into this."

No player in 1997 may have shown more heart in a single-game performance than defensive tackle Keith Traylor. On the day before the AFC Divisional playoff game against Kansas City, he learned his mother had passed away. Playing with a heavy heart, Traylor helped stuff Kansas City's rushing attack while registering two tackles for losses.

Traylor actually began his NFL career with the Broncos in 1991 as a linebacker, starting three games in his first two seasons. Traylor, though, was released because of off-field problems. After spending the 1994 season out of the football, Traylor played in the NFL's World League as a 300-plus-pound defensive tackle. He then signed with the Chiefs for two seasons before rejoining the Broncos with a six-year, $10.2 million contract.

Denver's fourth defensive line starter in Super Bowl XXXII was Maa Tanuvasa, who used his quickness to register 8.5 sacks during the 1997 season. He became a starter in mid-season after the play of Michael Dean Perry had dramatically declined, which led to his release later in the season.

Maa Tanuvasa saw increased playing time at defensive tackle in 1997, starting five games after mid-season. He finished with 21 tackles (20 solo). His 8.5 sacks were tied for the team lead and ranked 10th in the AFC.

Chapter 11

Special Teams

Upchurch Downfield!

Returners

Place-kickers

Punters

Since the inception of the Broncos in 1960, there have been plenty of special players who have made an impact on special teams. But maybe none more so than Rick Upchurch, who established himself as one of the greatest punt returners in National Football League history while playing in Denver from 1975-83. A fourth-round draft pick (the 95th player selected overall) by Denver in 1975 from the University of Minnesota, Upchurch didn't take long to make an impact.

During his rookie season, Upchurch assumed both punt and kickoff return duties. On punts, he replaced Billy Thompson, whose shoes were not easy to fill. Just like Upchurch, Thompson made an immediate impression as a rookie in Denver. In 1969, he became the only player in AFL-NFL history to lead the league in both punt and kickoff returns. Making that feat even more impressive was the fact Thompson also recorded a team-high three interceptions as Denver's starter at right cornerback, which is one of the most physically demanding positions in pro football. He averaged 11.5 yards on punt returns and 28.5 on kickoff returns in 1969. In 1974, Thompson averaged an impressive 13.5 yards on 26 punt return opportunities.

There was little drop-off, though, when Upchurch assumed the role the following season. Upchurch averaged 12.2 yards on his punt returns and 27.1 yards on his kickoff returns. He also caught 18 passes for 436 yards and two touchdowns, including a 90-yarder from quarterback Charley Johnson in a 37-33 victory over the Kansas City Chiefs in the 1975 season-opener at Mile High Stadium. The play equaled John McCormick's 1965 bomb to wide receiver Bob Scarpitto as the fifth-longest scoring pass in Broncos team history.

Rick Upchurch goes stride for stride with Cleveland's Bill Cowher in 1980.

COWHER
53
UPCHURCH
80

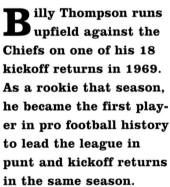

Billy Thompson runs upfield against the Chiefs on one of his 18 kickoff returns in 1969. As a rookie that season, he became the first player in pro football history to lead the league in punt and kickoff returns in the same season.

For the season, Upchurch averaged a team-leading 24.2 yards a reception. That would have been good enough to set another rookie record, but a minimum of 20 receptions is required by the Broncos to qualify for consideration.

After such a fast start, it wasn't much of a surprise when Upchurch was honored by the NFL Players Association as their AFC Offensive Rookie of the Year in March 1976. But what Upchurch accomplished on special teams during the 1976 season couldn't have been expected by anyone.

Upchurch was simply phenomenal as a returner en route to earning a trip to the Pro Bowl. He made a splash during the third game of the season against the Cleveland Browns at Mile High Stadium. To return one punt for a touchdown in a game is impressive enough, but Upchurch tied an NFL record by reaching the end zone twice in a 44-13 victory over the Browns on Sept. 26.

Upchurch remembers the game as if it were played yesterday.

"I never thought I'd ever, ever do anything like that," Upchurch said. "I knew we were playing Cleveland in a nationally televised game, so all the folks at home in Ohio where I grew up would be watching. That was kind of a unique game for me.

"I remember the first one I caught, the [blocking] wall was perfect. I remember just making couple of moves and all of a sudden everything opened up. I hit to the right, made my cut and the field was wide open. I had a couple of guys to beat, but

I made one miss and the other was caught when [running back] Lonnie Perrin blocked him.

"On the other one, I remember the [Cleveland punter] kicked the ball up real high. It just kept hanging and hanging and hanging. When it finally came down, it hit me right in the hands. There was a guy right in front of me, but I juked him. Then I cut to the right, headed toward the sideline and walked on in.

"I was like, 'Man, this is pretty easy.' Well, actually I didn't really think that. Everything just seemed to work that day. Everybody was blocking real well. It caught [the Browns] off guard. I remember when I went into the locker room after the game, they told me I tied a record with only two other guys who had ever done it. I was like, 'As long as we won the game, that was what was important.'"

Upchurch struck again the following week against San Diego with a 92-yard return, which was the longest in franchise history until the 1997 season. Upchurch then cemented his name in the NFL record books later in the month. During a win over Kansas City, 35-26, at Arrowhead Stadium, Upchurch returned his fourth punt

of the 1976 campaign for a touchdown to tie the NFL's single-season record. For the season, Upchurch averaged 13.74 yards on 39 returns.

Upchurch credits his success to his blockers and to assistant coaches Myrel Moore, Marv Braden and Fran Polsfoot.

"First of all, I had a lot of confidence in the guys I was playing with," he said. "When you have that, you have confidence [too]. I did a lot of film study with a lot of teams, which helped me learn where their weak points were. The coaches and I would break down the films and see what the other teams were doing.

"Another thing was that I [had been] doing this since high school. That gave me a lot of confidence," he added.

"I would say Rick Upchurch was very fast, and once I was in the open field, no one was going to catch me. I also had very good coaches in high school and college. They taught me how to study film and made me a student of the game. What also helped was that I was a running back in college and high school. When I got hit, it did not mean anything to me. I liked to get hit. I was big, and I was going to get right back up. The best returners aren't scared of that part of the game."

Rick Upchurch was best known as a returner, but he was a wide receiver as well. His 267 receptions in nine seasons ranks eighth on the Broncos' all-time list.

There was only one drawback to such success. Upchurch found himself a marked man on the field. With teams reluctant to kick to him, he never threatened to break the NFL's single-season punt return scoring record again. Upchurch scored once in 1977 (an 87-yard return in a 21-7 win over Pittsburgh) and again in 1978, but was then shut out the following two seasons. The same avoidance occurred on kickoffs.

"They would either kick it high to me or to the sidelines," said Upchurch, whose days as the primary kickoff returner ended after the '77 season. "There were all types of things they would do. They would even rather kick the ball out of bounds than kick to me. Even when I went to the Pro Bowl, I was talking to [place-kickers] Mark Moseley and Efren Herrera. They told me their coaches had told their team not to kick the ball to me. I was like, 'Man, I can't even touch the ball in the Pro Bowl.'"

In 1981, Upchurch was replaced on punt returns by Wade Manning, a rookie from Ohio State. Upchurch regained the job in 1982 and returned two punts for

touchdowns, including a 78-yarder in a 37-16 loss to visiting Kansas City late in the season. That return tied Upchurch for the NFL's all-time return record with eight career touchdowns. He yielded his punt return duties once again in 1983—this time to South Carolina State wide receiver Zach Thomas—before retiring at season's end.

Upchurch's return prowess often overshadows the fact he was a dangerous wide receiver for the Broncos. He caught 267 passes for 4,369 yards and 24 touchdowns, marks that rank him among the top 10 Denver receivers of all-time.

Like Upchurch, Darrien Gordon is another player whose punt return prowess has received more recognition than his capabilities at another position. A 1993 first-round draft pick from Stanford, Gordon was signed as a free-agent in 1997 from the San Diego Chargers. He was so successful on punt returns that the media seemed to forget that he had won the spot as Denver's starting right cornerback during training camp and was doing well, including a 32-yard interception return for a touchdown during the season's second game at Seattle.

Cornerback Darrien Gordon is the NFL's all-time leader in career punt return average. He returned two for touchdowns in the Broncos' 34-0 win over Carolina on Nov. 9, 1997.

"I think my skills as a corner are right up there with the top guys," said Gordon, who finished the 1997 season with four interceptions. "For that to be down played because of what I do as a returner is real disheartening. I want to be thought of as a Deion Sanders, where they know he's a great corner with the ability to return punts and kicks and play wide receiver. I think I have all those abilities also, but I primarily want to be known as a topflight corner."

Said secondary coach Ed Donatell: "He likes to be known as someone who does more than return punts. It just happens that he has done some great stuff there. When you score three touchdowns, they're going to talk about you as a punt returner."

In the third game of the season, Gordon exploded for the longest punt return in franchise history and the longest in the NFL in three seasons. Gordon sliced through the St. Louis Rams' coverage team to jaunt 94 yards for a touchdown in a 35-14 Broncos victory at Mile High Stadium.

Gordon then joined Upchurch as the only players in Broncos history to register two punt returns for a touchdown in the same game. It also made Denver only the second team in NFL history to record such an accomplishment on two separate occasions (Detroit's Jack Christiansen did it twice in 1951.)

Even more impressive, both of Gordon's returns came in the first quarter to set the foundation for Denver's 34-0 blowout of the Carolina Panthers at Mile High on Nov. 9. Gordon's first score was tougher than the second, as he initially struggled to corral a 54-yard punt by Ken Walker. Gordon caught the ball on Denver's 18-yard line and ran across the field toward the Broncos' sideline behind a wall of players. When Broncos cornerback Randy Hilliard tied up Walker past midfield, the sideline was clear for Gordon to give Denver a 7-0 lead.

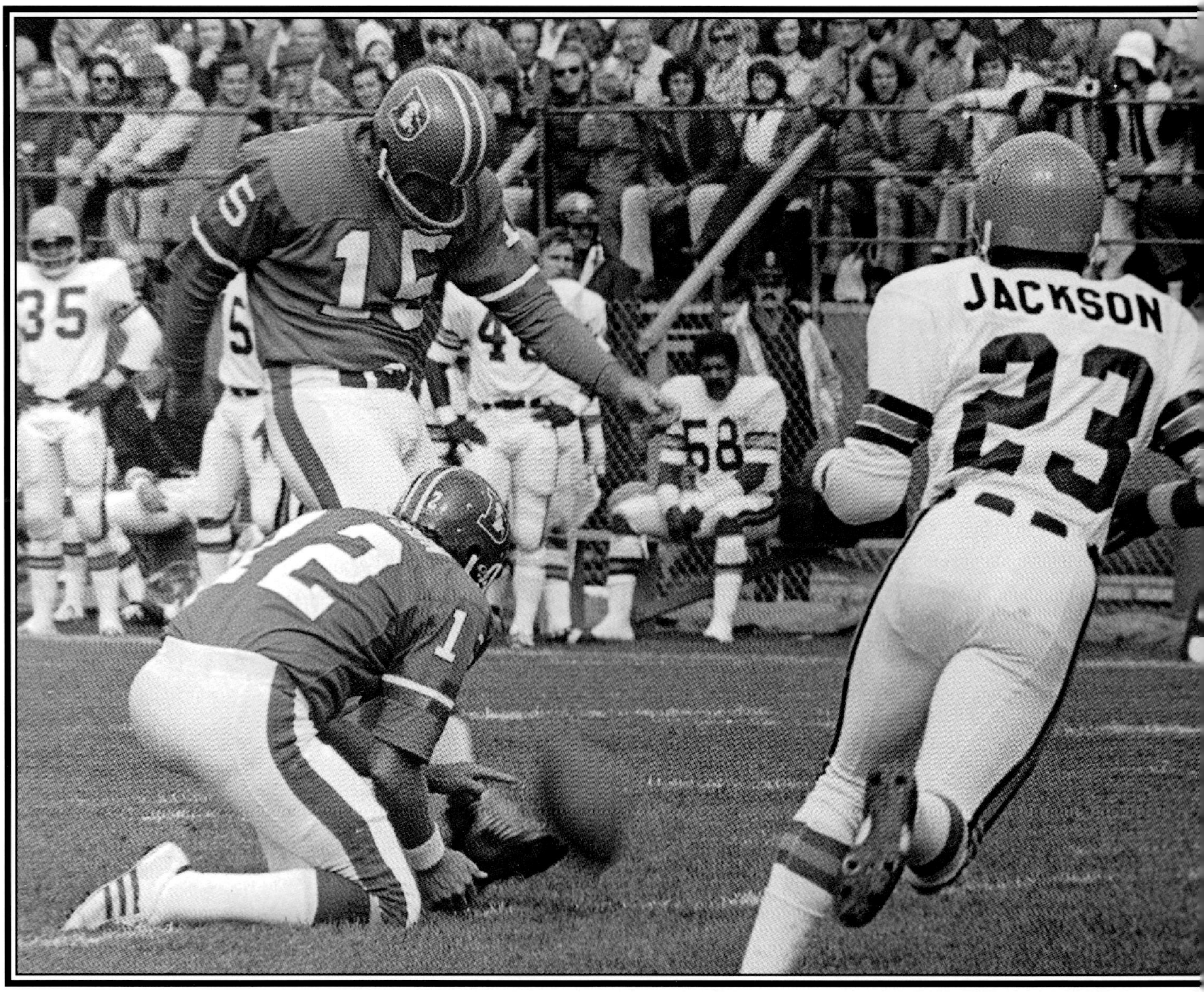

The second return wouldn't have happened without the help of a Carolina penalty, because a 64-yard Walker punt was nullified when an ineligible-man-downfield penalty was assessed. His next punt sailed 52 yards but gave Gordon the chance to dart through the middle of the Panthers' coverage.

Gordon avoided a Walker tackle at Carolina's 40-yard line and veered toward the Panthers' sideline, where he capped a 75-yard return by strutting into the end zone. Gordon finished the game with 168 return yards, a new Broncos record. To show his appreciation, he rewarded all special teams players with a cash bonus for their blocking on the two plays.

By averaging 13.6 yards a return in 1997 (the NFL's second-best figure behind Baltimore's Jermaine Lewis), Gordon retained his position as the league's all-time leader in punt return average—also 13.6. His six career returns for touchdowns ties him for third all-time behind Upchurch and Jack Christiansen (eight each); and Dave Meggett (seven).

The two best punt returners in Broncos history met for the first time after the Carolina game when Upchurch presented Gordon with the Miller Lite NFL Play-

Jim Turner demonstrates his straight-on kicking style, one of the last players in NFL history to employ the technique. He played nine seasons in Denver (1971-79) to become the Broncos' all-time scoring leader with 742 points. He also leads in field goals (151) and extra points (283).

er of the Week award. So who does Upchurch think is the better returner?

"If you look at sports, all kinds of standards are set year in and year out," Upchurch said. "You have different eras and things like that. When you set standards, that gives somebody else something to look for. And there's always somebody out there who's better. I don't know if he's better, but he sure is achieving some of the things I did in my day."

The most prolific kickoff returner in Broncos history is also the team's all-time leading rusher, running back Floyd Little, who holds the franchise record for all-time return yardage (2,523) in spite of being Denver's first-string returner for only the 1967 and '68 seasons.

Since the early 1970s, the Broncos have struggled to find a game-breaker on kickoff returns. The last time the Broncos scored on a kickoff came on Sept. 24, 1972, when Randy Montgomery traveled 94 yards against San Diego. His 201 yards that day remains a Broncos single-game mark.

Glyn Milburn, a second-round pick in 1993, showed promise when he set Denver's single-season yardage mark of 1,269 return yards in 1995. That same season, Milburn also had an 86-yard return against San Diego before being stopped short of the goal line. Milburn struggled to make the adjustment from running back to wide receiver and was traded before the 1996 season to Detroit.

The only player inducted into the Broncos Ring of Fame based solely on special teams accomplishments was place-kicker Jim Turner. Acquired from the New York Jets in 1971 for another kicker, Bobby Howfield, the deal became one of the best of the Lou Saban era. Turner had kicked three field goals to help the Jets beat the Baltimore Colts, 16-7, in Super Bowl III. His straight-on style (still considered the most reliable technique in those days), would be a good fit for the wide variety of weather conditions in Mile High Stadium.

Chris Norman (left) owns the longest punt in Broncos history, 83 yards against Kansas City in 1984. Jim Fraser (right) punted a pair of 75-yarders in 1962, the first of three straight seasons he would lead the AFL in punting.

Turner, though, wasn't just a kicker. He was also an excellent athlete, as proven by his stint as the Utah State quarterback in the early 1960s. By keeping himself in excellent physical condition, Turner never missed an NFL game and retired with 228 consecutive appearances, including 130 with the Broncos.

In nine years with Denver (1971-79), Turner scored a team-record 742 points. At retirement, he ranked second all-time in the NFL in points (1,439) and field goals (304). Turner also scored one touchdown and kicked 521 extra points, becoming only the fourth player in league history to surpass the 500 mark.

Because of the thin air in Denver, it's understandable why kickers and punters love to play in Mile High Stadium. There is a belief that the football travels further at 5,280 feet than at sea level, which seemed to be substantiated during the Broncos' formative years when Jim Fraser won three consecutive AFL punting titles from 1962-64. Fraser still holds franchise records for best career (45.2) and single-season (46.09 in 1963) averages.

More than 20 punts of 70-plus yards have traveled through the Mile High atmosphere. Chris Norman set the franchise record with an 83-yarder against Kansas City on Sept. 23, 1984, but that was barely a squib compared to Steve O'Neal's NFL-record-setting 98-yard boomer for the Jets against the Broncos on Sept. 21, 1969.

Fred Steinfort also took advantage of the mile-high air during the 1980 season. His 57-yard field goal in a 20-17 victory over visiting Washington was the third-longest in NFL history at the time.

However, not every Broncos specialist believes the altitude plays a major role in how far a kick travels.

"I don't think there's much of an advantage," said 1997 Broncos punter Tom Rouen, who joined the team in '93 after attending high school and college in Colorado. "It looks higher because there's less resistance going up, but there's also less resistance going down. I think they did a study when I was at [the University of Colorado] that said there was probably a four-inch difference in a kick with all things being equal. But when you take Denver in [the winter] and compare it to Seattle playing indoors or San Diego with warmer weather, what you're losing in the cold weather isn't being made up by altitude. You play half your games on the road and we've always done well there, too."

No place-kicker in Broncos history may have performed better in the clutch than Rich Karlis in the 1986 AFC Championship game against Cleveland. As a barefoot kicker, one can understand why Karlis's sole was filthy before his 33-yard field goal gave Denver a dramatic 23-20 overtime victory and its first trip to the Super Bowl in nine seasons. The playing surface at Cleveland Municipal Stadium included the dirt baseball infield used for Cleveland Indians games.

"They had sprinkled pieces of grass and sand down there to make it look good," said Karlis, who kicked field goals in six other post-season games during his seven-year Broncos career (1982-88). "The more I tried to do [to find a spot for holder Gary Kubiak], the deeper I was going into dirt. Nothing but dirt."

Billy Van Heusen is the Broncos' all-time punting leader with 574 in his nine-year career (1968-76). He also was a dependable pass receiver, averaging 20.54 yards per catch, also a Broncos career record.

Karlis managed to convert his third field goal of the game by a yard, prompting a wild post-game celebration among Broncos players.

"I remember going out on the field and looking for Rich, but I couldn't find him," Broncos coach Dan Reeves said. "He was down there under players in the mud somewhere."

Karlis finished his Broncos career ranked second all-time behind Jim Turner in points (742-655), field goals (151-137) and extra points (283-244). Karlis will also be remembered for his seven field goals against San Diego in 1988, equalling Gene Mingo's team record—also versus the Chargers—in 1963.

In the 1990s, Jason Elam, a third-round pick in 1993, has developed into one of the AFC's best kickers. He was erratic in 1997, but made amends for that in the biggest victory in franchise history. Elam kicked a 51-yard field goal—the second-longest in Super Bowl history—in Denver's 31-24 victory over Green Bay.

"We got a great snap and I got it down with the laces around," said Broncos holder Tom Rouen. "As soon as he hit it, it sounded good. It was going straight, but I just didn't know if it was going to be long enough. It just kept going and went through. I think it was just a huge moment in the game. It gave us a little bit of an advantage that we needed, and it was a morale booster. A lot of times, a long kick like that gets everyone pumped up. That certainly did that."

Rich Karlis is best known for kicking the game-winner in the 1986 AFC Championship game, but he also kicked at least one field goal in seven of the Broncos' eight post-season games during his seven-year NFL career (1982-88).

Fred Steinfort (left) kicked the longest field goal in Broncos history, 57 yards, against the Redskins in 1980. Jason Elam (right) booted the second longest field goal in Super Bowl history, a 51-yarder, against the Packers in Super Bowl XXXII.

When the National Football League adopted a free-agency system in 1993, players began to change teams like never before. Keeping an entire roster intact for more than one season has become almost impossible for most teams. Players now hop-scotch from franchise to franchise if the money is right. Some players today even joke that when they sign with a new team, they have to learn who their new rivals are.

But no matter how many faces change on a Denver Broncos roster, there will always be a hatred for the Oakland Raiders. That's because players in Denver quickly learn of a 38-year rivalry that is among the most heated in professional sports.

Chapter 12

The Rivalries

Shootouts in the AFC

Oakland-L.A. Raiders

Kansas City Chiefs

Cleveland Browns

"The Raiders have always been The Rival until recent years, when maybe the Chiefs have equaled them," said Jim Saccomano, the Broncos' senior director of public relations. "As a team, [Kansas City] has passed them. But the hatred is still there."

The Broncos and Raiders were two of the eight teams that played in the first season of the American Football League in 1960. Both clubs struggled in their formative years, but the Raiders began showing significant improvement with a 10-4 record in 1963, one win behind the Western Division champion Chargers. The Broncos, meanwhile, finished in the basement. That year also marked the start of a 15-year string of almost complete domination of the Broncos by the Raiders.

In fact, the Raiders should have considered moving to Denver because of how well they fared when playing in the mile-high city. From 1963 through '77, Oakland posted a 13-0-2 road record against the Broncos. Overall, the Broncos won only three of 30 regular-season games against the Raiders during that period.

Terrell Davis pulls away from a horde of silver and black attackers on Nov. 24, 1997.

29
42
BIEKE

Calvin Jones clutches Cliff Branch, but takes a stiff arm in the process in the fourth quarter of the 23-23 tie between the Broncos and the Raiders in 1973 on "Monday Night Football."

"They just came in and pummeled us year after year—and with attitude," Saccomano said. "We joked about that, even with the Raiders people. It was a hardcore rivalry."

But that's not to say the Broncos never enjoyed any success against the silver and black. In 1973, Denver could claim a moral victory over the Raiders in spite of not winning the game. Playing in the first Monday night game in franchise history, Denver rallied to post a 23-23 tie against Oakland at Mile High Stadium. After opening the season with a 2-3-1 mark, the Broncos went 5-2-1 in their final eight games to post the first winning record in the history of the franchise.

"When I played, there was no question that the Raiders were the top rival," said Broncos safety Billy Thompson, who battled against Oakland from 1969-81. "They were the top team in the AFC West for a long time. . . . I don't want to say they were the gangsters on the block, but they were the bullies. They were cocky and they made no bones about it. They were good and they had this intimidating factor they tried to use on everybody.

"The Broncos were, for quite some time, the doormats of the AFC West. In 1973, things started to change. We started to gain a little respect here and there. We were the upstarts challenging the kings. It was really exciting for us because the Broncos had never won. This was a new era for us. I thought we had a lot of exciting young players and I thought we had our best team in 1975. We didn't make it, but we got close. Then we came back in 1976, 1977 and '78 and turned everything around."

When recalling the 1973 Monday night game, Saccomano said, "It was a monumental moment. It really was. Denver wasn't what it is now. You had a [basketball] team that was in about its sixth season in the [American Basketball Association] and the Broncos. It was their first major prime-time appearance, and they came from behind and tied the Raiders. It was a huge game for the city and a big moment."

The stakes were even higher when the Raiders hosted the Broncos in the fifth game of the 1977 season. Denver had opened the campaign undefeated, but would not be regarded as a serious contender unless it could finally top the Raiders. Oakland had won Super Bowl XI the previous season by topping Minnesota, 32-14, and was on a 17-game winning streak.

"The Broncos believe we can win against Oakland, which I don't believe was true when we played them both times last year," Broncos backup quarterback Norris Weese said in *Orange Madness*.

Not only did the Broncos win the game, they embarrassed Oakland in a 30-7 victory. Raiders quarterback Ken Stabler was intercepted seven times, with three pass-

es getting snagged by linebacker Joe Rizzo. It was late in the game when Broncos linebacker Tom Jackson delivered one of the most famous lines in franchise history. Jackson made an obscene gesture to plump Raiders coach John Madden and said, "Hey fat man, take this. We got you fat man."

"Only a certain kind of guy would do that," Saccomano said. "T.J. was one of those kinds of guys."

The "Fat Man" and his team got their revenge two weeks later by once again defeating the Broncos at Mile High Stadium, this time by a 24-14 margin. So one could imagine the suspense gripping Denver when the Raiders returned for the AFC Championship game.

Gene Mingo's junction was the end zone on this touchdown in 1962. The 23-6 Broncos victory was their only win over the Raiders at Oakland in the first 12 years of the rivalry.

Riddell
RAIDERS

There was a string of memorable meetings in the mid-1980s. In a six-game stretch from November 1983 to September 1986, the margin of victory was three points or less each time, including three overtime games.

As it turned out, it was appropriate that the game was played on January 1, 1978. That's because the Broncos made a new start by topping Oakland, 20-17, to land a spot in Super Bowl XII.

The rivalry remained extremely competitive over the next decade, even after the Raiders moved to Los Angeles in 1982. There was a string of memorable meetings in the mid-1980s. In a six-game stretch from November 1983 to September 1986, the margin of victory was three points or less each time, including three overtime games.

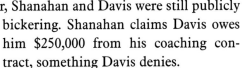

Randy Gradishar delivers a crushing tackle in 1977. Denver beat the Super Bowl champion Raiders twice that season, a 30-7 win at Oakland and in the AFC Championship game, 20-17, at Mile High.

The series took an interesting turn in 1988 when Mike Shanahan left his post as a Broncos assistant coach to become head coach of the Raiders. One can easily understand why Raiders owner Al Davis would want Shanahan with him rather than against him. The Broncos had posted four consecutive victories against the Raiders while scoring an average of 28 points in the 1986 and '87 seasons.

At first, the hiring paid dividends as the Shanahan-coached Raiders defeated Denver twice in the regular season. But there wasn't much else for the Raiders to celebrate in 1988. They finished with a 7-9 mark to miss the playoffs for a third straight year. The Broncos likewise missed the playoffs at 8-8.

Shanahan and Davis got along like oil and water. Shanahan grew frustrated by Davis meddling with his play-calling and personnel decisions. After a slow start in 1989, Davis fired Shanahan after only four games. Shanahan returned to Denver to become an assistant coach. Eight years later, Shanahan and Davis were still publicly bickering. Shanahan claims Davis owes him $250,000 from his coaching contract, something Davis denies.

Vance Johnson gets a twisted view of the Broncos-Raiders rivalry. While in Los Angeles from 1982 through 1994, the Raiders uncoiled on Denver, winning 18 of 26 games, including five out of six overtime contests.

There is just as intense a rivalry between one member of the Broncos and the head coach of another team, although this one is more competitive than personal. Broncos quarterback John Elway and Kansas City Chiefs coach Marty Schottenheimer are amicable enough that the duo speaks while playing golf together in celebrity tournaments.

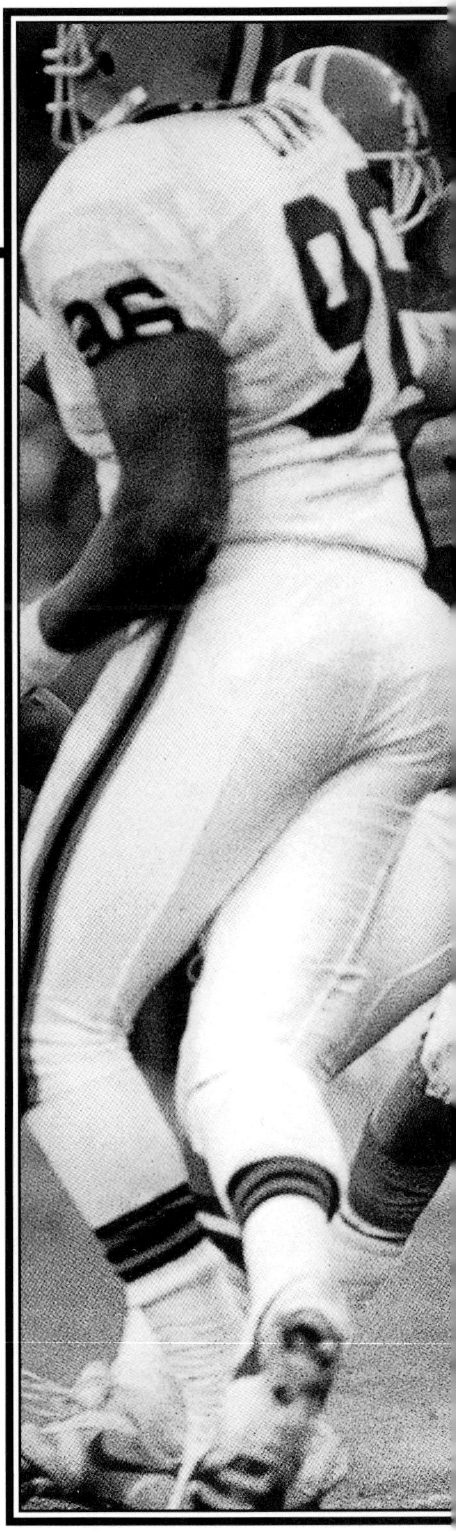

Broncos broadcaster Dave Logan gets a leg up on the Denver-Cleveland rivalry from Perry Smith in 1980. Logan was a wide receiver that season for the Browns, known as the "Kardiac Kids" for their heart-stopping finishes. They won nine games by seven points or less, but lost to Denver, 19-16.

"I've always said the quality about him that I think exceeds all others is his great competitive nature," Schottenheimer said. "That's the thing that has enabled him to be the great quarterback that he's been."

Kind words from a man who has been tormented by Elway more than any other NFL head coach. Were it not for Elway, Schottenheimer's fingers could very well be adorned with several Super Bowl rings.

Instead, Schottenheimer remains one of the most successful coaches in NFL history never to win a world title—and Elway deserves much of the credit (or blame) for that.

The Broncos and Cleveland Browns already had a competitive rivalry by the time they met in the 1986 AFC Championship game. By a scheduling quirk, the teams met 11 times from 1970 through '84 even though they were in separate divisions. The Broncos always seemed to have the edge, winning eight.

Examples: The final victory of Lou Saban's coaching tenure was a 27-0 shutout of the 1971 Browns who would win the AFC Central that season. And the 1980 Browns,

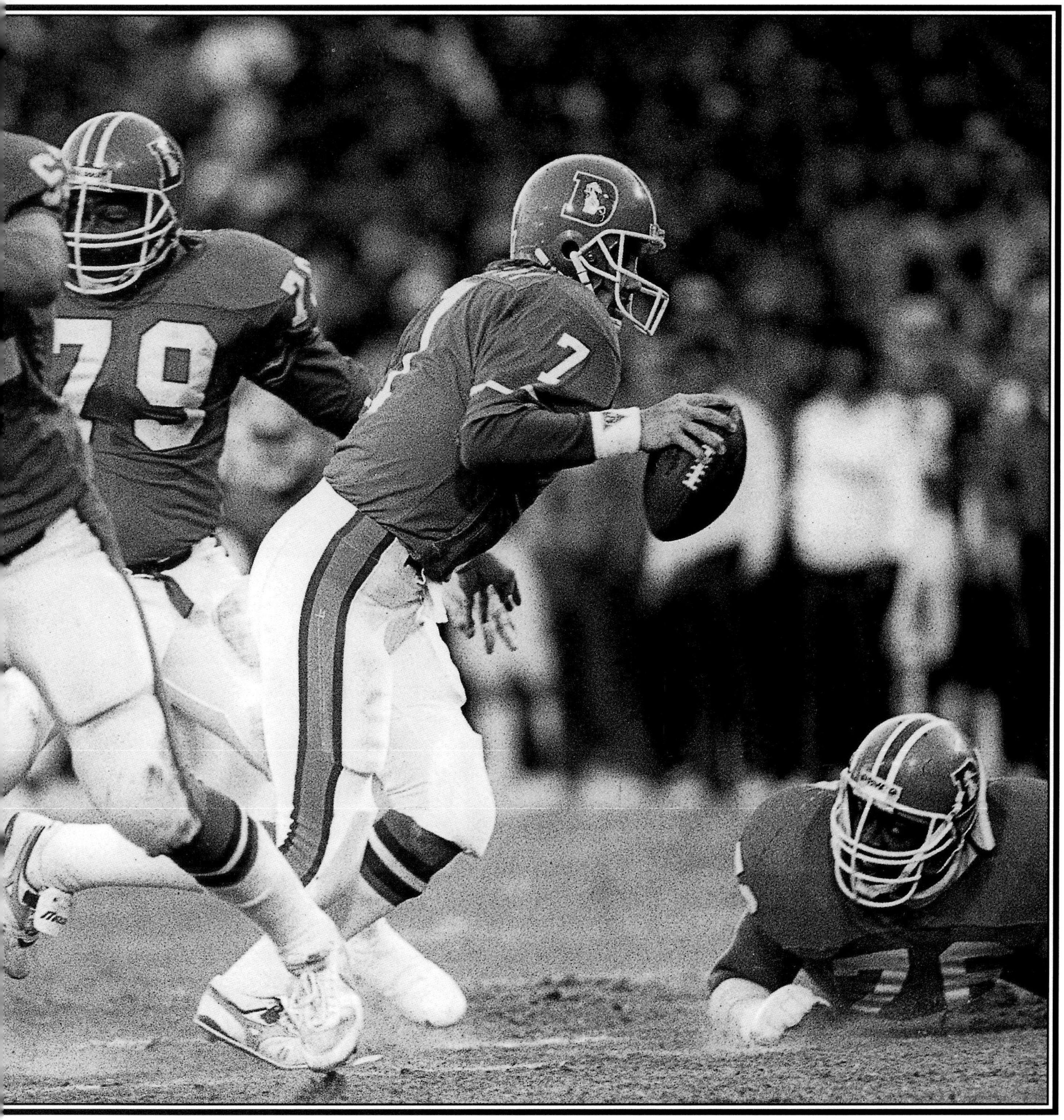

known as the "Kardiac Kids" for winning heart-stopping close games, were beaten by the Broncos, 19-16, in an otherwise forgetful season for Denver.

While those were painful losses for the Browns, nothing could compare to the misery Cleveland and its fans would experience when Elway and Schottenheimer met for the first time. Elway led "The Drive"—a 15-play, 98-yard series to tie the score late in the fourth quarter—en route to a 23-20 overtime victory to reach Super Bowl XXI. The Drive now lives forever in Broncos glory and Browns infamy.

John Elway escapes pursuit in the 1987 AFC Championship game at Mile High Stadium.

While coaching the Cleveland Browns, Marty Schottenheimer lost all three games against the Broncos.

Reflecting upon the 5-yard touchdown pass he threw to wide receiver Mark Jackson with 39 seconds left in regulation that tied the score at 20-20, Elway said, "I saw Mark get inside, and I've never thrown a ball that hard in my life. If Mark didn't catch it, nobody was going to catch it. And he did make a great catch. It was coming."

Schottenheimer was foiled again the following season in another crushing defeat just one game away from the Super Bowl. Denver cornerback Jeremiah Castille stripped the ball from Browns running back Earnest Byner near the goal-line and recovered the fumble in the final two minutes of a 38-33 Broncos victory at Mile High Stadium.

"I think it was more like we really earned it in the game in Cleveland," Elway said. "We were a little lucky the second year with the fumble. But the bottom line is, it's the playoffs and once you get there, it's do or die. The playoffs are a fun time, and you've got to make them a fun time."

Suffice to say, Marty Schottenheimer doesn't find either loss a laughing matter. He doesn't, however, allow himself to be tortured by either defeat.

"Frankly, those situations back in Cleveland, in terms of the NFL today, are another lifetime," Schottenheimer said a decade after both losses. "We turn around as coaches and players in a far shorter length of time than that."

The Browns made the playoffs again in 1988 (the Broncos didn't), but Schottenheimer resigned after a dispute with owner Art Modell over the coach's refusal to hire an offensive coordinator for 1989. (Schottenheimer had handled the duties himself in '88.) Schottenheimer was quickly hired by the Kansas City Chiefs. That added life to a rivalry that hadn't had much spark in recent years, as the Broncos had won 17 of their previous 25 games against the Chiefs.

Schottenheimer immediately made the Chiefs a contender, but Elway continued to be a thorn in his side, leading fourth-quarter comebacks in one game

Rulon Jones celebrates a sack of quarterback Bernie Kosar. The Broncos won 16 of 21 games versus Cleveland from 1970-94, including three AFC title games. The rivalry will be rekindled in 1999 when the Browns rejoin the NFL.

75
75 BIKE
U 42

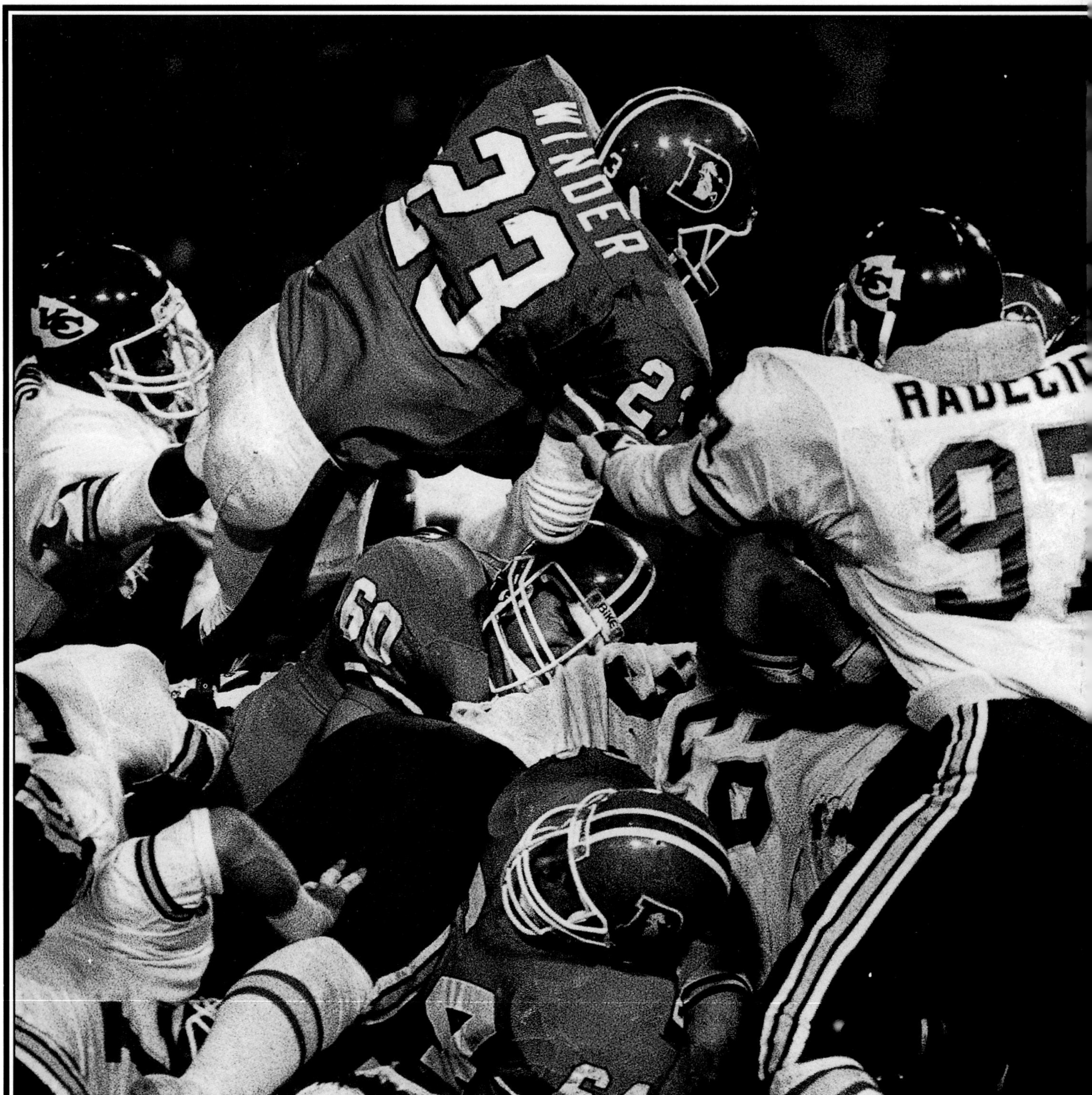

Sammy Winder goes over the top against Kansas City. Through 1997, the Chiefs were on top in the rivalry, 43-33.

each season from 1990 to '93. Overall, Schottenheimer has an 8-14 record against the Broncos. His record against the rest of the NFL in his 13 and a half years as an NFL head coach is 135-73-1.

Schottenheimer entered the 1998 season as the second-winningest active coach in the NFL behind the Atlanta Falcons' Dan Reeves, but Schottenheimer's first victory against Elway and the Broncos did not come until the 1990 season, 31-20, at Arrowhead Stadium.

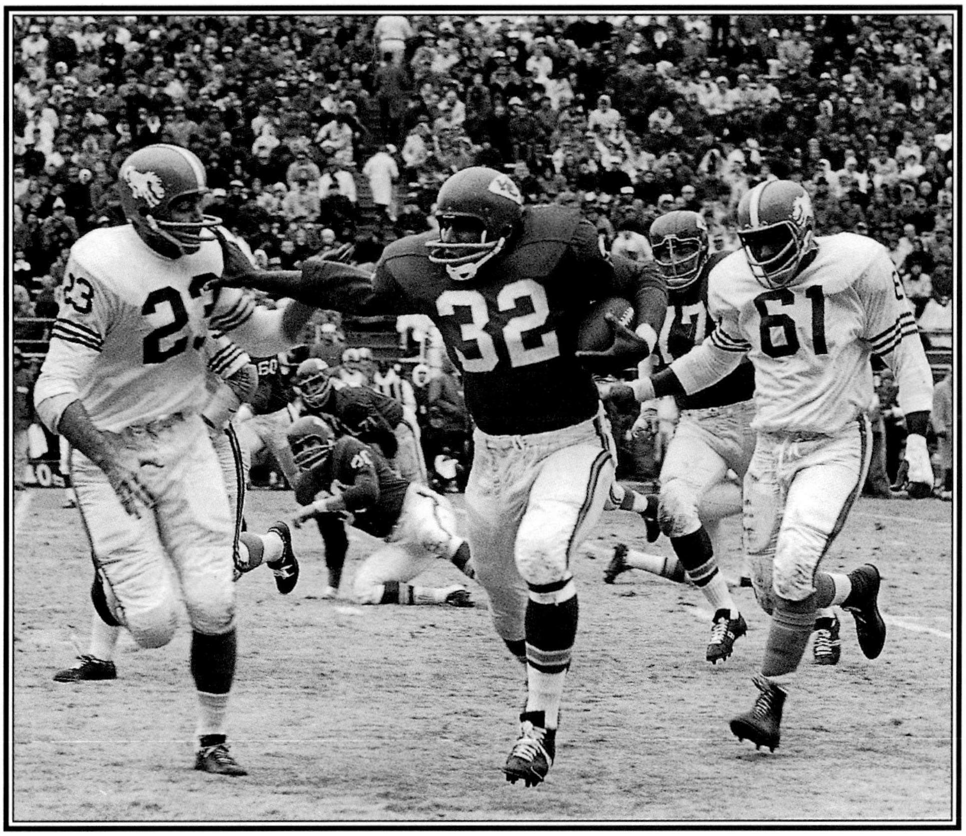

Goose Gonsoulin gets a hand in the face mask from Kansas City running back Curtis McClinton in 1963. The Chiefs handed Denver a 52-21 loss, its eighth straight to the Texans-Chiefs since the rivalry began in 1960.

"Marty couldn't beat John," said Reeves, who coached the Broncos against both the Schottenheimer-led Browns and Chiefs. "Even in the game they finally ended up beating us, Marty did something he shouldn't have done strictly because he was worried about Elway. He ended up going for it on fourth down because he didn't want John to get the ball back. . . . In the back of his mind, he's thinking, 'I can't give the ball back to John.'"

Schottenheimer also gained some revenge in a 31-28 victory on Oct. 17, 1994. An Elway touchdown pass had put the Broncos ahead with 1:29 remaining, but another future Hall-of-Fame quarterback, Joe Montana, led the Chiefs to the game-winning touchdown with eight seconds left. In a 1997 poll of media members conducted by the NFL, the game was voted the eighth best in league history.

The Broncos-Chiefs rivalry began in 1960 as a Broncos-Texans rivalry. The Dallas Texans—league founder Lamar Hunt's entry in the new American Football League—played three seasons in Dallas, but lost the popularity contest to the Cow-

Alfred Williams wraps up Chiefs quarterback Elvis Grbac in the 1997 season opener at Mile High Stadium, won by the Broncos, 19-3.

boys and were relocated to Kansas City for the 1963 season.

Through the first 15 seasons of the rivalry, the Broncos won just four of 30 games. But as Denver approached playoff status in the mid-1970s, the tide turned in its favor. From 1975-97, including the 1997 playoff game, the Broncos have won 29 of 46. Entering 1998, the series stood at Chiefs 43, Broncos 33.

The rivalry turned ugly during the 1996 season. Kansas City is notorious for having its wide receivers deliver chop blocks at the knees of defensive backs and linebackers, a legal but controversial tactic that sparked major controversy during a 34-7 Broncos victory. Cornerback Lionel Washington suffered a torn knee ligament after being chop-blocked by Kansas City's Dale Carter in the third quarter. Carter infuriated the Broncos even more by laughing after heading to the Chiefs' sideline.

Denver never expected the ferocity of the Chiefs' chop-blocking. In another incident, Carter—a Pro Bowl cornerback who also played wide receiver in 1996—went after the knees of Broncos cornerback Darrius Johnson 25 yards downfield on a pass play. Mike Shanahan was infuriated that Carter had never turned around to look for a pass. He even showed footage of the play to the Denver media in response to Schottenheimer defending his players with videotape during a news conference one day earlier.

Although Carter was never fined by the NFL, Schottenheimer apologized to Shanahan for the block on Johnson. "If you have to use that tactic, especially when the game is over, it tells you the type of character you have," Johnson said.

It turned just as ugly when Denver beat Kansas City, 19-3, in the 1997 season opener. Chiefs safety Jerome Woods was fined $7,500 after hitting Elway outside the pocket, even though a flag was not thrown on the play. Woods was then fined $10,000 the next time the two teams met for using his helmet to bust open the chin of Broncos wide receiver Ed McCaffrey.

The Chiefs won the second game, 24-22, at Arrowhead Stadium in one of the wildest finishes of the '97 season. The Broncos had a 22-21 lead after a Jason Elam field goal with under 90 seconds to play, but Denver's prevent defense could not stop the Chiefs from driving into field-goal range. That allowed Pete Stoyanovich to kick a 54-yard field goal to win the game with no time remaining. It was the longest game-winning field goal on the final play since New Orleans kicker Tom Dempsey booted an NFL-record 63-yarder in 1970.

> ***The coach denied the charge and the NFL was unable to prove any wrongdoing, but Broncos defensive end Neil Smith said he wouldn't be surprised if bounties were placed on his teammates.***

Before the game, a Chiefs player claimed that Schottenheimer said he would pay for any fines his players incurred for hard hits on the Broncos. The coach denied the charge and the NFL was unable to prove any wrongdoing, but Broncos defensive end Neil Smith said he wouldn't be surprised if bounties were placed on his teammates. "It could have been said easily," said Smith, who played for Schottenheimer from 1989-96. "He gets very caught up. He knew how important the game was."

The Chiefs went on to finish the regular season 13-3, win the AFC West title and claim home-field advantage throughout the playoffs. But once again, Schottenheimer couldn't top Elway and Co. The Broncos held on for a 14-10 victory in an AFC Divisional playoff game at Arrowhead Stadium. Schottenheimer and the entire Kansas City region was crushed, as most felt this was the Chiefs' best chance to reach the Super Bowl because of how well the team plays in the NFL's biggest stadium.

The Broncos' rivalries with their two other AFC West foes—San Diego and Seattle—aren't as intense as those with the Raiders and Chiefs. But that's not to say there isn't heated competition each time the Broncos play either squad. Plus, since

The 1997 Broncos felt the thrill of victory and the agony of defeat at Arrowhead Stadium. John Elway (left) avoids Reggie Tongue in the Broncos' 14-10 AFC Divisional playoff win on Jan. 4, 1998. Rod Smith (right) loses possession in a 24-22 Chiefs victory on Nov. 16, 1997.

A new rivalry was born when Dan Reeves took the reigns at Atlanta in 1997. The Broncos beat the Falcons and their former coach, 29-21, in the Georgia Dome on Sept. 28.

the inception of free-agency, each AFC West team tries to sign players from other divisional foes to improve themselves while weakening a rival.

As the Broncos entered the 1998 season, they had two additional rivals outside of their division. That's because two ex-Broncos coaches now have jobs elsewhere in the NFL.

Dan Reeves, who led Denver to three Super Bowl berths between 1981 and '92, is the head coach of the Atlanta Falcons. And Wade Phillips, Denver's head coach from 1993-94, entered his first season as head coach of Buffalo in 1998 following the retirement of Marv Levy.

The Broncos played against Reeves during the 1997 season, scoring a 29-21 victory over the Falcons. But because the Broncos had changed their jersey colors from the traditional orange worn in the Reeves era to ones that were largely white and navy blue, Reeves said the game didn't make him that nostalgic.

"When I saw the uniform, it wasn't like I got the feel that this was the team I had coached for 12 years," Reeves said. "And I'd been gone for so long. But it was weird, because they've got six or seven players from when I was there and a lot of the coaches and front office people are there. It was a weird feeling."

Shanahan and Reeves didn't end their relationship in Denver on the best of terms. Reeves fired Shanahan after the 1991 season for what he believed was insubordination. But it became evident during the first half of the game that Shanahan still has respect for Reeves.

The Falcons entered the game with a winless record and fell behind, 23-0, midway through the second quarter. The Broncos successfully went for two-point conversions on their second and third touchdowns because kicker Jason Elam had injured his groin, something that shocked and infuriated Reeves until he learned why Denver wasn't kicking extra points.

"I thought they were trying to run the score up," said Reeves, whose Atlanta team posted a 7-9 record in 1997 after opening the season 1-7. "They go for it on fourth-and-three, make it and score a touchdown. Then they line up and they're not kicking an extra point. They're going for two. I'm really mad, but then they kicked off and [Elam] didn't kick. They sent a message over saying their field goal kicker was injured. At least that sounds good. It didn't look like he got hurt, but it sounds good."

Denver Broncos

Records and Statistics

Otis Armstrong

All-Time Results

Regular Season

Season	W	L	T	Finish	Division
1960	4	9	1	fourth	AFL West
1961	3	11	0	third	AFL West
1962	7	7	0	second	AFL West
1963	2	11	1	fourth	AFL West
1964	2	11	1	fourth	AFL West
1965	4	10	0	fourth	AFL West
1966	4	10	0	fourth	AFL West
1967	3	11	0	fourth	AFL West
1968	5	9	0	fourth	AFL West
1969	5	8	1	fourth	AFL West
1970	5	8	1	fourth	AFC West
1971	4	9	1	fourth	AFC West
1972	5	9	0	third	AFC West
1973	7	5	2	second	AFC West
1974	7	6	1	second	AFC West
1975	6	8	0	second	AFC West
1976	9	5	0	second	AFC West
1977	12	2	0	first	AFC West
1978	10	6	0	first	AFC West
1979	10	6	0	second	AFC West
1980	8	8	0	fourth	AFC West
1981	10	6	0	first	AFC West
1982	2	7	0	fifth	AFC West
1983	9	7	0	third	AFC West
1984	13	3	0	first	AFC West
1985	11	5	0	second	AFC West
1986	11	5	0	first	AFC West
1987	10	4	1	first	AFC West
1988	8	8	0	second	AFC West
1989	11	5	0	first	AFC West
1990	5	11	0	fifth	AFC West
1991	12	4	0	first	AFC West
1992	8	8	0	third	AFC West
1993	9	7	0	third	AFC West
1994	7	9	0	fourth	AFC West
1995	8	8	0	fourth	AFC West
1996	13	3	0	first	AFC West
1997	12	4	0	second	AFC West

Post-Season

Season	Game	Score		Date	Location
1977	AFC Divisional	Denver 34	Pittsburgh 21	12-24-77	Mile High Stadium, Denver, Colo.
1977	AFC Championship	Denver 20	Oakland 17	1-01-78	Mile High Stadium, Denver, Colo.
1977	Super Bowl XII	Dallas 27	Denver 10	1-15-78	Louisiana Superdome, New Orleans, La.
1978	AFC Divisional	Pittsburgh 33	Denver 10	12-30-78	Three Rivers Stadium, Pittsburgh, Pa.
1979	AFC Wild Card	Houston 13	Denver 7	12-23-79	Astrodome, Houston, Texas
1983	AFC Wild Card	Seattle 31	Denver 7	12-24-83	Kingdome, Seattle, Wash.
1984	AFC Divisional	Pittsburgh 24	Denver 17	12-30-84	Mile High Stadium, Denver, Colo.
1986	AFC Divisional	Denver 22	New England 17	1-04-87	Mile High Stadium, Denver, Colo.
1986	AFC Championship	Denver 23	Cleveland 20	1-11-87	Cleveland Stadium, Cleveland, Ohio
1986	Super Bowl XXI	N.Y. Giants 39	Denver 20	1-25-87	Rose Bowl, Pasadena, Calif.
1987	AFC Divisional	Denver 34	Houston 10	1-10-88	Mile High Stadium, Denver, Colo.
1987	AFC Championship	Denver 38	Cleveland 33	1-17-88	Mile High Stadium, Denver, Colo.
1987	Super Bowl XXII	Washington 42	Denver 10	1-31-88	Jack Murphy Stadium, San Diego, Calif.
1989	AFC Divisional	Denver 24	Pittsburgh 23	1-07-90	Mile High Stadium, Denver, Colo.
1989	AFC Championship	Denver 37	Cleveland 21	1-14-90	Mile High Stadium, Denver, Colo.
1989	Super Bowl XXIV	San Francisco 55	Denver 10	1-28-90	Louisiana Superdome, New Orleans, La.
1991	AFC Divisional	Denver 26	Houston 24	1-04-92	Mile High Stadium, Denver, Colo.
1991	AFC Championship	Buffalo 10	Denver 7	1-12-92	Rich Stadium, Buffalo, N.Y.
1993	AFC Wild Card	L.A. Raiders 42	Denver 24	1-09-94	L.A. Coliseum, Los Angeles, Calif.
1996	AFC Divisional	Jacksonville 30	Denver 27	1-04-97	Mile High Stadium, Denver, Colo.
1997	AFC Wild Card	Denver 42	Jacksonville 17	12-27-97	Mile High Stadium, Denver, Colo.
1997	AFC Divisional	Denver 14	Kansas City 10	1-04-98	Arrowhead Stadium, Kansas City, Mo.
1997	AFC Championship	Denver 24	Pittsburgh 21	1-11-98	Three Rivers Stadium, Pittsburgh, Pa.
1997	Super Bowl XXXII	Denver 31	Green Bay 24	1-25-98	Qualcomm Stadium, San Diego, Calif.

Team Records

CHAMPIONSHIPS

Super Bowls
1 1997
American Football Conference
5 1977, 1986, 1987, 1989, 1997
AFC Western Division
8 1977, 1978, 1984, 1986, 1987, 1989, 1991, 1996
Playoff Berths
12 1977, 1978, 1979, 1983, 1984, 1986, 1987, 1989, 1991, 1993, 1996, 1997

STREAKS

Most Wins, One Season
13 1996
13 1984
Most Consecutive Wins
10 1984 (3rd through 12th)
Most Consecutive Games Without A Loss
10 1984
Most Consecutive Home Wins
16 9-1-96 through 12-21-97 (current)
Most Consecutive Road Wins
7 12-12-76 through 12-4-77
Most Consec. Preseason Wins
9 8-22-81 through 8-20-83
Most Consecutive Preseason Home Wins
6 8-22-81 through 8-20-83
Most Consecutive Preseason Road Wins
3 many (last 8-15-87 through 8-3-88)
Most Consec. Postseason Home Wins
6 (1-4-87 through 1-4-92)
Most Consecutive Losses
11 1963-1964
Most Consec. Games Without Win
14 1963-1964
Most Consecutive Home Losses
7 9-24-67 through 9-29-68
Most Consecutive Road Losses
12 11-9-63 through 9-11-65
Most Consec. Preseason Losses
6 twice (last 8-17-68 through 8-16-69)
Most Consecutive Preseason Home Losses
4 8-7-65 through 8-28-66
Most Consecutive Preseason Road Losses
7 8-25-90 through 8-16-93
Most Consecutive Home Games without a Win
7 9-24-67 through 9-29-68
7 11-1-70 through 10-10-71
Most Consecutive Road Games without a Win
17 12-2-62 through 9-11-65

SCORING

Most Points Scored
Season
472 1997
Game
50 vs. San Diego, 10-6-63

Largest Margin of Victory
43 vs. New York Jets, 9-19-76 (46-3)

Most Points, One Half
38 vs. Seattle, 11-26-89
38 vs. New England, 11-11-79
38 vs. Tampa Bay, 11-7-76

Most Points, One Quarter
26 at New York Jets, 12-3-67

Most Touchdowns Scored
Season
55 1997
Game
6 11 times (last vs. Balt., 10-20-96)

Most Field Goals Made
Season
31 1995
Game
5 at Kansas City, 11-16-97
5 vs. Buffalo, 9-3-95
5 vs. Seattle, 11-20-83

Best Percentage on PAT Attempts
1.000 12 times, most recent 1997 (50 of 50)

Fewest Points Scored
Season
148 1982 *(players strike; 9-game season)*
196 1966
Game (times Denver shutout: 9)
0 at L.A. Raiders (24-0) 11-22-92
0 at Philadelphia (30-0) 9-20-92
0 at New Orleans (42-0) 11-20-88
0 at Chicago (27-0) 9-9-84
0 at San Diego (23-0) 10-8-78
0 at San Diego (17-0) 12-15-74
0 at Kansas City (16-0) 12-6-70
0 at Oakland (51-0) 9-10-67
0 at San Diego (37-0) 10-29-61

TOTAL OFFENSE

Most Total Plays
Season
1,152 1985
Game
95 at Green Bay (Milw.), 9-20-87

Most Yards Total Offense
Season
6,040 1995
Game
548 vs. Baltimore, 10-20-96

Highest Average Gain Per Play
Season
5.70 1995
Game
8.56 vs. San Diego, 9-7-62

Fewest Yards Total Offense
Season
2,837 1982 *(players strike; 9-game season)*
3,168 1966
Game
5 at Oakland, 9-10-67

RUSHING

Most Rushes
Season
601 1978
Game
60 vs. San Diego, 11-30-75

Most Yards Rushing
Season
2,451 1978
Game
356 at Chicago, 12-12-76

Best Average Gain Per Rush
Season
4.57 1997
Game (min. 10 rushes)
7.66 vs. Cincinnati, 9-21-97

Fewest Yards Rushing
Season
1,018 1982 *(players strike; 9-game season)*
1,991 1961
Game
13 at Oakland, 10-22-72

PASSING

Most Pass Attempts

Season
626 1994
Game
59 at Green Bay, 10-10-93

Most Completions

Season
388 1994
Game
36 vs. San Diego 9-4-94

Best Completion Percentage

Season
.633 1993

Most Yards Passing (net yards)

Season
4,260 1995
Game
459 vs. Kansas City, 11-18-74

Fewest Yards Passing (net yards)

Season
1,682 1967
Game
–53 at Oakland, 9-10-67

Most Touchdown Passes Thrown

Season
27 1997
27 1995
27 1993
27 1981
Game
5 vs. Minnesota, 11-18-84
5 vs. Buffalo, 10-28-62

Most Interceptions Thrown

Season
45 1961
Game
8 at Houston, 12-2-62

Best Int. Avoidance Pct.

Season
.018 1993
Game
.000 many times

Highest Avg. Gain Per Attempt

Season
8.23 1981

Highest Avg. Gain Per Comp.

Season
14.94 1976

Fewest Times Denver Passer Sacked

Season
22 1971
Game
0 many times

Most Times Denver Passer Sacked

Season
63 1963
Game
11 vs. Oakland, 11-5-67
11 vs. Buffalo, 12-13-64

Most Yardage Lost on Sacks

Season
590 1963
Game
95 vs. Oakland, 11-5-67

FIRST DOWNS

Most First Downs

Season
346 1994
Game
34 vs. Oakland, 11-5-67

Most First Downs Rushing

Season
138 1997
Game
19 at Chicago, 12-12-76
19 vs. San Diego, 11-30-75

Most First Downs Passing

Season
205 1995
Game
25 vs. Kansas City, 11-24-74

Most First Downs by Penalty

Season
43 1994
Game
11 vs. Houston, 10-6-85

Fewest First Downs

Season
170 1982 *(players strike; 9-game season)*
171 1966
Game
0 at Houston, 9-3-66

PUNTING

Most Punts

Season
105 1967
Game
12 at Buffalo, 10-25-81
12 vs. Cincinnati, 10-6-68
12 at Oakland, 9-10-67

Fewest Punts

Season
45 1982 *(players strike; 9-game season)*
54 1995
Game
0 at Minnesota, 11-4-90
0 vs. Dallas, 10-8-61

Best Punting Average

Season
45.2 1966
Game (min. 4 punts)
57.2 vs. Los Angeles Raiders, 9-26-88

Lowest Punting Average

35.1 1976

Best Net Punting Average

Season (category started in 1976)
38.5 1990
Game (min. 4 punts)
52.8 vs. Los Angeles Raiders, 9-26-88

PUNT RETURNS

Most Punt Returns

Season
63 1970
Game
8 vs. San Diego, 12-27-87
8 vs. Baltimore, 10-22-78
8 vs. San Diego, 11-30-75
8 at Kansas City, 10-6-74
8 at Buffalo, 9-20-70

Most Punt Return Yards

Season
712 1977
Game
168 vs. Carolina, 11-9-97

Best Punt Return Average

14.5 1982

KICKOFF RETURNS

Most Kickoff Returns

Season
78 1963
Game
10 at Indianapolis, 10-31-88
10 vs. Boston, 10-4-64
10 at San Diego, 12-22-63

Best Kickoff Return Average

26.9 1966

Most Kickoff Return Yards

Season
1,801 1963
Game
295 vs. Boston, 10-4-64

FUMBLES

Most Fumbles

Season
40 1961
Game
6 vs. Philadelphia, 11-29-89
6 vs. Cleveland, 10-19-75
6 at Boston Patriots, 11-6-66
6 vs. L.A. Chargers, 10-16-60

Most Fumbles Lost
Season
23 1961
Game
5 vs. Cleveland, 10-19-75
5 vs. Chicago, 9-30-73

Fewest Fumbles
Season
15 1969
Game
0 many times

Fewest Fumbles Lost
Season
8 1985
8 1964
Game
0 many times

PENALTIES

Most Penalties
Season
132 1978
Game
15 vs. Tampa Bay, 11-7-76

Most Yards Penalized
Season
1,097 1978
Game
160 vs. Tampa Bay, 11-7-76

Fewest Penalties
Season
48 1967
Game
0 at Chicago, 12-18-93
0 vs. Kansas City, 12-17-67

Fewest Yards Penalized
Season
501 1960
Game
0 at Chicago, 12-18-93
0 vs Kansas City, 12-17-67
0 at Boston, 9-21-62

Giveaway-Takeaway Ratio (1970-97)
+21 1984

TOTAL DEFENSE

Fewest Points Allowed
Season
148 1977
Game (List of Denver Shutouts)
Denver 34, Carolina 0, 11-9-97
Denver 27, Oakland 0, 10-16-95
Denver 12, at Cleveland 0, 9-27-92
Denver 37, at Phoenix 0, 12-16-89
Denver 12, at San Diego 0, 10-2-88
Denver 24, San Diego 0, 12-27-87
Denver 34, Detroit 0, 11-1-87
Denver 21, Kansas City 0, 10-23-84
Denver 17, at Oakland 0, 10-4-81
Denver 7, San Diego 0, 10-7-79
Denver 10, Cincinnati 0, 9-2-79
Denver 7, St. Louis 0, 9-18-77
Denver, 17, at San Diego 0, 11-14-76
Denver 26, San Diego 0, 10-3-76
Denver 27, Cleveland 0, 10-24-71
Denver 13, San Diego 0, 11-2-69

Most Points Allowed
Season
473 1963
Game
59 vs. Cleveland, 9-7-63

Fewest Touchdowns Allowed
Season
18 1977
Game
0 many times

Fewest Field Goals Allowed
Season
8 1977
Game
0 many times

Fewest Total Plays Allowed
Season
616 1982 *(players strike; 9-game season)*
826 1971
Game
40 vs. San Diego, 10-6-63

Fewest Total Yards Allowed
Season
3,169 1982 *(players strike; 9-game season)*
3,705 1970
Game
60 at Cleveland, 10-24-71

Lowest Average Yield Per Play
Season
4.01 1977

Rulon Jones

Game
1.12 vs. Chicago, 12-5-71

RUSHING DEFENSE

Fewest Rushes Allowed
Season
293 1982 *(players strike; 9-game season)*
345 1996
Game
9 at New England, 11-17-96

Fewest Rushing Yards Allowed
Season
935 1982 *(players strike; 9-game season)*
1,331 1996
Game
0 at Kansas City, 12-19-65

Lowest Average Yield Per Rush
Season
3.19 1982
Game
0.00 at Kansas City, 12-19-65

PASSING DEFENSE

Fewest Pass Attempts Allowed
Season
307 1982 *(players strike; 9-game season)*
348 1975
Game
10 at Kansas City, 9-24-78 (OT)

Fewest Completions Allowed
Season
150 1971
Game
2 at Chicago, 12-12-76

Lowest Completion Pct. Allowed
Season
.421 1971
Game
.118 at Chicago, 12-12-76 (2 of 17)

Fewest Net Yards Allowed
Season
1,985 1971
Game
–7 vs. Chicago, 12-5-71

Fewest Touchdown Passes Allowed
Season
8 1976
Game
0 many times

Most Opponent Passes Intercepted
Season
32 1964
Game
7 at Detroit, 10-7-84
7 at Oakland, 10-16-77
7 vs. Seattle, 11-20-83
7 at Oakland, 10-4-81
7 vs. Buffalo, 12-13-64

Highest Pct. Of Opponent Passes Intercepted
Season
.073 1964

Most Yards on Int. Returns
Season
510 1984
Game
133 at Buffalo, 9-18-60

Most Sacks
Season
57 1984
Game
10 at Cincinnati, 10-19-69

Most Yardage on Sacks
Season
459 1986
Game
95 vs. New York Jets, 11-15-64

Lowest Average Yield Per Pass Attempt
5.00 1964

Lowest Avg. Yield Per Completion
10.60 1976

PUNTING

Lowest Opponent Punting Average
Season
37.3 1973
Game (min. 4 punts)
30.0 vs. Buffalo, 11-27-60

PUNT RETURNS

Lowest Opponent Punt Return Average
4.81 1978

KICKOFF RETURNS

Lowest Opponent Kickoff Return Average
17.14 1961

FUMBLES

Most Opponent Fumbles Recovered
Season
24 1984
Game
6 at Buffalo, 12-2-79

Most Total Opponent Fumbles
Season
46 1983
Game
7 vs. Green Bay, 10-15-84

Fewest Opponent Fumbles Recovered
Season
7 1982 *(players strike; 9-game season)*
9 1996
Game
0 many times

FIRST DOWNS

Fewest Opponent First Downs
Season
176 1982 *(players strike; 9-game season)*
199 1970
Game
3 vs. San Diego, 11-30-75

Fewest Opponent Rushing First Downs
Season
53 1982 *(players strike; 9-game season)*
67 1996
Game
0 vs. Carolina, 11-9-97
0 vs. Kansas City, 10-27-96
0 vs. Oakland, 10-16-95

Fewest Opponent Passing First Downs
Season
91 1971
Game
1 vs. San Diego, 11-30-75
1 at Chicago, 12-12-76

Fewest Opponent First Downs by Penalty
Season
12 1968
Game
0 many times

PENALTIES

Most Opponent Penalties
Season
138 1983
Game
20 vs. Oakland, 12-15-96

Most Opponent Penalty Yards
Season
1,118 1997
Game
188 vs. Houston, 10-6-85

Fewest Opponent Penalty Yards
Season
516 1963
Game
0 at Oakland, 12-19-71

Individual Records

SCORING

Most Touchdowns Scored

Career

54	Floyd Little, 1967-75

Season

15	Terrell Davis, 1997
15	Terrell Davis, 1996

Game

3	19 times (last by Davis, vs. Oakland, 11-24-97)

Most TDs Scored by Rookie

Season

12	Lionel Taylor, 1960 (12 pass)

Game

3	Davis, vs. Washington, 9-17-95 (2 r, 1 p)
3	Taylor, vs. Buffalo, 11-27-60 (3 pass)

Most Consec. Games Scoring, Non-Kicker

6	Taylor, 1960-61; Denson, '69; Little '72, V. Johnson, '87

Most Points Scored

Career

742	Jim Turner, 1971-79

Season

137	Gene Mingo, 1962

Game

21	Mingo, at L.A., 12-10-60

Most Points Scored by Rookie

Season

123	Gene Mingo, 1960

Game

21	Mingo, at L.A. Chargers, 12-10-60

Most PAT Attempts

Career

304	Jim Turner, 1971-79

Season

46	Jason Elam, 1997
46	Jason Elam, 1996

Game

6	Elam, vs. Baltimore, 10-20-96
6	David Treadwell, vs. Cin., 9-1-91
6	Rich Karlis, vs. Minn., 11-18-84
6	Fred Steinfort, vs. S.D., 9-27-81
6	Turner, (6 times: vs. N.E., 11-11-79, vs. Tampa Bay, 11-7-76, vs. Cleveland, 9-26-76, vs. N.Y. Jets, 9-19-76, at Houston, 10-14-73,vs. N.E., 12-17-72)

Most PATs Made

Career

283	Jim Turner, 1971-79

Season

46	Jason Elam, 1997
46	Jason Elam, 1996

Game

6	Elam, vs. Baltimore, 10-20-96
6	Treadwell, vs. Cincinnati, 9-1-91
6	Karlis, vs. Minnesota, 11-18-84
6	Steinfort, vs. San Diego., 9-27-81
6	Turner, New England, 11-11-79
6	Turner, vs. Tampa Bay, 11-7-76
6	Turner, at Houston, 10-14-73
6	Turner, vs. N.E., 12-17-72

Most PATs Made by Rookie

Season

41	Jason Elam, 1993 (42 attempts)

Best PAT Percentage

Career (min. 20 attempts)

*.995	Jason Elam, 1993-97 * *NFL Record*

Season (min. 14 attempts)

1.000	12 times, last by Jason Elam, 1997 (46 of 46)

Most Consecutive PATs Made

177	Jason Elam (9th in '93-current)

Most Field Goals Attempted

Career

233	Jim Turner, 1971-79

Season

39	Gene Mingo, 1962

Game

7	Karlis, at San Diego, 10-2-88
7	Mingo, vs. San Diego, 10-6-63

Most Field Goals Made

Career

151	Jim Turner, 1971-79

Season

31	Jason Elam, 1995

Game

5	Elam, at Kansas City, 11-16-97
5	Elam, vs. Buffalo, 9-3-95
5	Karlis, vs. Seattle, 11-20-83
5	Mingo, vs. San Diego, 10-6-63

Most Field Goals Made by Rookie

Season

27	David Treadwell, 1989

Game

4	Elam, at N.Y. Jets, 9-5-93
4	Treadwell, at Buffalo, 9-18-89

Best Field Goal Percentage

Career (min. 20 attempts)

.780	David Treadwell, 1989-92

Season (min. 10 attempts)

.846	Rich Karlis, 1982 (11 of 13)

Longest Field Goal

57	Fred Steinfort, vs. Wash., 10-13-80

Most Consecutive Games with a Field Goal

15	Rich Karlis (13th in '84–11th in '85)

Most Consecutive Field Goals Made

13	Rich Karlis (last 4 in '84 - first 9 in '85)

Most Consecutive Games Scoring

79	Jason Elam, 1993-97 (current)

TOTAL OFFENSE

Most Total Plays

Career

8,251	John Elway, 1983-97

Season

656	John Elway, 1985

Game

64	Elway, at Green Bay, 10-10-93

Most Yards Total Offense (Combined Rushing and Passing)

Career

51,982	John Elway, 1983-97 (3,313-48,669)

Season

4,183	John Elway, 1993

Game

447	Frank Tripucka, at Buf., 9-15-62

Most Total Yds. from Scrimmage (Rushing and Receiving)

Career

8,741	Floyd Little, 1967-75 (6,323-2,418)

Season

2,037	Terrell Davis, 1997 (1,750-287)

Game

236	Davis, at Buffalo, 10-26-97 (207-29)

Most Total Yds. from Scrim. by Rookie (Rushing and Receiving)

Season

1,484	Terrell Davis, 1995 (1,117-367)

Game
199 Lionel Taylor, vs. Buf., 11-27-60 (0-199)

Most Combined Yardage (Rushing-Receiving-Returns)

Career
12,157 Floyd Little, 1967-75 (6,323-2,418-3-416)
Season
2,080 Glyn Milburn, 1995 (266-191-1,623)
Game
*404 Milburn, vs. Seattle, 12-10-95 (131-45-228) **NFL Record*

Most Comb. Yardage by Rookie (Rushing-Receiving-Returns)

Season
1,929 Rick Upchurch, 1975 (97-436-1,396)
Game
284 Upchurch, vs. K.C., 9-21-75 (13-153-118)

Best Average Gain Per Play

Career (min. 200 plays)
7.30 Craig Morton, 1977-82
7.30 Charley Johnson, 1972-75
Season (min. 125 plays)
8.37 Craig Morton, 1981
Game (min. 10 plays)
15.70 Morton, vs. San Diego, 9-27-81

RUSHING

Most Attempts

Career
1,641 Floyd Little, 1967-75
Season
369 Terrell Davis, 1997
Game
42 Davis, at Buffalo (OT), 10-26-97

Most Attempts by Rookie

Season
294 Bobby Humphrey, 1989
Game
31 Humphrey, at L.A. Raiders, 12-3-89
31 Humphrey, at Washington, 11-20-89

Most Rushing Yards

Career
6,323 Floyd Little, 1967-75
Season
1,750 Terrell Davis, 1997
Game
215 Davis, vs. Cincinnati, 9-21-97

Most Rushing Yards by Rookie

Season
1,151 Bobby Humphrey, 1989
Game
176 Davis, vs. San Diego, 11-19-95

Best Rushing Average

Career (min. 100 carries)
4.60 Terrell Davis, 1995-97
Season (min. 100 carries)
5.35 Otis Armstrong, 1974
Game (min. 8 rushes)
11.00 Dave Rolle, vs. Oak., 10-2-60

Best Rushing Average by Rookie

Season (min. 100 carries)
4.71 Terrell Davis, 1995
Game (min. 8 rushes)
10.38 Billy Joe, at Boston, 10-18-63

Most Rushing Touchdowns

Career
43 Floyd Little, 1967-75
Season
15 Terrell Davis, 1997
Game
3 Terrell Davis, vs. Oakland, 11-24-97
3 Gaston Green, vs. S.D., 9-22-91
3 Otis Armstrong, vs. Hou., 12-8-74
3 Jon Keyworth, vs. Kansas City, 11-18-74
3 Little, vs. Cincinnati, 9-16-73

Most Rushing TDs by Rookie

Season
7 Terrell Davis, 1995
7 Bobby Humphrey, 1989
Game
3 Keyworth, vs. K.C., 11-18-74

Most Consecutive Games Scoring by Rush

5 Davis, 1997
5 Sammy Winder, 1985

Longest Scoring Run

82 Gene Mingo, vs. Oakland, 10-5-62

Longest Scoring Run by Rookie

68 Billy Joe, at Boston, 10-18-63

Longest Non-Scoring Run

68 Henry Bell, vs. Los Angeles, 10-16-60

Long. Non-Scoring Run by Rookie

68 Henry Bell, vs. L.A., 10-16-60

PASSING

Most Passing Yards

Career
48,669 John Elway, 1983-97
Season
4,030 John Elway, 1993
Game
447 Frank Tripucka, at Buf., 9-15-62

Most Passing Yards by Rookie

Season
1,689 Mickey Slaughter, 1963
Game
345 Elway, vs. Baltimore, 12-11-83 (23-34)

Most Attempts

Career
6,894 John Elway, 1983-97
Season
605 John Elway, 1985
Game
59 Elway, at Green Bay, 10-10-93

Most Attempts by Rookie

Season
259 John Elway, 1983
Game
44 Elway, vs. Baltimore, 12-11-83

Most Completions

Career
3,913 John Elway, 1983-97
Season
348 John Elway, 1993
Game
36 Elway vs. San Diego, 9-4-94

Most Completions by Rookie

Season
123 John Elway, 1983
Game
23 Elway, vs. Baltimore, 12-11-83

Best Completion Percentage

Career (min. 100 passes)
.626 Hugh Millen, 1994-95
Season (min. 50 passes)
.632 John Elway, 1983
.632 Norris Weese, 1978
Game (min. 10 passes)
.944 Morton, vs San Diego, 9-27-81

Most Touchdown Passes

Career
278 John Elway, 1983-97
Season
27 John Elway, 1997
Game
5 Elway, vs. Minnesota, 11-18-84
5 Tripucka, vs Buffalo, 10-28-62

Most Touchdown Passes Thrown by Rookie

Season
14 Marlin Briscoe, 1968
Game
4 Elway, vs. Baltimore, 12-11-83
4 Briscoe, vs. Buffalo, 11-24-68

Most Interceptions Thrown

Career
216 John Elway, 1983-97
Season
34 Frank Tripucka, 1960
Game
6 Don Horn, at Green Bay, 9-26-71
6 George Herring, at Hou., 11-26-61

Most Interceptions Thrown by a Rookie

Season

14 John Elway, 1983
14 Mickey Slaughter, 1963

Game

5 Slaughter, vs. Houston, 10-13-63

Best Interception Avoidance

Career (min. 100 passes)

.018 Hugh Millen, 1994-95

Season (min. 50 passes)

.013 Gary Kubiak, 1984

Best Average Gain Per Attempt

Career (min. 100 attempts)

7.52 Norris Weese, 1976-79

Season (min. 50 attempts)

8.65 Jacky Lee, 1965

Game (min. 12 attempts)

17.10 Morton vs. San Diego, 9-27-81

Best Avg. Gain Per Completion

Career (min. 100 passes)

17.09 Marlin Briscoe, 1968

Season (min. 50 passes)

17.93 John Hufnagel, 1975

Game (min. 12 passes)

33.64 Lee at Oakland, 12-5-65

Highest Passer Rating

Career (min. 500 passes)

79.2 John Elway, 1983-97

Season (min. 200 passes)

92.8 John Elway, 1993

Highest Passer Rating by Rookie

Season (min. 200 passes)

67.2 Mickey Slaughter, 1963

Most Consec. Games With a TD

15 Elway, 1995-96 (last 12 games of 1995, first three of 1996)

Most Consecutive Completions

20 Millen, last 7 at L.A. Raiders, 12-11-94 and first 13 at S.F., 12-17-94

Longest Scoring Pass

97 George Shaw–Jerry Tarr, at Boston, 9-21-63

Longest Non-Scoring Pass

86 John Elway–Vance Johnson, vs. L.A. Raiders, 9-26-88

Longest Completion by Rookie

81 Arthur Marshall–Cedric Tillman vs. Dallas, 12-6-92 (TD)

RECEIVING

Most Receptions

Career

543 Lionel Taylor, 1960-65

Season

100 Lionel Taylor, 1961

Game

13 Shannon Sharpe, vs. S.D., 10-6-96
13 Bob Anderson, vs. Chi., 9-30-73
13 Taylor, vs. Oakland, 11-29-64

Most Receptions by Rookie

Season

92 Lionel Taylor, 1960

Game

11 Taylor, vs. New York, 12-4-60

Most Receiving Yards

Career

6,872 Lionel Taylor, 1960-66

Season

1,244 Steve Watson, 1981

Game

199 Taylor, vs. Buffalo, 11-27-60

Most Receiving Yards by Rookie

Season

1,235 Lionel Taylor, 1960

Game

199 Taylor, vs. Buffalo, 11-27-60

Most Touchdown Receptions

Career

44 Lionel Taylor, 1960-66
44 Haven Moses, 1972-81

Season

14 Anthony Miller, 1995

Game

3 Ed McCaffrey, vs. Balt., 10-20-96
3 Sharpe, vs. San Diego, 10-6-96
3 Miller, at Dallas, 9-10-95
3 Sharpe, vs. Kansas City, 12-12-93
3 Watson, vs. Baltimore, 9-20-81
3 Moses, at Houston, 10-14-73
3 Bob Scarpitto, at Buf., 12-18-66
3 Taylor, vs. Buffalo, 11-27-60

Most TD Receptions by Rookie

Season

12 Lionel Taylor, 1960

Game

3 Taylor, vs. Buffalo, 11-27-60

Best Average Gain Per Reception

Career (min. 50 receptions)

20.54 Bill Van Heusen, 1968-76

Season (min. 20 receptions)

22.05 Bob Scarpitto, 1963

Game (min. 4 receptions)

41.3 Little vs. Buffalo, 11-24-68

Best Avg. Gain Per Rec. by Rookie

Season (min. 20 receptions)

20.32 Ricky Nattiel, 1987

Game (min. 4 receptions)

24.00 Vance Johnson, at Atl., 9-22-85

Most Consecutive Games with TD

6 Anthony Miller, 1995
6 Lionel Taylor, 1960-61 (last 4 games of 1960, first 2 of '61)
6 Vance Johnson, 1987
6 Al Denson, 1969

Most Consec. Games. with a Reception

62 Lionel Taylor, 1960-64

Longest Reception by Rookie

90 Rick Upchurch, (from Charley Johnson), vs. Kansas City, 9-21-75

PUNTING

Most Punts

Career

574 Bill Van Heusen, 1968-76

Season

105 Bob Scarpitto, 1967

Game

12 Luke Prestridge, at Buf., 10-25-81
12 Van Heusen, vs. Cincinnati, 10-6-68
12 Scarpitto, at Oakland, 9-19-67

Best Average Per Punt

Career (min. 50 punts)

45.2 Jim Fraser, 1962-64

Season (min. 50 punts)

46.09 Jim Fraser, 1963

Game (min. 4 punts)

57.20 Mike Horan, vs. L.A. Raiders, 9-26-88

Longest Punt

83 Chris Norman, vs. K.C., 9-23-84

PUNT RETURNS

Most Punt Returns

Career

248 Rick Upchurch, 1975-83

Season

51 Rick Upchurch, 1977

Game

8 Upchurch, vs. Balt., 10-22-78

Most Yards on Punt Returns

Career

3,008 Rick Upchurch, 1975-83

Season

653 Rick Upchurch, 1977

Game

168 Darrien Gordon, vs. Carolina, 11-9-97

Best Average Per Punt Return

Career (min. 15 punts)

13.58 Darrien Gordon, 1997

Season (min. 10 punts)

16.88 Floyd Little, 1967

Longest Non-Scoring Punt Ret.

60 Billy Thompson, at Baltimore, 11-10-74

KICKOFF RETURNS

Most Kickoff Returns

Career
104 Ken Bell, 1986-89
104 Floyd Little, 1967-75

Season
47 Glyn Milburn, 1995
47 Odell Barry, 1964

Game
7 Milburn, at Houston, 1-26-95
7 Milburn, at L.A. Raid., 12-11-94
7 Bell, at Pittsburgh, 10-23-88
7 Barry, at Kansas City, 11-1-64

Most Yards on Kickoff Returns

Career
2,523 Floyd Little, 1967-75

Season
1,269 Glyn Milburn, 1995

Game
201 Randy Montgomery, at San Diego, 9-24-72

Best Average Per Kickoff Return

Career (min. 40 returns)
26.28 Abner Haynes, 1965-66

Season (min. 14 returns)
28.50 Billy Thompson, 1969

Longest Scoring Kickoff Return

100 Goldie Sellers, vs. Hous., 9-3-66
100 Nemiah Wilson, at K.C., 10-8-66

Longest Non-Scoring Kickoff Ret.

89 Little, vs. Oakland, 11-10-68

DEFENSE

Most Interceptions

Career
44 Steve Foley, 1976-86

Season
11 Goose Gonsoulin, 1960

Game
4 Willie Brown, vs. N.Y., 11-15-64
4 Gonsoulin, at Buffalo, 9-18-60

Most Interceptions by Rookie

Season
11 Goose Gonsoulin, 1960

Game
4 Gonsoulin, at Buffalo, 9-18-60

Most Yards on Interception Returns

Career
784 Billy Thompson, 1969-81

Season
179 Mike Harden, 1986

Game
93 Randy Gradishar, at Clev., 10-5-80

Best Interception Return Average

Career (min. 10 returns)
23.73 Wymon Henderson, 1989-92

Most Consecutive Games with an Interception

4 Tyrone Braxton (gms. 12-15 in '96)

Longest Scoring Interception Return

93 Gradishar, at Cleveland, 10-5-80

Longest Non-Scoring Int. Return

70 Leroy Moore, at Boston, 11-20-64

Longest Scoring Fumble Return

88 Bob Swenson, at S.F., 11-18-79

Most Sacks

Career
97.5 Simon Fletcher, 1985-95

Season
16.0 Simon Fletcher, 1992

Game
4 Rich Jackson, at Cin., 10-19-69
4 Dave Costa, at Buffalo, 9-7-70
4 Barney Chavous, at Sea., 12-21-80
4 Karl Mecklenburg, vs. N.O., 9-15-85
4 Karl Mecklenburg, at Pittsburgh, 12-1-85
4 Simon Fletcher, at San Diego, 11-11-90

Most Sacks by Rookie

Season
11.5 Rulon Jones, 1980

Game
3 Jones, vs. Oakland, 12-14-80

Most Multi-Sack Games

Career
20 Simon Fletcher

Most Consecutive Games with a Sack

10 Fletcher (games 10-16 '92; 1-3 '93)
10 Fletcher (games 9-16, 1991)

Rick Upchurch

All-Time Roster

A

81	Bob Adams	TE	Pacific	1975
73	Scott Adams	T	Georgia	1997
60	Kenneth M. Adamson	G	Notre Dame	1960-62
57	Allen Adridge	LB	Houston	1994-97
68	Steve Alexakos	G	San Jose St.	1970
58	Elijah Alexander	LB	Kansas St.	1993-95
40	Jeff Alexander	RB	Southern	1989, 1992
80	Ray Alexander	WR	Florida A&M	1984
25	Ted Alflen	RB	Springfield Col.	1969
22	Elihu (Buddy) Allen	HB	Utah St.	1961
24	Donald R. Allen	FB	Texas	1960
57	Ty Allert	LB	Texas	1990
73	Henry Allison	T	San Diego St.	1977
62	Vaughn S. (Buddy) Alliston	LB	Mississippi	1960
77	Lyle Alzado	DE	Yankton Col.	1971-78
22	David R. Ames	HB	Richmond	1961
11	Robert Anderson	HB	Colorado	1970-73
83	Willie "Flipper" Anderson	WR	UCLA	1997
86	Mitch Andrews	TE	Louisiana St.	1987
84	Lou Andrus	LB	Brigham Young	1967
24	Otis Armstrong	RB	Purdue	1973-80
65	LeFrancis Arnold	G-C	Oregon	1974
73	Mike Askea	T	Stanford	1973
28	Billy Atkins	DB	Auburn	1964
74	Frank Atkinson	DE	Stanford	1964
47	George Atkinson	S	Morris Brown	1979
27	Steve Atwater	S	Arkansas	1989-97
67	John Ayers	G	West Texas St.	1987

B

56,65	Jay Bachman	C	Cincinnati	1968-71
75	Bill Bain	T	Southern Calif.	1976, 1978
74	Jerry Baker	T	Tulane	1983
85	Mike Barber	TE	Louisiana Tech	1985
62	Ernie Barnes	G	North Car. Col.	1963-64
73	Walter Barnes	DE	Nebraska	1969-71
86	Dean Barnett	TE	Nevada-L.V.	1983
42	Odell Barry	HB	Findlay	1964-65
52	James Barton	C	Marshall	1961-62
54	Rick Baska	LB	UCLA	1976-77
46	Norman Bass	DB	Pacific	1964
64	Scott Beavers	G	Georgia Tech	1990
85	Tom Beer	TE	Houston	1967-69
56	Dave Behrman	C	Michigan St.	1967
73	Kevin Belcher	T	Wisconsin	1987
20	Henry Bell	HB	No college.	1960
35	Ken Bell	RB-WR	Boston Col.	1986-89
3	Scott Bentley	PK	Florida St.	1997
43	Frank Bernardi	DB	Colorado	1960
74	Lee Bernet	T	Wisconsin	1965-66
33	Rod Bernstine	RB	Texas A&M	1993-95
54	Keith Bishop	C-G	Baylor	1980, 1982-89
24	Tony Boddie	RB	Montana St.	1986-87
82,83	Melvin Bonner	WR	Baylor	1993-94
89	Gordon Bowdell	WR	Michigan St.	1971
65	Walt Bowyer	DE	Arizona St.	1983-84, '87-88
77	Greg Boyd	DE	San Diego St.	1980-82
52	Greg Bracelin	LB	California	1980
23	Ronnie Bradford	DB	Colorado	1993-95
24	Phil Brady	S	Brigham Young	1969
56	John Bramlett	LB	Memphis St.	1965-66
32	Melvin Bratton	RB	Miami, Fla.	1989-90
34	Tyrone Braxton	DB	N. Dakota St.	1987-93, '95-97
19	Don Breaux	QB	McNeese St.	1963
76	Bob Breitenstein	T	Tulsa	1965-67
26	Chris Brewer	RB	Arizona	1984
15	Marlin Briscoe	QB	Omaha	1968
6	Bubby Brister	QB	Northeast La.	1997
36	John W. (Red) Brodnax	FB	Louisiana St.	1960
56	Michael Brooks	LB	Louisiana St.	1987-92
87	Boyd Brown	TE	Alcorn St.	1974-76
89	Clay Brown	TE	Brigham Young	1983
34,46	Hardy Brown	LB	Tulsa	1960
70	Jamie Brown	T	Florida A&M	1995-97
55	Ken Brown	LB	Virginia Tech	1995
55	Ken Brown	C	New Mexico	1979
82	Laron Brown	WR	Texas	1987
24	Willie Brown	DB	Grambling	1963-66
72	Sam Brunelli	G	Colorado St.	1966-71
82	Larry Brunson	WR	Colorado	1980
64	Bill Bryan	C	Duke	1977-88
95	Steve Bryan	DE-LB	Oklahoma	1987-88
80	Tom Buckman	TE	Texas A&M	1969
33	Fred Bukaty	FB	Kansas	1961
60	Joe Burch	C	Texas Southern	1994
21	Bobby Burnett	RB	Arkansas	1969
56	Keith Burns	LB	Oklahoma St.	1994-97
41	George Burrell	S	Pennsylvania	1969
58	Steve Busick	LB	Southern Calif.	1981-85
21,22	Gerry Bussell	DB	Georgia Tech	1965
51	Bill Butler	LB	San Fernando Valley	1970
28	Butler By'not'e	CB	Ohio St.	1994
24	George (Butch) Byrd	DB	Boston University	1971

C

59	Glenn Cadrez	LB	Houston	1995-97
28	Scott Caldwell	RB	Texas-Arlington	1987
79	Carter Campbell	DE	Weber St.	1971
86	Jeff Campbell	WR	Colorado	1994
67	Mark Campbell	DT	Florida	1996
35	Larry Canada	FB	Wisconsin	1978-79, 1981
40	Albert R. Carmichael	HB	Southern Calif.	1960-61
40	Paul Carmichael	HB	El Camino J.C.	1965
86	Don Carothers	E	Bradley	1960
89	Kenneth L. Carpenter	E	Oregon St.	1960
92	Alphonso Carreker	DE	Florida St.	1989, 1991
29	Darren Carrington	CB	Northern Ariz.	1989

Billy Thompson

89	Dwayne Carswell	TE	Liberty	1994-97
68	Rubin Carter	DT	Miami, Fla.	1975-86
51	Tim Casey	LB	Oregon	1969
66	John E. Cash	E	Allen	1961-62
45	Tom Cassese	DB	C.W. Post	1967
28	Jeremiah Castille	CB	Alabama	1987-88
40	Grady Cavness	CB	Texas-El Paso	1969
86	Byron Chamberlain	TE	Wayne St.	1995-97
79	Barney Chavous	DE	South Car. St.	1973-85
15	Max Choboian	QB	San Fernando St.	1966
78	Tom Cichowski	T	Maryland	1968-69
54	Ralph Cindrich	LB	Pittsburgh	1974
78	Brian Clark	T	Clemson	1982
43	Derrick Clark	RB	Evangel Col.	1994
20,27	Kevin Clark	DB	San Jose St.	1987-88, '90-91
73	Kelvin Clark	T	Nebraska	1979-81
15	Mike Clendenen	K	Houston	1987
26	Don Coffey	E	Memphis St.	1963
76	Steve Coleman	DE	Delaware St.	1974
69	Tony Colorito	NT	Southern Calif.	1986
59	Darren Comeaux	LB	Arizona St.	1982-86
80	Ed Cooke	DE	Maryland	1964-65
63	Mark Cooper	G-T	Miami, Fla.	1983-87
25	Kip Corrington	S	Texas A&M	1989-90
63	Dave Costa	DT	Utah	1967-71
66	Bill Cottrell	G	Delaware Valley	1972
66,77	Larry Cox	DT	Abilene Christian	1966-68
41	Eric Crabtree	FL	Pittsburgh	1966-68
68	Gary Crane	LB	Arkansas St.	1969
29	Aaron Craver	RB	Fresno St.	1995-96
33	Willis Crenshaw	FB	Kansas St.	1970
53,78	Ken Criter	LB	Wisconsin	1969-74
39	Ray Crockett	CB	Baylor	1994-97
51	Mike Croel	LB	Nebraska	1991-94
54	Ed Cummings	LB	Stanford	1965
50	Carl Cunningham	LB	Houston	1967-70
74	Mike Current	T	Ohio St.	1967-75
58	Scott Curtis	LB	New Hampshire	1989-90

D

5	Brad Daluiso	K	UCLA	1992
75	Eldon V. Danenhauer	T	Pittsburg (Kan.)	1960-65
76	William A. Danenhauer	E	Emporia Col.	1960
62	Jeff Davidson	G-T	Ohio St.	1990-92
32	Dick Davis	RB	Nebraska	1970
62	Jack T. Davis	T	Arizona	1960
73	Marvin Davis	DT	Wichita St.	1966
30	Terrell Davis	RB	Georgia	1995-97
33	Joe Dawkins	RB	Wisconsin	1971-73
84	Albert E. Day	T	Eastern Michigan	1960
17	Steve DeBerg	QB	San Jose St.	1981-83
39	Robert Delpino	RB	Missouri	1993
55	Rick Dennison	LB	Colorado St.	1982-90
88	Al Denson	FL	Florida A&M	1964-70
65	John Denvir	G	Colorado	1962
63	David Diaz-Infante	G-C	San Jose St.	1996-97
71	Wallace Dickey	T	SW Texas St.	1968-69
35	Richard L. (Bo) Dickinson	FB	Southern Miss.	1962-63
10	Doug (Bucky) Dilts	P	Georgia	1977-78
29	Charles Dimry	CB	Nevada-L.V.	1991-93
30	Hewritt Dixon	FB-TE	Florida A&M	1963-65
31	Zachary Dixon	RB	Temple	1979
2	Joe DiVito	QB	Boston Col.	1968
33	Dedrick Dodge	S	Florida St.	1997
59	Kirk Dodge	LB	Nevada-L.V.	1987
82	Jack Dolbin	WR	Wake Forest	1975-79
76	Tom Domres	DT	Wisconsin	1971-72
54	Mitch Donahue	LB	Wyoming	1993-94
33	Tony Dorsett	RB	Pittsburgh	1988-89
45	Gary Downs	RB	North Car. St.	1995
14	Richard A. (Skip) Doyle	HB	Ohio St.	1960
99	Shane Dronett	DE	Texas	1993-95
76	Tom Drougas	T	Oregon	1974
97	Darren Drozdov	DT	Maryland	1993-94
32	Joe Dudek	RB	Plymouth St.	1987
4	Rick Duncan	K	Eastern Montana	1967
21	Myron Dupree	CB	N. Carolina Central	1983
55	Pete Duranko	DE	Notre Dame	1967-70, '72-74

E

24	Booker Edgerson	CB	Western Illinois	1970
85	Ron Egloff	TE	Wisconsin	1977-83
1	Jason Elam	K	Hawaii	1993-97
62	Jim Elfrid	LB	Colorado St.	1961
7	John Elway	QB	Stanford	1983-97
89	John Embree	WR	Compton J.C.	1969-70
14	George Hunter Enis	QB	Texas Christian	1962
88	Pat Epperson	E	Adams St.	1960
53	Tom Erlandson	LB	Washington St.	1962-65
16	Mike Ernst	QB	Cal. St. Fullerton	1972
46	Terry Erwin	HB	Boston Col.	1968
40	Jay Dale Evans	HB	Kansas City	1961
88	Jerry Evans	TE	Toledo	1993-95
56	Larry Evans	LB	Mississippi Col.	1976-82
35	Blake Ezor	RB	Michigan St.	1990

F

86	Stan Fanning	DE	Idaho	1964
44	Miller Farr	DB	Wichita St.	1965
63	Sean Farrell	G	Penn St.	1990-91
37	Steve Fitzhugh	DB	Miami (Ohio)	1987
20	Billy Ray Fletcher	E	Memphis St.	1966
73	Simon Fletcher	LB-DE	Houston	1985-95
61	Eric Floyd	OL	Auburn	1995
43	Steve Foley	DB	Tulane	1976-86
32	Garrett Ford	FB	West Virginia	1968
57	Fred Forsberg	LB	Washington	1968, '70-73
84	Jason Franci	E	Santa Barbara	1966
31	Mike Franckowiak	RB	Central Michigan	1975-76
51,55	Jim Fraser	LB-P	Wisconsin	1962-64
42	Al Frazier	HB	Florida A&M	1961-63
86	Marv Frazier	WR	Cheyney St.	1973-75
62	Mike Freeman	G	Arizona	1984, 1986-87
68	Russell Freeman	T	Georgia Tech	1992-94
24	Randy Fuller	CB	Tennessee St.	1994
2	Will Furrer	QB	Virginia Tech	1994

G

64	George Gaiser	T	Southern Methodist	1968
28	Bob Gaiters	HB	New Mexico St.	1963
99	David Galloway	DE	Florida	1990
82	David Gamble	WR	New Hampshire	1997
52	Dave Garnett	LB	Stanford	1995
66	Scott Garnett	NT	Washington	1984
23	Drake Garrett	DB	Michigan St.	1968-70
61	Charles E. Gavin	DE	Tennessee St.	1960-63
92	Ron Geater	NT	Iowa	1992
79	Jumpy Geathers	DT	Wichita St.	1996-97
57	Bob Geddes	LB	UCLA	1972
40	Jack Gehrke	WR	Utah	1971
6	Ralph Giacommaro	P	Penn St.	1987
90	Freddie Gilbert	DE	Georgia	1986-88

2,30	Cookie Gilchrist	FB	No College	1965, 1967
17	Scotty Glacken	QB	Duke	1966-67
49	Glenn Glass	DB	Tennessee	1966
62	Tom Glassic	G	Virginia	1976-83
67	George Goeddeke	G	Notre Dame	1967-72
45,23	Austin (Goose) Gonsoulin	DB	Baylor	1960-66
79	John Gonzaga	G	No College	1966
62	Brian Goodman	G	UCLA	1975
64	Harvey Goodman	G	Colorado	1976
28	Cornell Gorden	CB	North Car. A&T	1970-72
23	Darrien Gordon	CB	Stanford	1997
83	Sam Graddy	WR	Tennessee	1987-88
52,53	Randy Gradishar	LB	Ohio St.	1974-83
58	Tom Graham	LB	Oregon	1972-74
35	John Granby	S	Virginia Tech	1992
63	John Grant	DT-DE	Southern Calif.	1973-79
72	Marsharne Graves	T	Arizona	1984
28	Gaston Green	RB	UCLA	1991-92
87	Paul Green	TE	Southern Calif.	1989
85	Willie Green	WR	Mississippi	1997
20	Charles Greer	DB	Colorado	1968-74
85	James D. Greer	E	Elizabeth City St.	1960
46	John Griffin	HB	Memphis St.	1964-66
29	Howard Griffith	FB	Illinois	1997
89	Bill Groman	HB-E	Heidelberg	1963
77	Dick Guesman	T-K	West Virginia	1964
37	Kevin Guidry	CB	Louisiana St.	1988
53	Donald Gulseth	LB	North Dakota	1966
63	Melwood N. (Buzz) Guy	G	Duke	1961-62

H

75	Brian Habib	G	Washington	1993-97
48	Dale Hackbart	S	Wisconsin	1973
85	Joey Hackett	TE	Elon Col.	1986
84	Mike Haffner	E	UCLA	1968-70
54	Britt Hager	LB	Texas	1995-96
22	Steve Haggerty	DB	Colorado	1975
26	Chris Hale	DB	Southern Calif.	1993
93	Ronnie Haliburton	LB	Louisiana St.	1990-91
40	Darryl Hall	S	Washington	1993-94
69	Darrell Hamilton	T	North Carolina	1989-91
72	Wayne Hammond	DT	Montana St.	1976
23	Billy Hardee	DB	Virginia Tech	1976
31	Mike Harden	CB-S	Michigan	1980-88
78	Archie Harris	OL	William & Mary	1987
47	Tony Harris	WR	Toledo	1972
82	Dwight Harrison	WR	Texas A&I	1971-72
27	Maurice Harvey	DB	Ball St.	1978, 1980
52	Richard Harvey	LB	Tulane	1994
96	Harald Hasselbach	DE	Washington	1994-97
67	Johnny Ray Hatley	T	Sul Ross St.	1960
37	Tim Hauck	S	Montana	1995-96
71	Arthur A. Hauser	T	Xavier	1961
29,33	Wendell Hayes	HB	Humboldt St.	1965-67
28	Abner Haynes	HB	North Texas St.	1965-66
36	Mark Haynes	CB	Colorado	1986-89
23	Alfred Haywood	RB	Bethune-Cookman	1975
22	Vaughn Hebron	RB	Virginia Tech	1996-97
24	Wymon Henderson	CB	Nevada-L.V.	1989-92
86	Jerry Hendren	WR	Idaho	1970
68	Brad Henke	DE-NT	Arizona	1989
89	Gary Henson	E	Colorado	1964
43	Lonnie Hepburn	CB	Texas Southern	1974
16	George W. Herring	QB,P	Southern Miss.	1960-61
10	Mark Herrmann	QB	Purdue	1981-82
50	Jon Hesse	LB	Nebraska	1997
31	Bo Hickey	FB	Maryland	1967
28	Clifford Hicks	CB	Oregon	1995
56,65	Walter Highsmith	C	Florida A&M	1968-69
84	Jack Hill	HB	Utah St.	1961
21	Randy Hilliard	CB	NW Louisiana St.	1994-97
23	George Hoey	DB	Michigan	1975
87	John Hoffman	DE	Hawaii	1972
64	John Hohman	G	Wisconsin	1965-66
34	Gus Holloman	DB	Houston	1968-69
73	Shawn Hollingsworth	T	Angelo St.	1983
90	Ron Holmes	DE	Washington	1989-92
73,74	Gordon Holz	DT	Minnesota	1960-63
74,78	Winford Hood	G-T	Georgia	1984-88
50	Jerry Hopkins	LB	Texas A&M	1963-66
2	Mike Horan	P	Long Beach St.	1986-92
13	Don Horn	QB	San Diego St.	1971-72
60	Paul Howard	G	Brig. Young	1973-75, '77-86
3	Bobby Howfield	K	No College	1968-70
57	John Huard	LB	Maine	1967-69
53	Robert Hudson	LB	Clemson	1960-61
14,16	John Hufnagel	QB	Penn St.	1974-75
26	Bobby Humphrey	RB	Alabama	1989-91
2	Bob Humphreys	K	Wichita St.	1967-68
79	Stefan Humphries	G	Michigan	1987-88
98	Ricky Hunley	LB	Arizona	1984-87
25	Daniel Hunter	CB	Henderson St.	1985-86
65,67	Glenn Hyde	G-T	Pittsburgh	1976-81, '84-85

I

73	Martin Imhof	DE	San Diego St.	1976
62	Jerry Inman	DT	Oregon	1966-71, '73

J

29	Bernard Jackson	DB	Washington St.	1977-80
68	Larron Jackson	G	Missouri	1971-74
78	Larry Jackson	DE	Texas A&M	1995
80	Mark Jackson	WR	Purdue	1986-92
87	Richard Jackson	DE	Southern	1967-72
25,28	Roger Jackson	DB	Beth-Cookman	1982-85, '87
57	Tom Jackson	LB	Louisville	1973-86
52	Frank Jackunas	C	Detroit	1963
50	Ray Jacobs	LB	North Carolina	1994-95
83	Ray Jacobs	DT	Howard Payne	1963-66
20	Tory James	CB	Louisiana St.	1996-97
70	Charlie Janerette	DT	Penn St.	1964-65
26	Tom Janik	DB-P	Texas A&I	1963-64
43	Pete Jaquess	DB	Eastern N.M.	1967-70
81,82	Patrick Jeffers	WR	Virginia	1996-97
30	Jim Jensen	RB	Iowa	1977, 1979-80
81	William Jessup	E	Southern Calif.	1960
51	Eugene Jeter	LB	Arkansas AM&N	1965-67
3	William (Billy) Joe	FB	Villanova	1963-64
86	Barry Johnson	WR	Maryland	1991
86	Butch Johnson	WR	Cal-Riverside	1984-85
12	Charley Johnson	QB	New Mexico St.	1972-75
66	Chuck Johnson	T	Texas	1992-93
25	Darrius Johnson	CB	Oklahoma	1996-97
21	Earl Johnson	DB	South Carolina	1987
87	Jason Johnson	WR	Illinois St.	1988
89	Reggie Johnson	TE	Florida St.	1991-93
82	Vance Johnson	WR	Arizona	1985-93, 1995
95	Tim Joiner	LB	Louisiana St.	1987
26	Calvin Jones	CB	Washington	1973-76
53	Danté Jones	LB	Oklahoma	1995
69	David Jones	OL	Texas	1987
20	Daryll Jones	DB	Georgia	1987

72	Ernest Jones	DE	Oregon	1996-97
35	Henry Jones	RB	Grambling	1969
93	James Jones	DT	Northern Iowa	1995
80	Jimmy Jones	WR	Wisconsin	1968
	K.C. Jones	C	Miami, Fla.(IR)	1997
32	Leonard Jones	DB	Texas St.	1987
31	Rondell Jones	S	North Carolina	1993-96
75	Rulon Jones	DE	Utah St.	1980-88
	Selwyn Jones	CB	Colorado St. (IR)	1997
77	Tony Jones	T	Western Carolina	1997
31	Victor Jones	RB	Louisiana St.	1992
54	Larry Jordan	E-LB	Youngstown	1962-64
83	Donald G. Joyce	E	Tulane	1962
66	Jim Juriga	T-G	Illinois	1988-90

K

55	John Kacherski	LB	Ohio St.	1992
59	Larry Kaminski	C	Purdue	1966-73
72	Bob Kampa	DT	California	1974
12	Ken Karcher	QB	Tulane	1987-88
3	Rich Karlis	K	Cincinnati	1982-88
72	Keith Kartz	C-T	California	1987-94
88	Clarence Kay	TE	Georgia	1984-92
61	Bill Keating	DT	Michigan	966-67
32	Mike Kellogg	FB	Santa Clara	1966-67
86,87	Pat Kelly	TE	Syracuse	1988-89
68	Crawford Ker	G	Florida	1991
32	Jon Keyworth	RB	Colorado	1974-80
33	Jim Kiick	RB	Wyoming	1976-77
80,82	Tony Kimbrough	WR	Jackson St.	1993-94
81	Todd Kinchen	WR	Louisiana St.	1996
70	Donald W. King	E	Kentucky	1960
84	Vince Kinney	WR	Maryland	1978-79
97	Bruce Klostermann	LB	South Dakota St.	1987-89
16	Jeff Knapple	QB	Northern Colo.	1980
99	Shawn Knight	NT	Brigham Young	1988
56	Mike Knox	LB	Nebraska	1987
73	Robert E. Konovsky	E	Wisconsin	1961
71	Greg Kragen	NT	Utah St.	1985-93
86	Jim Krieg	WR	Washington	1972
12	Gary Kroner	K	Wisconsin	1965-67
52	Ray Kubala	C	Texas A&M	1964-67
8	Gary Kubiak	QB	Texas A&M	1983-91
52	Frank W. Kuchta	C	Notre Dame	1960
22	Aaron Kyle	DB	Wyoming	1980-82

L

40	Ron Lamb	FB	South Carolina	1968
51,76	Gordon Lambert	LB	Tenn.-Martin	1968-69
50	Pat Lamberti, Jr.	LB	Richmond	1961
33	Gene Lang	RB	Louisiana St.	1984-87
21	Le-Lo Lang	CB	Washington	1990-93
67,76	Ken Lanier	T	Florida St.	1981-92, '94
80	Dan LaRose	DE	Missouri	1966
77	Carl James Larpenter	G	Texas	1960-61
87	Bill Larson	TE	Colorado St.	1980
45	Bill Laskey	LB	Michigan	1973-74
73	Isaac T. Lassiter	E	St. Augustine	1962-64
75	Kit Lathrop	DE	Arizona St.	1979
72	Don Latimer	DT	Miami, Fla.	1978-83
10	Jim Leclair	QB	C.W. Post	1967-68
53	Roger LeClerc	C	Trinity (Conn.)	1967
15	Jacky Lee	QB	Cincinnati	1964-65
68	Larry Lee	C-G	UCLA	1987
81	Max Leetzow	DE	Idaho	1965-66
54	Mike Lemon	LB	Kansas	1975
28	Jack Lentz	S	Holy Cross	1967-68
26	Darrell Lester	FB	McNeese St.	1965-66
20,41	Greg Lewis	RB	Washington	1991-92
48	Herman Lewis	DE	Virginia Union	1968
8	Jeff Lewis	QB	Northern Ariz.	1996-97
22	Tony Lilly	S	Florida	1984-87
13	Hub Lindsey	HB	Wyoming	1968
14	Pete Liske	QB	Penn St.	1969-70
44	Floyd Little	HB	Syracuse	1967-75
74	Bill Lobenstein	DL	Wisc.-Whitewater	1987
89	Kerry Locklin	TE	New Mexico St.	1987
97	Mike Lodish	DT	UCLA	1995-97
89	Dave Logan	WR	Colorado	1984
31	Derek Loville	RB	Oregon	1997
58,59	Tim Lucas	LB	California	1987-93
21	Tommy Luke	LB	Mississippi	1968
22	Fran Lynch	HB	Hofstra	1967-76
37	Anthony Lynn	RB	Texas Tech	1993, 1997
61	Tom Lyons	G	Georgia	1971-76
41	Rob Lytle	TE-RB	Michigan	1977-83

M

52	Dan MacDonald	LB	Idaho St.	1987
8	Tommy Maddox	QB	UCLA	1992-93
78	Don Maggs	G-T	Tulane	1993-94
33	Ernest G. (Pete) Mangum	LB	Mississippi	1960
83	Wade Manning	WR	Ohio St.	1981-82
66	Brison Manor	DE	Arkansas	1977-84
50	Bobby Maples	C	Baylor	1972-78
86	Arthur Marshall	WR	Georgia	1992-93
43	Charles E. Marshall	HB	Oregon St.	1962
29	Warren Marshall	RB	James Madison	1987
47	Paul Martha	S	Pittsburgh	1970
83,85	Rick Massie	WR	Kentucky	1987-88
81	Billy Masters	TE	Louisiana St.	1970-74
73	Pat Matson	G	Oregon	1966-67
55	Archie Matsos	LB	Michigan St.	1966
76,77	Jack Mattox	T	Fresno St.	1961-62
55	Marv Matuszak	LB	Tulsa	1964
74	Andy Maurer	T	Oregon	1977
14	Dean May	QB	Louisville	1987
56	Ray May	LB	Southern Calif.	1973-75
87	Ed McCaffrey	WR	Stanford	1995-97
40	Brendan McCarthy	FB	Boston Col.	1968-69
10,11	John McCormick	QB	Mass.	1963, '65-66, '68
96	Jake McCullough	DE	Clemson	1989-90
67	Robert V. McCullough	G	Colorado	1962-65
33	Lawrence McCutcheon	RB	Colorado St.	1980
54	Ed (Wahoo) McDaniel	LB	Oklahoma	1961-63
82	Orlando McDaniel	WR	Louisiana St.	1982
68	Reggie McElroy	G-T	West Texas St.	1995-96
64	Lewis B. (Bud) McFadin	DT	Texas	1960-63
47	John McGeever	DB	Auburn	1962-65
89	Keli McGregor	TE	Colorado St.	1985
16	Monte McGuire	QB	Texas Tech	1987
58	Bill McKoy	LB	Purdue	1970-72
26	Tim McKyer	CB	Texas-Arlington	1997
68	Ron McLean	DL	Cal. St. Fullerton	1987
45	James R. McMillin	DB	Colorado St.	1960-62, '64-65
41	Robert McNamara	HB	Minnesota	1960-61
77,97	Karl Mecklenburg	LB-DE	Minnesota	1983-94
61	Bob Meeks	C	Auburn	1992-94
64	Jon Melander	G	Minnesota	1993-94
59	Mark Merrill	LB	Minnesota	1981-82
46,87	Bobby Micho	RB-TE	Texas	1986-87
22	Glyn Milburn	RB	Stanford	1993-95

17	Hugh Millen	QB	Washington	1994-95
83	Anthony Miller	WR	Tennessee	1994-96
52	Jeff Mills	LB	Nebraska	1990-93
21	Eugene Mingo	HB-K	No College	1960-64
71	Claudie Minor	T	San Diego St.	1974-82
20	Tommy Earl Minter	HB	Baylor	1962
67	Dean Miraldi	T	Utah	1985
75	Rex Mirich	DE	Northern Arizona	1967-69
49	Alvin Mitchell	S-WR	Morgan St.	1970
27	Charlie Mitchell	HB	Washington	1963-67
41	Leroy Mitchell	CB	Texas Southern	1971-73
51	John Mobley	LB	Kutztown	1996-97
89	Orson Mobley	TE	Salem Col. (W.V.)	1986-90
22	Alton Montgomery	S-CB	Houston	1990-92
78	Marv Montgomery	T	Southern Calif.	1971-76
21	Randy Montgomery	CB	Weber St.	1971-73
52	Mike Montler	C	Colorado	1977
2	Alex Moore	HB	Norfolk St.	1968
87	Bob Moore	TE	Stanford	1978
78	Leroy Moore	DE	Fort Valley St.	1964-65
76	Randy Moore	DT	Arizona St.	1976
12	Shawn Moore	QB	Virginia	1991-93
86	Emery Moorehead	WR-RB	Colorado	1980
7	Craig Morton	QB	California	1977-82
25	Haven Moses	WR	San Diego St.	1972-81
85	John Mosier	TE	Kansas	1971
86	Bobby Moten	TE	Bishop Col.	1968
51	Marc Munford	LB	Nebraska	1987-90
57	Mark Murray	LB	Florida	1991
14	Bill Musgrave	QB	Oregon	1995-96
29	Wilbur Myers	S	Delta St.	1983
39	Jesse Myles	RB	Louisiana St.	1983-84
54	Chip Myrtle	LB	Maryland	1967-72

N

58	Rob Nairne	LB	Oregon St.	1977-80
66	Tom Nalen	C	Boston Col.	1994-97
84	Ricky Nattiel	WR	Florida	1987-92
62	Dan Neil	C-G	Texas	1997
80	Ron Nery	E	Wisconsin	1963
76	Tom Neville	T	Mississippi St.	1978
51	Lee (Mike) Nichols	C	Arkansas A&M	1960-61
43	John Nocera	LB	Iowa	1963
68	Tom Nomina	T	Miami (Ohio)	1963-65
38	Ben Norman	RB	Colorado St.	1980
1,4	Chris Norman	P	South Carolina	1984-86
15	Philip H. Nugent	HB	Tulane	1961

O

27	Tom Oberg	S	Portland St.	1968-69
88	Riley Odoms	TE	Houston	1972-83
42	Muhammad Oliver	DB	Oregon	1992
58	Phil Olsen	C	Utah St.	1975-76
76	Harold Olson	T	Clemson	1963-64
0	John Olszewski	FB	California	1962
66	Jim O'Malley	LB	Notre Dame	1973-75
91	Willie Oshodin	DE	Villanova	1993-95

P

23	Chris Pane	DB	Chico St.	1976-79
56	Don Parish	LB	Stanford	1972
60	Ernie Park	G	McMurray Col.	1967
60	Charlie Parker	G	Southern Miss.	1965
1	Daren Parker	P	South Carolina	1992
74	Scott Parrish	T	Utah St.	1976
24	Rick Parros	RB	Utah St.	1981-84
12	Al Pastrana	QB	Maryland	1969-70
88	Russell Payne	TE	Appalachian St.	1987
71	Jack Peavey	OL	Troy St.	1987
12	Craig Penrose	QB	San Diego St.	1976-79
71	James W. Perkins	T	Colorado	1962-64
33,35	Lonnie Perrin	RB	Illinois	1976-78
60	Gerald Perry	G-T	Southern U.	1988-90
95	Michael Dean Perry	DT	Clemson	1995-97
33	Robert Perryman	FB	Michigan	1991-92
77	Anton Peters	T	Florida	1963
26	Lyle Pickens	DB	Colorado	1987
48	John Pitts	S	Arizona St.	1973-75
82	Dave Pivec	TE	Notre Dame	1969
38	Bruce Plummer	DB	Mississippi St.	1987-88, '90
22	Bobby Ply	DB	Baylor	1967
21	Randy Poltl	DB	Stanford	1975-77
47	David Poole	DB	Carson-Newman	1993
34	Nathan Poole	RB	Louisville	1982-83, '85, '87
31	Kerry Porter	RB	Washington St.	1990
23	Dickie Post	RB	Houston	1971
91	Warren Powers	DE	Maryland	1989-91
88	Eugene Prebola	E	Boston U.	1961-63
23	Steve Preece	S	Oregon St.	1972
46	Dave Preston	HB	Bowling Green	1978-83
11	Luke Prestridge	P	Baylor	1979-83
56	James Price	LB	Auburn	1964
25	Errol Prisby	DB	Cincinnati	1967
81	Mike Pritchard	WR	Colorado	1994-95
93	Trevor Pryce	DT	Clemson	1997
83	John J. Pyeatt	HB	No College	1960

Q

26	Frank Quayle	RB	Virginia	1969

R

78	Bruce Radford	DE	Grambling	1979
10	Steve Ramsey	QB	North Texas St.	1971-76
	Leo T. Reed	T	Colorado St.	1961
32	Tony Reed	RB	Colorado	1981
74	Dan Remsberg	T	Abilene Christian	1986-87
40	Randy Rich	DB	New Mexico	1977
43	Bob Richardson	DB	UCLA	1966
99	David Richie	DT	Washington	1997
58	Frank Richter	LB	Georgia	1967-69
26	Larry Riley	DB	Salem Col. (W.V.)	1977
38	Reggie Rivers	RB	SW Texas St.	1991-96
59	Joe Rizzo	LB	Merch. Marines	1974-80
48	Randy Robbins	DB	Arizona	1984-91
36	Frank Robinson	CB	Boise St.	1992-93
94	Jeff Robinson	DE	Idaho	1993-96
95	Jeroy Robinson	LB	Texas A&M	1990
17	Matt Robinson	QB	Georgia	1980
77	Alden Roche	DE	Southern U.	1970
4	Ruben Rodriguez	P	Arizona	1992
68	William E. Roehnelt	LB	Bradley	1961-62
73	Stan Rogers	T	Maryland	1975
35	David S. Rolle	FB	Oklahoma	1960-61
53	Bill Romanowski	LB	Boston Col.	1996-97
42	Albert Romine	HB	Florence St.	1960
81	Barry Rose	WR	Wisc.-Stevens Pt.	1993
30	Oliver Ross	RB	Alabama A&M	1973-75
11	Tobin Rote	QB	Rice	1966
16	Tom Rouen	P	Colorado	1993-97
33	Justin D. Rowland	HB	Texas Christian	1962
46	John Rowser	DB	Michigan	1974-76
11	T.J. Rubley	QB	Tulsa	1996

40	Martin Rudolph	DB	Arizona	1987
57	Mike Ruether	C	Texas	1988-89
58	Steve Russ	LB	Air Force	1997
39	Darryl Russell	DB	Appalachian St.	1987
85	Derek Russell	WR	Arkansas	1991-94
42	Leonard Russell	RB	Arizona St.	1994
50	Jim Ryan	LB	William and Mary	1979-88
80	Tom Rychlec	E	American Int.	1963

S

26	George Saimes	S	Michigan St.	1970-72
74	Harvey Salem	T	California	1991
84	Clint Sampson	WR	San Diego St.	1983-86
55	Glenell Sanders	LB	Louisiana Tech	1994
83	John Sawyer	TE	Southern Miss.	1983-84
54	Ron Sbranti	LB	Utah St.	1966
82	Robert Scarpitto	WR-P	Notre Dame	1962-67
67	Carl Schaukowitch	G	Penn St.	1975
67	Steve Schindler	G	Boston Col.	1977-78
69	Mark Schlereth	G	Idaho	1995-97
64	Mike Schnitker	G	Colorado	1969-74
74	Bill Schultz	T	Southern Calif.	1995
84,86	John Schultz	WR	Maryland	1976-78
45	Lew Scott	DB	Oregon St.	1966
76	Kirk Scrafford	T	Montana	1993-94
35	James H. Sears	HB	Southern Calif.	1960-61
21	Goldie Sellers	DB	Grambling	1966-67
45	Jeff Severson	DB	Long Beach St.	1975
30	Steve Sewell	RB-WR	Oklahoma	1985-92
65	Don Shackelford	G	Pacific	1964
75	Rick Sharp	T	Washington	1972
81,84	Shannon Sharpe	WR	Savannah St.	1990-97
17	George H. Shaw	QB	Oregon	1962
45	Richard Shelton	CB	Liberty	1989
84	Rod Sherman	WR	Southern Calif.	1972
88	Mike Sherrard	WR	UCLA	1996
75	Roger T. Shoals	T	Maryland	1971
63	Laval Short	DT	Colorado	1980
80	Jerry Simmons	WR	Beth.-Cookman	1971-74
51	Leon Simmons	LB	Grambling	1963
51	Mike Simone	LB	Stanford	1972-74
67	Jack M. Simpson	LB	Mississippi	1961
45	John Sklopan	HB	Southern Miss.	1963
7,14	Milton (Mickey) Slaughter	QB	Louisiana Tech	1963-66
39	Tom Smiley	RB	Lamar Tech	1969
56	Aaron Smith	LB	Utah St.	1984
55	Art Smith	LB	Hawaii	1980
26	Ben Smith	CB	Georgia	1994
20	Daniel Eugene Smith	HB	NE Oklahoma	1961
49	Dennis Smith	S	Southern Calif.	1981-94
42	Detron Smith	FB	Texas A&M	1996-97
14	Don Smith	G	Florida A&M	1967
75	Ed Smith	DE	Colorado Col.	1973-75
28	Elliott Smith	CB	Alcorn A&M	1990
72	Harold Smith	T	UCLA	1960
	Hugh B. Smith	E	Kansas	1962
47	James Smith	S	Utah St.	1969
57	Matt Smith	LB	West Virginia	1987
65	Monte Smith	G	North Dakota	1989
90	Neil Smith	DE	Nebraska	1997
70	Paul Smith	DT-DE	New Mexico	1968-78
45	Perry Smith	DB	Colorado St.	1980-81
80	Rod Smith	WR	Missouri Southern	1995-97
32	Sammie Smith	RB	Florida St.	1992
71	Willie Smith	G	Michigan	1960
84	Matt Snorton	TE	Michigan St.	1964
70	Brian Sochia	NT-DE	NW Okla. St.	1991-92
39	Roland Solomon	CB	Utah	1981
51	Henry Sorrell	LB	Chattanooga	1967
78	Rich Stachowski	DT-NT	California	1983
62	Jerry N. Stalcup	LB	Wisconsin	1961-62
85	Tim Stallworth	WR	Washington St.	1990
14	Scott Stankavage	QB	North Carolina	1984, 1986
46	Bruce Starling	HB	Florida	1963
23	Larry Steele	P	Santa Rosa	1974
19	Fred Steinfort	K	Boston Col.	1979-81
36	James E. Stinnette	FB-LB	Oregon St.	1961-62
21	Jesse Stokes	DB	Corpus Christi	1968
34	Don E. Stone	FB	Arkansas	1961-64
82	Otto Stowe	WR	Iowa St.	1974
22	Robert J. Stransky	HB	Colorado	1960
63	David Strickland	T-G	Memphis St.	1960
41	Deon Strother	RB	Southern Calif.	1994
70	Dave Studdard	T	Texas	1979-88
72	Jerry G. Sturm	C-T-G	Illinois	1961-66
60	Nick Subis	G-C	San Diego St.	1991
50	John Sullins	LB	Alabama	1992
46	Don Summers	TE	Boise St.	1984-85
85	Jim Summers	DB	Michigan St.	1967
25	Charles Swann	WR-DB	Indiana St.	1994
80	Shane Swanson	WR	Nebraska	1987
74	Harry Swayne	T	Rutgers	1997
49	Neal Sweeney	FL	Tulsa	1967
51	Bob Swenson	LB	California	1975-79, '81-83
23	Gene Sykes	DB	Louisiana St.	1967
94	Jim Szymanski	DE	Michigan St.	1990-91

T

64	Ralph Tamm	G-C	West Chester	1995-96
98	Maa Tanuvasa	DT	Hawaii	1995-97
65	George Tarasovic	DE	Louisiana St.	1967
41	Jerry L. Tarr	E	Oregon	1962
95	Alphonso Taylor	DT	Temple	1993
81	Kitrick Taylor	WR	Washington St.	1993
87	Lionel T. Taylor	E	N.M. Highlands	1960-66
13	Steve Tensi	QB	Florida St.	1967-70
84	Jim Thibert	LB	Toledo	1965
32	Calvin Thomas	RB	Illinois	1988
48	Earlie Thomas	DB	Colorado St.	1975
26	Eric Thomas	CB	Tulane	1995
26	J. T. Thomas	S	Florida St.	1982
82	Zach Thomas	WR-PR	South Carolina St.	1983-84
53	Anthony Thompson	LB	East Carolina	1990
61	Arland Thompson	G	Baylor	1980
36	Bill Thompson	DB	Maryland St.	1969-81
76	Broderick Thompson	T	Kansas	1995-96
77	Jim Thompson	DT	Southern Illinois	1965
4	Robert Thompson	WR	Youngstown St.	1987
87	Cedric Tillman	WR	Alcorn St.	1992-94
51	Dave Tobey	LB	Oregon	1968
61	Andre Townsend	DE-NT	Mississippi	1984-90
54,94	Keith Traylor	LB	Central St. (Ok.)	1991-92, '97
20	Jerry Traynham	HB	Southern Calif.	1961
9	David Treadwell	K	Clemson	1989-92
37	Steve Trimble	DB	Maryland	1981-83
18	Frank Tripucka	QB	Notre Dame	1960-63
91	Jeff Tupper	DL	Oklahoma	1987
55	Godwin Turk	LB	Southern	1976-78
35	Clem Turner	RB	Cincinnati	1970-72
15	Jim Turner	K	Utah St.	1971-79
23	Maurice Tyler	S	Morgan St.	1973-74
72	Richard Tyson	G	Tulsa	1967

U

67 ....Keith Uecker .... T .... Auburn 1982-83
80 ....Rick Upchurch .... WR .... Minnesota 1975-83
50 ....Olen Underwood .... LB .... Texas 1971

V

42 ....Bill Van Heusen .... WR-P ..... Maryland 1968-76
61 ....Bob Vaughan .... G .... Mississippi 1968
32 ....Tony Veland .... S .... Nebraska 1997
86 ....Chris Verhulst .... TE .... Chico St. 1990
65 ....Lloyd Voss .... T .... Nebraska 1972

W

37 ....Bob Wade .... CB .... Morgan St. 1970
30 ....Clarence Walker .... HB .... Southern Ill. 1963
96 ....Kenny Walker .... DE .... Nebraska 1991-92
59 ....Brett Wallerstedt .... LB .... Arizona St. 1994
83 ....Dave Washington .... LB .... Alcorn A&M 1971
56 ....Dave Washington .... E .... Southern Calif. 1968
84 ....Gene Washington .... WR .... Michigan St. 1973
48 ....Lionel Washington .... CB .... Tulane 1995-96
98 ....Ted Washington .... NT .... Louisville 1994
81 ....Steve Watson .... WR .... Temple 1979-87
14 ....Norris Weese .... QB .... Mississippi 1976-79
40 ....Ted Wegert .... FB .... No College 1960
13 ....Jack Weil .... P .... Wyoming 1986
29 ....Bill West .... CB .... Tennessee St. 1972
40,42 ...Charlie West .... DB .... Texas-El Paso 1978-79
20 ....Willie West .... DB .... Oregon 1964
89 ....Max Wettstein .... E .... Florida St. 1966
83 ....Jim Whalen .... TE .... Boston Col. 1970-71
89 ....Andre White .... TE .... Florida A&M 1967
78 ....Jim White .... DE .... Colorado St. 1976
79 ....Dave Widell .... C-G .... Boston Col. 1990-94
67 ....Doug Widell .... G .... Boston Col. 1989-92
47 ....Gerald Willhite .... RB .... San Jose St. 1982-88
91 ....Alfred Williams .... DE .... Colorado 1996-97
90 ....Dan Williams .... DE .... Toledo 1993-96
Harold Williams .... HB .... Miami (Ohio) 1961
29 ....Wandy Williams .... RB .... Hofstra 1969-70
85 ....Jeff Wilner .... TE .... Wesleyan (Ct.) 1995
48 ....Nemiah Wilson .... DB .... Grambling 1965-67
91 ....Troy Wilson .... DE .... Pittsburg St. 1995
88 ....Sir Mawn Wilson .... WR .... Syracuse 1997
45 ....Steve Wilson .... CB .... Howard 1982-88
23 ....Sammy Winder .... RB .... Southern Miss. 1982-90
55 ....Bryant Winn .... LB .... Houston 1987
16 ....Dick Wood .... QB .... Auburn 1962
52 ....Ken Woodard .... LB .... Tuskegee Inst. 1982-86
99 ....Ray Woodard .... DE .... Texas 1987
85 ....Chris Woods .... WR .... Auburn 1989
58 ....Jack Work .... DB .... Denver 1960
87 ....James Earl Wright .... HB .... Memphis St. 1964
87 ....Jim Wright .... TE .... Texas Christian 1980-85
42 ....Lonnie Wright .... DB .... Colorado St. 1966-67
20 ....Louis Wright .... CB .... San Jose St. 1975-86
57,92 ...Dave Wyman .... LB .... Stanford 1993-95

Y

76 ....William G. Yelverton .... E .... Mississippi 1960
65 ....Joseph A. Young .... E .... Arizona 1960-61
83 ....Michael Young .... WR .... UCLA 1989-92
60 ....Robert Young .... G .... Howard Payne 1966-70

Z

46 ....Bob Zeman .... DB .... Wisconsin 1962-63
65 ....Gary Zimmerman .... T .... Oregon 1993-97

(IR): Injured Reserve

All-Time Head Coaches

Frank Filchock .... 1960-1961 .... 7-20-1 .... .268
Jack Faulkner .... 1962-1964 .... 9-22-1 .... .297
Mac Speedie .... 1964-1966 .... 6-19-1 .... .250
Ray Malavasi .... 1966 .... 4-8-0 .... .333
Lou Saban .... 1967-1971 .... 20-42-3 .... .331
Jerry Smith .... 1971 .... 2-3-0 .... .400
John Ralston .... 1972-1976 .... 34-33-3 .... .507
Red Miller .... 1977-1980 .... 42-25-0★ .... .627
Dan Reeves .... 1981-1992 .... 117-79-1★ .... .596
Wade Phillips .... 1993-1994 .... 16-17★ .... .485
Mike Shanahan .... 1995-1997 .... 37-16-0★ .... .698

★ ***Includes post-season games***

Bibliography

Carroll, Bob. *When the Grass Was Real, The Ten Best Years of Pro Football.* Simon & Schuster, 1993.

Carroll, Bob; Gershman, Michael; Neft, David; and Thorn, John. *Total Football, The Official Encyclopedia of the National Football League.* Harper Collins, 1997.

Connor, Dick. *The Denver Broncos.* Prentice-Hall, 1974.

Denver Broncos. *1997 Denver Broncos Media Guide.*

Denver Broncos. *1997 Postseason Review.*

Diddlebock, Bob and Mecklenburg, Karl. *Meck For the Defense.* McGraw-Hill Book Company, 1988.

Hession, Joseph and Spence, Michael. *Broncos: Three Decades of Football.* Foghorn Press, 1987.

Latimer, Clay. *John Elway: Armed and Dangerous.* Addax Publishing Group, 1997.

Meserole, Mike. *1997 Sports Almanac.* Houghton Mifflin, 1997.

Moon, Bob. *The Cleveland Browns, A 50-Year Tradition.* SporTradition Publications, 1997.

National Football League. *The Official National Football League 1997 Record & Fact Book,* Workman Publishing Co., 1997.

Orr, Jack. *We Came of Age, A Picture History of the American Football League.* The Lion Press, Inc., 1969.

Paige, Woodrow Jr. *Orange Madness.* Thomas Y. Crowell, 1978.

Sahadi, Lou. *Broncos!* Stein and Day, 1978.

Sports Illustrated. *John Elway: The Drive of a Champion.* Simon and Schuster, 1998.

Photography Credits

Allsport: page 154.

AP Wide World Photos: page 130.

John Betancourt: pages iii, 62, 63, 75, 78, 91, 110, 112, 120, 133, 148 R, 155 L, 156, 166, 170, 171 R, 175, 176, 182, 196 L, 201, 204, 209, 210, 214, 215.

Chance Brockway: pages i, iv, vi, 1, 20, 22 L-R, 23, 24, 26, 28, 32, 33, 34, 36, 37 L-R, 40, 41, 46, 48, 49, 57, 58, 60, 61, 65, 67 L-R, 68, 69, 70 L-R, 72, 73, 76 L-R, 77, 85 L, 88, 89, 136, 137, 139, 140 L-R, 142, 143, 144 L-R, 145 L, 149 L-R, 151 L, 158, 160 L-R, 161, 163, 164, 168, 169, 172, 174, 177, 180, 181, 183, 184, 185, 189, 190 L-R, 191, 192, 197, 199 L, 205, 216, 220, 225, 226.

Browns News/Illustrated: pages 74, 90, 102, 103, 106 L-R, 107 L-R, 115, 135, 155 R, 157 L, 159, 186, 187, 194, 198, 199 R, 206, 207, 208.

Corbis-Bettmann: pages 2, 4, 5, 6, 8, 10, 12, 13, 15, 17, 18, 27, 30, 31 L, 35, 39, 50, 53, 54, 59, 66, 71, 79, 80, 82, 83, 84, 86, 87, 92, 93, 95, 96, 97, 99, 121, 123, 124, 127, 162, 167, 173, 202, 203, 211, 212, 213 L-R.

Denver Broncos Football Club: pages 7, 11, 14, 19, 21 L-R, 31 R, 109, 114, 118, 119 L-R, 122, 125, 138, 145 R, 148 L, 150, 151 R, 153, 157 R, 171 L, 193, 196 R.

Diamond Images: pages 108, 178.

Pete Groh: pages 85 R, 100, 104, 105, 111, 134, 146, 147, 179.

Ernie Leyba: pages 42, 47, 52, 152.

PRO-File Collection: page 25.

Tony Tomsic: pages 44, 56, 116, 117, 128, 129, 131, 141.

Records and Statistics courtesy of Denver Broncos Media Relations Office